PEER
TRAINING

PEER TRAINING

Improved Performance One by One

CAROLYN NILSON

PRENTICE HALL
Englewood Cliffs, New Jersey 07632

Prentice-Hall International (UK) Limited, *London*
Prentice-Hall of Australia Pty. Limited, *Sydney*
Prentice-Hall Canada, Inc., *Toronto*
Prentice-Hall Hispanoamericana, S.A., *Mexico*
Prentice-Hall of India Private Limited, *New Delhi*
Prentice-Hall of Japan, Inc., *Tokyo*
Simon & Schuster Asia Pte. Ltd., *Singapore*
Editora Prentice-Hall do Brasil, Ltda., *Rio de Janeiro*

© 1994 by

PRENTICE-HALL, Inc.

Englewood Cliffs, NJ

10 9 8 7 6 5 4 3 2 1

Library of Congress Cataloging-in-Publication Data
Nilson, Carolyn D.
    Peer training : improved performance one by one / Carolyn Nilson.
        p.   cm.
    Includes bibliographical references and index.
    ISBN 0-13-104639-X
    1. Employees—Training of.   I. Title.
  HF5549.5.T7N5268   1994
658.3'124—dc20

94-165
CIP

ISBN 0-13-104639-X

PRENTICE HALL
Career and Personal Development
Englewood Cliffs, NJ 07632

Simon & Schuster, A Paramount Communications Company

Printed in the United States of America

DEDICATION

This book is dedicated to Lisa, Carla, Andrew, Magdalena, Matthaeus, Hannah, Chrystal, Scotty, Nicky, Ian, Bobby, Scott, Meagan, Ashley, Sari, Michael, Dylan, Shelby, Rosey, Benjamin, and Ryan whose workplaces will be different from those of their parents and grandparents—whose learning, one by one, is our sacred trust and urgent responsibility.

The graphic format of the book is based on this model:

Problem:

Plan of Action:

Examples:

ABOUT THE AUTHOR

Carolyn Nilson, Ed.D, is a veteran trainer with a wide experience base in traditional and state-of-the art training assignments. Among the corporations and agencies she has served as consultant in training design are: American Management Association, The ARINC Companies, AT&T, Chemical Bank, Chevron, Dun & Bradstreet, Martin-Marietta, Nabisco, National Institute of Education, National Occupational Competency Testing Institute, National Westminster Bank, New Jersey Bell, New Jersey State Department of Education, US Department of Education Office of Vocational and Adult Education, and The World Bank.

Dr. Nilson was a Member of the Technical Staff at AT&T Bell Laboratories where she was part of the Standards, Audits, and Inspections Group of the Systems Training Center. In this capacity, she developed, implemented, and promoted quality standards in course design and delivery throughout AT&T; she was the Bell Labs' representative on a corporate instructional design team. At Bell Labs, she received commendations for her work one-to-one with technical professionals for whom English was a second language. She also taught the Bell Labs' train-the-trainer course.

She also held the position of Manager of Simulation (CBT) Training at Combustion Engineering, where she managed the training operation and created high-level computer-based training for an international base of clients in various fields of the chemical process industry. At CE, she was a member of a corporate training design team where her specific contribution was design of an expert system in learner evaluation.

Dr. Nilson was Director of Training for a systems consulting firm with a broad-based Fortune 500 clientele in the New York City metropolitan area. In this position, she supervised a staff of training consultants and was responsible for training analysis, design, development, implementation, and evaluation across a range of corporations.

She is the author of numerous articles, papers, speeches, and manuals in training design, delivery, evaluation, and management, and is a popular conference speaker and seminar leader. She is an active member of the American Society for Training and Development (ASTD), where she recently was part of the first grass-roots planning task force in the area of human resources development skills and strategies. Her work has been featured in *Training* magazine, *Training & Development*, *Entrepreneur*, and *Fortune*.

Her other books include:

Training Program Workbook & Kit, Prentice Hall, 1989;

Training for Non-Trainers, Amacom, 1990;

How to Manage Training, Amacom, 1991;

How to Start a Training Program in Your Growing Business, Amacom, 1992;

Trainer's Complete Guide to Management and Supervisory Development, Prentice Hall, 1992; and

Team Games for Trainers, McGraw Hill, 1993.

Carolyn Nilson received her doctorate from Rutgers University, with a specialty in measurement and evaluation in vocational and technical education.

WHAT THIS BOOK WILL DO FOR YOU

This book's major contribution is that it codifies and organizes the many and varied principles and practices of person-to-person teaching and learning that go on in the workplace. It shows how to do peer training in ways that are sensible, interesting, efficient, and even fun. It shows what to do and why it should be done.

The book updates teaching and learning methods based on what we know about the nature of workplace learning in post-industrial society, about the special teaching and learning challenges of information-intensive work environments, about the new realities of global competitiveness, and about the economic pulls and tugs of major institutional changes in American life that affect work and workers.

The book presents information in easily comprehended bits and chunks that guide the user in logical step-by-step approaches to solving training problems at this one-to-one level. It is a book for trainers and training planners especially. It is also a hands-on manual and guidebook for any manager, supervisor, field worker, office worker, or line employee who has to teach another employee. It is a book that addresses major upheavals in human resources development, and especially in training, in industries such as health care, manufacturing, banking and finance, hospitality, transportation, and communications, where customer satisfaction and employee empowerment very forcefully affect the management of people on the job interacting with their markets. It is a book that is equally relevant for the account rep, the systems analyst, the drafter, the assembler, the clerk, the meat cutter, the driver, the mechanic, the engineer, the market researcher, and the technical writer. It is for hourly and salaried workers, union agents and corporate officers, new hires and old timers, consultants and CEOs. It is a book for every department and every team, a rich source of ideas and tools to help every person who must function as a trainer as part of his or her job. It is a book of particular relevance for students in college or university programs in human resources development or training management, who deal in the currency of ideas and creativity.

The graphic elements of the book include a structured format for identifying and defining a specific problem area, presenting the outline of a plan of action, and describing examples of the problem, its effects, or its solution. The reader will find narrative text followed by "problem boxes" and worksheets of various kinds. This applications bias in the design of the book is meant to encourage the immediate use of the book and promote success of the new technique or idea introduced.

INTRODUCTION

This book is for people who believe in people. More than this, it is a practical book that guides people at work in helping each other to learn. It is a comprehensive do-it-yourself handbook, workbook, and reference source for people on the job who consider themselves associates, colleagues, partners, teammates, and buddies—PEERS—with fellow workers. It is for people who feel or who want to feel that what they know and can do will make a difference to the company for which they work. Ultimately, this is a book for people who truly believe in the power of one individual interacting with another.

Trainers will find this book a familiar starting place for consideration of methods and strategies for developing an organization whose collective strength will be based on the strength of its individuals at work. Supervisors, team leaders, and managers of all sorts will see immediately how they can become informed, sensitive, and competent on-the-job trainers—as they are called on so frequently to do. This book is designed to empower, facilitate, and enable anyone who takes the job of teaching and learning on the job seriously. It is especially meant for those who have the responsibility for training added to the job they already do. It is a boon to the change makers in organizations of all sorts—to those charged with the daunting tasks of leading their companies into a new era of human resources development.

It is a book for people who believe in the possibility that business growth will be strongest and longest by developing the capabilities of workers at every level and in every job description—that the true test of competitiveness will be made on the longevity of a company's collective intellect and will. The focus of the book's many methods and techniques for analysis, design, development, implementation, and evaluation is peer to peer training, and through it, the enormous power of one person teaching and learning.

The assumptions upon which this book is crafted are that:

- *continuous improvement* in products and services is possible through business organizations that value individuals;
- *empowered employees* require and respond to work situations that challenge, stretch, and encourage their strengths;
- the rich *diversity of the workforce* must be nurtured at the individual level in order to achieve the flexibility necessary for innovation and creativity; and that

- the *learning organization* can flourish only where self-mastery is built upon measurement systems and evaluation results originating with individuals and returning to individuals for implementation of improvements.

This book is a response to the reality that old forms of hierarchical and authoritarian management no longer work, that old formulas for capital growth need to be replaced with new formulas that realize the financial value of human capital, and that today's knowledge workers require their own kinds of methods for maximizing their contributions to work. Corporate commitments to training in this new organizational world must be greater than ever before and must challenge and develop the individual in innovative and business-wise ways that fit the learner and more flexible business organizations across the corporate landscape.

FORMAT OF THE BOOK

This book is built upon the framework of the classic Instructional System Design (ISD) approach which begins with analysis, proceeds through design, development and implementation, and concludes with evaluation—all forming a conceptual systems design loop that fosters action from results of evaluation, and then returns to the analysis phase for continuation. The book is laid out so that narrative text is followed by structured problem statements, examples, forms, checklists, and worksheets to facilitate peer to peer workplace learning and business growth. Sample transparency masters, templates, and industry-specific case applications are included for illustration.

The macro-themes of the last years of this century are folded into the trainer's standard systems approach to facilitating change:

ISD phase	*Dealing mostly with:*
Section I: Analysis	continuous improvement
Section II: Design, Development and Implementation	empowered individuals and a flexible workforce
Section III: Evaluation	learning organization

CONTENTS

SECTION III. EVALUATION OF PEER TRAINING 281

SYSTEMS ANALYSIS AND SUPPORT FOR PEER TRAINING

This section includes guidelines, forms, and worksheets to help you figure out how systems can work for you in introducing or enhancing your peer training program. The business analysis tools presented here will allow you to take a look at various traditional business functions—operations, finance, marketing, research and development (R&D)—and see how this new, personalized view of human resources development can work in your enterprise. This section addresses the organizational issues that surround the person-to-person interactions on the job and either undermine these interactions or support them. Tools in the section are designed to help you understand the systems and support structures you'll need for peer training to flourish.

THE VALUE OF CONTINUOUS IMPROVEMENT

In order to approach any front-end analysis with a problem-solving mindset, it's probably a good idea to adopt some overarching value which can guide and sustain your probing and investigations. "Continuous improvement" is one such value that can be your beacon as you search for new pathways through old organizations.

Analysis work is always difficult. Human nature seems to resist the pulling apart that inevitably accompanies analysis of procedures, structures, and interactions. Workers don't like their work to be scrutinized or their assumptions to be opened to question. People don't want their filing systems disturbed or their routines changed. Managers don't like the time spent on activities without an immediate effect on the bottom line. Holding that value up high during analysis work can help everyone involved to get through it with their old culture intact but with the beginning of a glimmer of how the old ways can evolve into something better.

It has taken several generations of management practice to even begin to institutionalize the notion of continuous improvement. Quality guru, W. Edwards Deming, nearly fifty years ago began advocating designing quality *into* the work processes that produced products, taking the measurement science of statistical quality control out of the end-of-process inspection where it had been so comfortable during the mass production heydays of the 1940s and early 1950s. Deming came up with formulas to determine the cost of quality, or more precisely, the cost of poor quality, and showed through numerous consultancies and experiments how building quality into product development through in-process inspections at many points during development, in fact, cost less than inspecting it out at the end of development. Deming started the great hunt for faults, failures, flaws, defects, and errors at the micro level in product development.

Deming also at the same time began preaching that work should be joyous, and that fear should not be the motivator for productivity. Driving fear out of the workplace became a corollary to building quality into work processes. Unfortunately, American businesses in the '50s and '60s were not ready to listen to what Deming had to say. Buoyed by wartime success, growing families, and a technology-based psychological boost to the frontier mentality, American business seemed at that time to feel that more was better and faster was greater. Expansion and growth meant gathering headcounts, increasing span of controls, shipping products, building bigger plants, getting the numbers up. Productivity was driven by the fear of small numbers. Many university MBA programs grew up during these years around the concept of managing the numbers—the big numbers; tax law for decades has reflected the value American society places on big number management.

But times have changed, and the business world is looking inward. In recent decades, the total quality management movement has taken hold of the imaginations of a great many American businesses of all types and sizes, and great strides have been made in many companies to make a transition from old command and control environments to new more collegial ones. Recent changes to the Malcolm Baldrige Quality Award's categories reflect what's happening: In the 1993 guidelines, for the first time, the human resources development area includes an employee development and employee satisfaction category, a corporate citizenship category, and a category that focuses on connection with invention, innovation, and creativity. All of these new items reflect a looking inward requirement, suggesting that total organizational quality needs not just big numbers but also demands that organizations pay attention to people's capacity for individual contribution to a greater good.

Process and system improvement can seem like very fuzzy terms, and posters, slogans, and company songs won't make it happen. Deming says workers must "create constancy of purpose"—that is, it doesn't magically appear. Having a vision of continuously improving planning, operations, production, and service is a good place to start, but the vision must be followed by implementation through finding and fixing problems at the most basic levels throughout the business and in the work of every single worker from the new-hire hourly worker to the CEO.

Real quality improvement has been such a long time coming because it is hard work at a close personal level, it can be tedious and expensive, and it requires that individuals give up some of their personal investment in their way of doing things to the shared common good. The comfortable security of a tight job description, a union contract, a clear reporting chain and a well-defined box on the organization chart are structures we have come to expect and enjoy at work. We don't feel very good when these familiar and secure artifacts of working life are challenged and modified; we are uncomfortable when continuous improvement means that business at every level and in every activity changes from the way we've gotten used to functioning. We find it hard to accept new measurement ideas and standards. We find it hard to believe that the man who works on the loading dock can creatively design continuous improvements to his work that equal the value of continuous improvements made by the woman who spends her day in the executive suite.

A COMMUNITY OF BELIEVERS

Sociologists, psychologists, politicians, and organization development specialists alike talk of the need for a new sense of community in the American workplace. The term "commitment" has entered the mainstream of our language whenever we speak of the effectiveness of group endeavor. In our neighborhoods, families, town halls, and workplaces we search for a commitment to community that transcends the commitment to self. But like continuous improvement, commitment and viable community don't happen just because we want them to happen. This, too, takes a lot of hard work at very "small" levels and with a very personal focus. The basic American values of sharing, fairness, responsibility, reasonableness, individual achievement, and equal opportunity are being challenged by the call to fit one's specialized, educated, experienced self into a more community-minded mold.

In a macro-view, the economics of the right-sizing of American corporations require that companies redefine growth from bigness to smallness, to a working environment that encourages individuals to compete against themselves in the search for excellence and quality, and to one that translates a traditional protective, rigid, and rugged individualism into a sharing, open, and flexible community of peers.

RE-ENGINEERING HUMAN RESOURCES

The re-engineering of a company's financial and capital bases, its strategic planning, operational, and budgeting processes, and its departments' functional relationships needs to expand into a re-engineering of the concepts and structures upon which its human resources are developed. Continuous improvement and joy in working are seldom-seen results of current re-engineering attempts. Indeed, the time seems right for new ways of thinking about the development of human resources that are more in tune with the realities of smaller worker enrollments, greater management spans of control, "pushed down" responsibilities, smaller and more specialized product and service outputs. Even our government bureaucracy wants to "re-invent" itself.

There is an urgent wake-up call for corporate America to march with these different drummers of change. Legions of unemployed managers, lack of growth in middle-income jobs, millions of American adults who are functionally illiterate, sick cities, swelling numbers of homeless persons, the working poor as a political force—all are signs that our value system for living and working is under fire and that our measurements need to be redefined. Workplace leadership is critical if we are to come to grips with any of these manifestations of breakdown in the economic drivers of our society.

New leadership, however, must be different from old style command and control leadership. "The Boss" is a dying breed and deserves the finality of a well-attended funeral. Leaders today, at minimum, must be flexible, facilitative, multi-skilled, and collegial. This is a far cry from the recent past where the brilliant engineer, attorney, or accountant climbed the corporate ladder to the top. Vertical metaphors no longer seem to work; today's workplace is more like a spider web or bubbling stew.

In today's workplace, leaders must be found everywhere. Vision and competency must be seen as resident in each person on the payroll. Training and education must be directed at helping each person be all they can be. Those responsible for training must revolutionize the workplace to make it a learning place. This is the challenge and opportunity of peer training—each person on the job teaching and learning from the other.

Those responsible for this critical process of growth and foundation of organizational strength initially will probably be trainers and managers or supervisors. Ultimately, it is their job to help all employees become better teachers and learners through skill development, attitude changes, and additions to their knowledge bases. This book is a tribute to the power of one person at work—a single employee with enormous capacity for contribution. It is addressed especially to the legions of responsible souls who are called upon in these changing times to be trainers regardless of your job title or type of organization.

The analysis tools in this chapter are focused entirely on analysis of systems and structures that can support such a re-engineering of human resources. Systems and structures addressed here include:

- planning and goal-setting, including quality goals and business objectives;
- the personnel management system including training, motivation, rewards, and opportunity within a diverse workforce;
- physical plant and learning spaces;
- information, graphics, and clerical support;
- management leadership; and
- learning organization requirements.

CHAPTER **1**

OVERVIEW OF PLANNING AND GOAL-SETTING: QUALITY GOALS

One of the facts of organizational life these days seems to be that work processes, service deliverables, and products are getting scrutinized for their effectiveness in the name of "quality." If you're not planning to go to a Crosby or Juran seminar or trying for the Baldrige Award or ISO 9000 certification, at least you are probably using some of the quality criteria made popular by these sources.

Organizations throughout the United States are involved at some level in quality assessment and implementation. The quality movement sets up peer training very nicely, and those who would become involved in any kind of one-to-one training can find within "total quality management" many ideas and techniques that support in-house, person-to-person training development, and just-in-time training delivery.

Quality goal-setting must be done at many levels—systemic, cognitive, and emotional, to name just a few options. At the emotional level, beliefs are being challenged and value systems about work and working are being changed; at the cognitive level, new procedures, technologies, and concepts are being learned and practiced; and at the systemic level, new ways of measuring cost and effectiveness are being instituted, and new communications tools and practices are being tried. Individuals are being empowered and being made responsible and accountable for more and more business processes that directly affect profit and company viability.

Total quality management demands a structure and a strategy for capitalizing on this "individual worth" foundation of organizational reinvention if the employee empowerment movement can be expected to work. The era of simple work and simple workers, of huge production runs and plenty of customers willing to wait for them, and of paternalistic lifetime employment security is over.

7

Those reflections of an earlier industrialized, brawny America need to evolve into an image of work that reflects the highly networked character of information and work tasks, the complexity, proximity, and impatience of global markets, and, in short, a brainier and more creative workforce. America's historic value of the "can do" individualist will stand us in good stead as we wrestle and grapple with the tough adversaries that accompany cultural change in the workplace.

Some of the key quality principles that must be reexamined from this individualistic perspective are:

- **Quality is a company-wide commitment.** This means that no one is excluded. Job titles, salary step, size of office, longevity, and other trappings of importance must be overlooked when quality leaders seek commitment from other employees. All employees must adopt a belief that each other employee is knowledgeable about his or her job and that each other employee can become even more valuable to the total organization through learning. Commitment at the personal level means that all persons are equally valued for who they are and who they can become. This is tough going in traditional top-down, hierarchical, command- and control-organizations.

- **Quality implementation requires strong leadership.** Leadership here is contrasted with management, supervision, or being in charge. Leadership is more than these, and is necessary if quality work is to follow quality posturing and "sloganeering." Writing the vision statement is the easy part—making it work is where leadership happens. Work systems and support structures often require radical revision in order for quality to be built into an organization, and this demands knowledgeable, sensitive, flexible, patient, and unswerving leadership. It is tempting, during implementation of total quality management, for many upper level managers to say "Let the workers handle it from now on," essentially abdicating their leadership roles. Individuals who are risking their jobs and their reputations by being open to change must have leaders guiding and continuously supporting them.

- **Quality requires appropriate measurements.** One of the hardest exercises in the quality quest is to identify and define the right measures. All people at work are guided by measures—numbers that motivate and reward their actions. Often, as organizations search for quality in processes, products, and services, the current numbers are deemed to be inadequate or irrelevant. Tossing out old numbers often gets people very upset, and great care must be taken during the pursuit of appropriate measures to include in the decision-making all of the individuals whose livelihood depends on the numbers.

- **Quality means that problems are your friends.** A rigorous "find and fix" cycle must be incorporated into everyone's thinking and practice in order for continuous improvement to happen. Workers need to adopt an attitude of continuous self-improvement, passionate pride in their own ever-better work output, and become restless searchers and learners for a better way to do everything about their jobs. In the traditional business as usual mentality, workers try to hide their mistakes, ''look out for #1,'' and politick around problems. In the mindset that quality requires, problems, errors, failures, and bad decisions become your friends—targets for focused assault of the best thinking that individuals and problem solving teams can muster.

• **Quality means that employees, board members, stockholders, suppliers, and customers are all in it together.** Implementation of a total quality system requires a structure and strategy throughout the company that directly links all of the internal and external parts of the company together under the same vision and towards the same goals. In old style business dealings, a great deal of ''us versus them'' happens; the new world of quality sees ''all of us in this together.'' In the new way of doing business, individuals matter because each constituent of a company is valued for his or her potentially unique or specialized contribution to the company's success. Above all, managers must manage these often new structures and strategies.

Setting goals for quality products, processes, and services should be done within the context of these important, broad quality principles.

QUALITY GOALS

Individual Quality Climate Assessment

Problem: The fundamental problem in setting realistic quality goals is to be sure that every individual employee embraces quality at a personal level. That is, quality should not be seen as "something the managers do" or "something in which I have no training" or "problems for which I have no resources." Quality goal setting must be seen as everyone's Job #1.

The first task is employee buy-in to the idea that management wants everyone to be involved in quality improvement and will support everyone's involvement, even when individuals make mistakes in their judgment or implementation actions. A host of climate indicators require individual analysis—those at the emotional level, the cognitive level, and at the systemic level.

Plan of Action: In order to level the playing field regarding employees' perceptions about the climate for quality, management must take the lead to spell out the possibilities in a non-threatening way. Great care at the goal setting stage must be taken to prod employees to think broadly and express themselves honestly. Managers must find ways to encourage each person on the payroll to speak up in the name of quality and to ensure that each will have a chance to be heard.

The objective in climate assessment is to achieve input from each employee at emotional, cognitive, and systemic levels. Savvy managers will figure out what kinds of devices—team meetings, vertical conferences, golf or tennis games, dinners out, e-mail, quality circles, focus groups, individual interviews, questionnaires, weekend retreats, simulations, management by walking around—turn on the communications juices among employees, and will use a variety of assessment devices to gather information. Individual quality climate assessment should not be a one-shot deal.

As management's plan of climate assessment begins its implementation phase, it should become readily apparent that the rule of "equal and all" applies. That is, all employees have equal access to those asking questions and evaluating results, and equal opportunity for contribution; all persons' opinions and suggestions are valued equally. The same questions should be asked of all persons.

Worksheets on the following pages provide some guidance.

Examples: The following examples illustrate quality climate assessment at three levels: emotional, cognitive, and systemic. Note that at each level, the individual's contribution to the assessment is paramount.

Emotional Level. The Families and Work Institute, a New York-based research and advocacy group sponsored by a group of large corporations and foundations, recently completed a survey of approximately 3,000 hourly and salaried workers to find out "what workers want" from working in this era of change and turmoil in the workplace. The assumptions of the study were that layoffs and corporate restructuring, increasing workplace diversity, and decline in real pay were affecting workers at an emotional level.

The study found that American workers:

1. measure their success through personal satisfaction on the job,
2. want respect from supervisors and peers,
3. value management and supervisory support,
4. care about how work affects their family,
5. expect open communications throughout the workplace, and
6. value autonomy on the job.[1]

This is a vastly different profile of worker values than we have seen when our parents came into the workforce a generation ago—a time then of employer loyalty, higher pay, job security, and getting ahead. Setting quality goals based on this kind of assessment at an emotional level will be a very different kind of exercise than we might have originally expected; managers seeking an accurate reading of employee job satisfaction indicators must ask questions that address workers' feelings, values, and attitudes. Quality goals must include a correct emotional foundation.

Another example of an assessment technique at the emotional level is that used by US Secretary of Labor, Robert B. Reich. In an article in *The Washington Post*, "A 'We' Company," Secretary Reich tells how he likes to visit a company's "front lines" and ask workers a few simple questions about the company—questions like, 'how do you get this to work?' or 'who's in charge around here?' He says that front line workers will either talk mostly in terms of "they" and "them," or of "we" and "us." His simple "pronoun test," he believes, gives him some immediate and important information about the emotional base of a company and its climate for becoming a high performance workplace.[2] At the emotional level, companies must come to grips with a new definition and practice of management control and trust within employment contracts. Driving fear out of the workplace, a key quality goal articulated by W. Edwards Deming, is hard work and must begin at the emotional level with valid employee assessments. Management by wandering around asking a few key questions is another way to conduct such an assessment.

Cognitive Level: Assessments at the cognitive level are conducted to find out what employees need to know in order to do things differently and to improve. In the quality arena, some of these knowledge-based items might be: new policies, new procedures, new measurement techniques, new reporting relationships, use of new tools, etc. Organizations seeking to define quality goals must first find out, at the individual employee level, exactly what people need to know.

Quality programs are doomed to failure if trainers assume that everyone needs to know the same things and if training is presented on too broad a scale. Training will fail the "transfer" test if trainers fall into the trap of doing "the information dump" of all the latest and greatest quality concepts, list of the gurus' key points, and the way to draw all of the important quality charts.

Richard Y. Chang, an examiner for the Malcolm Baldrige National Quality Award and President/CEO of a management consulting company in California that bears his name, reported at the 1993 National Conference of the American Society for Training and Development (ASTD) in Atlanta that of 500 American manufacturing and service companies recently surveyed, only one-third said they have experienced significant impact from their quality improvement effort, and of 100 British firms surveyed, only one-fifth believed they had achieved tangible results.[3] Results such as these suggest, among other things, that faulty assessments at the cognitive level might have been done prior to training. Teaching everybody everything is a waste of time and money, and it often has the effect of squelching people's enthusiasm or sending them the message that what they already know as individuals doesn't really count.

Sometimes, people don't know what they don't know—that is, a case can be made for managers and trainers to suggest possibilities and options for further study, and to lead employees into exploration of pathways for self-improvement. For example, if someone has never heard of a Pareto Diagram, obviously that person doesn't know he or she needs to know how to use one.

In a project sponsored by the US Department of Education's Office of Vocational and Adult Education (OVAE), The Greenville Technical College, Greenville, SC developed an instructional guide on introductory statistical process control (SPC) for use in post-high school quality courses and for use in industrial settings. This particular SPC Guide is part of the overall Project T.E.A.M. (Technical Education Advancement Modules).

The Guide contains succinct presentations of most of the basic SPC cognitive elements—concepts and definitions one might need to know in order to use statistics in process control. For example, three classes of SPC use are described: 1) using SPC to adjust a machine or process, 2) using SPC to improve a process, and 3) using SPC as a way to run a company.[4]

Employees who use SPC only to adjust the machine they work on might not know that a refinement to the way they use SPC might be exactly the thing that the operations manager needs in order to run the entire operation. Use of such a manual might be helpful in sparking employees' imaginations about what they as individuals could benefit from the most, and can help employees see that what they already know can be built upon for exponentially improved processes, not only within their own jobs but also within the larger company. The wise trainer or manager will use some kind of "cue card" to prompt employees' creative self-assessments, in the cognitive area especially.

Systemic Level: In the assessment of systemic problems, as in the cognitive level, it is tempting to paint with too broad a brush and fall into the trap of talking to everyone yet talking to no one in particular. The following example shows how individual quality climate assessment at the systemic level was done in an organization where one would least expect such effort.

The Department of the Navy's Naval Publications and Forms Center (NPFC) in Philadelphia, PA recently embarked on a massive, systemic quality improvement effort aimed at operations at the Center. Significant improvements were made in the areas of customer satisfaction, communications, personnel, and productivity. One of the elements of assessment and quality goal setting that made it all happen was employees' willingness to suggest changes in the civil service performance appraisal system and the production quota incentive awards program, both "sacred cows" in the Navy scheme of things. Although constrained by law and the inability to throw out these systems, the quality improvement effort resulted in a re-write of the employee performance standards, including writing into the standards a measure of customer satisfaction at the individual employee level.

Managers report that people are listening to each other and freely making recommendations for improvements in work processes. Cultural change at NPFC is palpable, and they say it feels good.[5] The systemic level assessment worked, in part, because individuals knew how the system should have worked to make it better for them as they did their jobs. Individuals are willing to be involved with standards, incentives, and rewards that matter to them personally.

WORKSHEET 1-1

QUALITY CLIMATE PERSONAL ASSESSMENT SURVEY

Note to the participant: This quality climate survey will help us determine where our priorities should be in terms of organizational re-design for continuous improvement in our products and services. The composite results of these personal surveys will be shared with all employees and will be the topic of an open discussion as soon as they have been tallied and distributed. Thank you for your thoughtful and honest responses.

Please return your completed survey by _____ to _____ .
Since results will be compiled for our open discussion session, you might want to make a copy of your completed survey for your own records.

| name of respondent | | | date | | | |

	disagree				agree	
		1	2		3	4

Instructions:
Circle the number that best indicates your personal assessment of each item. Items 1-5 represent the emotional level, items 6-10 represent the cognitive level, and items 11-15 represent the systemic level of the climate for quality.

1. My manager/supervisor trusts me.	1	2	3	4
2. My manager/supervisor wants to hear what I have to say.	1	2	3	4
3. Top management is willing to accept change.	1	2	3	4
4. Top management is more interested in "good numbers" than in productive people.	1	2	3	4
5. Competition is valued more than collaboration.	1	2	3	4
6. My organization's rate of error/re-work/scrap/failure/defect is higher than that of other organizations.	1	2	3	4
7. I need to know how to use statistical analysis tools to improve my work.	1	2	3	4
8. I know when a problem occurs in a process or product.	1	2	3	4
9. I know the causes of problems.	1	2	3	4
10. I know how to fix the problems I see.	1	2	3	4
11. Quality is really some other organization's job.	1	2	3	4
12. Communication is open around this company.	1	2	3	4
13. Promotions, assignments, and terminations are fair around this company.	1	2	3	4
14. The right things are measured around this company	1	2	3	4
15. Corporate politics gets in the way of good decision-making.	1	2	3	4

WORKSHEET 1 - 2

"HOW DO YOU DO YOUR JOB?" (OR, THE PRONOUN TEST)

Instructions:

Use this form to record tally marks. The purpose of the exercise is for a facilitator (someone from human resources staff, a supervisor, or an outside consultant) to interview a wide variety of employees about "the way work is done in this company," recording not only the substance of the employee's answer but, more importantly, the choice of pronouns used in dialogue with the facilitator. Be sure to spend an equal amount of time with each person questioned, so that results are valid and not affected by additional time for "drawing out" or "clamming up." Use the same interview techniques and dialogue facilitation techniques with each person interviewed.

Tell employees that you are doing interviews with a wide variety of employees over the next few days to find out how they really do their jobs. Do not tell them that you are analyzing their speech patterns for "correct" use of pronouns.

Ask the same questions of each person. Add other questions of interest to your particular company. Record a tally mark in the appropriate column, either the negative "they and them" indicating someone else higher up is in control, or the positive "we and us" indicating that employees on the front lines are in control. Make brief notes as you see fit about the substance of the employee's answer.

Use this exercise to collect information. Make this tally sheet a frequency count by making a tic mark each time a person's response clearly fits into either column, that is, an individual respondent can have many tic marks or very few. Save the feedback for a brainstorming session the following week.

	they and them	*we and us*
1. Who verifies the accuracy of your results?		
2. Who monitors time you allocate to your various work tasks?		
3. Who accounts for resource costs in the work you do?		
etc.		

WORKSHEET 1 - 3

COST OF QUALITY FACTORS

Note to the supervisor or team leader: This questionnaire is for you to do yourself. It will help you to identify and define the specific places to look for the factors that affect the cost of quality in your operation. In doing this, you must remember that errors can be your friends and you must be relentless in searching for and finding them so that focused organizational resources can be applied to them to fix them.

Depending on the kind of organization you have, look for these kinds of errors: scrap, defects, re-work, failure, downtime, fault, returns, rejections, missed deadlines, inaccurate projections, irate customers, cancellations, uninformed decisions, rumors, etc. Be willing to take a hard look at each problem area in your business; then, start fresh with new standards and procedures for fixing each one.

Here are some questions to ask yourself; take the time to write down your responses:

In my organization/project:

1. What are the most frequent errors?

2. What are the apparent causes of each of these errors?

3. Who is responsible for each cause?

4. Am I directly responsible for any of these errors? Which ones?

5. What is the effect of each error? That is, how do I know that an error exists?

6. How does each error affect specific other people? Who are these people and what is the effect?

7. Who are or can be my allies in fixing this error? When can I meet with them?

8. Who is the best person to fix each error?

9. What are the organizational costs for fixing each error?

10. What are the estimated dollar costs for fixing each error?

11. If I could solve just two of these errors, which ones should I choose?
    (1)
    (2)

12. This is the priority listing of all other errors:
    (3)
    (4)
    (5)
    ( ) etc.

FACE THE FACTS GROUP PROFILE

Note to the Supervisor/Team Leader: One of the obstacles in change management is the individual's sense of psychological inertia, or general preference for the status quo. The concept of a hierarchy of human needs articulated by A.H. Maslow has pervaded organizational and industrial psychology for several decades.[6] Followers of Maslow were particularly fond of structuring workplaces to ensure worker safety, both physically and psychologically, of creating work flows and support systems that helped individuals feel that they belonged to a group or a company, and of encouraging and rewarding individuals' contributions to work in order to foster self-esteem within persons at work. Maslow's model seems appropriate for organizations that are built upon internal competition between people and that reward high individual success and achievement.

One of the problems today is that as familiar structures and relationships change at work, the notions of safety, belonging, and self-esteem are all challenged. With empowerment, business decision-making at the front lines, levels of influence disappearing, profit sharing, and team work replacing hierarchical control, a new collaboration model is replacing the competition model. During times of change from one way of doing business to the other, individuals can be expected to have a hard time overcoming their psychological inertia which typically works to preserve the old order. Until individuals overcome their fears about their personal roles in the change, their new responsibilities and authority, and the potentially new consequences of their actions, they will be largely unable to get on with behaving in a collaborative way.

Wise leaders will take the time to encourage individuals caught in change to face their fears in open and honest ways. Caring leaders will demonstrate that they can be trusted to hear employees' concerns. One exercise that can help everyone openly get their feelings out on the table in front of everyone else is this FACE THE FACTS exercise. Use this group exercise with employees who are going through organizational change and who want to understand the current climate for quality.

Instructions:
Do this exercise using a white board or flipchart to focus respondents' attention and to record their responses. This exercise can be somewhat confrontational because it is so public. The leader, therefore, must take care to be supportive of all responders and to value each response.

Develop a list of ideas or assumptions about work that represent the current or old way of doing things. Write this list on the board or paper so that all in the group can see it. Lead the group through a voting exercise by show of hands, and create a group profile.

Don't spend too much time on each question. The idea is to encourage a gut-level, honest response from each person so that you get a good assessment of attitudes. Making it a public exercise resulting in a group profile will help each person see that there is a range of attitudes among the group members. This exercise, although an expression of individual attitudes, provides a general profile of the group.

FACE THE FACTS GROUP PROFILE

Voting is done by raising hands. Read each item, ask for a show of hands on each, and record the vote by a tic mark in the appropriate column. Make up your own list of "facts" about the organization. Begin with these items:

	I disagree	I'm neutral	I agree
1. More is better.			
2. Change is chaotic.			
3. Details guarantee security.			
4. The boss is always right.			
5. Procedures are sacred.			
6. Customers are always right.			
7. Promotion is the reward for success.			
8. If it's in writing, it's true.			
9. Task always wins over process.			
10. Feedback is valued.			

11.

12.

13.

14.

15.

P = O/I
(PRODUCTIVITY EQUALS OUTPUT DIVIDED BY INPUT)

Note to Supervisor/Team Leader: Use this overhead transparency master to focus a group's attention on the simple productivity formula. Use a simple math calculation to show how the result increases when the input denominator is reduced (for example, 4/4 is greater than 4/8). Lead a brainstorming session focusing on the reduction of the input denominator as a way of helping employees figure out the areas in which they can be directly involved in decreasing the costs of doing business, thereby making improvements that can lead to quality in processes or products.

Suggest that they begin by assessing waste in these areas. Use examples from your own business products, systems, and organizations.

procedures	*policies*	*work flow*	*products/services*
timeliness	sufficiency	efficiency	defects
accuracy	reliability	inclusivity	fit for use
clarity	validity	effectiveness	scheduling
ease of use	necessity	logic	inventory
completeness	fairness	orderliness	shipping

$$\text{PRODUCTIVITY} = \frac{\text{OUTPUT}}{\text{INPUT}}$$

WORKSHEET 1 - 6

NITS AND LICE

Instructions:

Use this worksheet in a team meeting or group session as a "cue card" to start your analytical juices flowing. Use this list of beginnings of sentences to get a group discussion going about what really gets under your skin about things around your organization. This is like the old school exercise of "fill in the blank." Take notes if you want to see how your "nits and lice" compare with those of your colleagues. One member of the group should read the items to get folks thinking. Answers can be rapid and discussion free-flowing and noisy. The objective is to "get it all out"—and to realize that often what "bugs" people can be the prescription for real cleansing and healing. Use the energy generated by this exercise to propel the group or specific individuals into healthy change.

1. The most unrealistic goal around here is _____ .

2. The budget for _____ is outrageous.

3. She should never be responsible for _____ .

4. He should never be responsible for _____ .

5. Her behavior regarding _____ was totally inappropriate.

6. His behavior regarding _____ was totally inappropriate.

7. The worst thing about politics around here is _____ .

8. I'd really like the whole story about _____ .

9. The most unreasonable customer we have is _____ .

10. The biggest waste of time is _____ .

WORKSHEET 1 - 7

KILLER COMMENTS

Note to Supervisor/Facilitator: This list of killer comments should remind you that at times of conflict, change, and learning, very often you'll hear folks make what seem to be obstructive comments. What you need to realize is that some of these killer comments are not really meant to sabotage, but are actually a reaction to a moment of insecurity at the beginning of a new awareness. Your task as a leader is to not necessarily fight back and counter the killer word or phrase, but to use it as a red flag signalling a potential breakthrough in understanding on the part of the individual making the comment. Read this list before you go into a new team meeting or group session. This review can help you become sensitive to the individual's locus within the spectrum of readiness for change.

KILLER COMMENTS

You've gotta be kidding!
That's not my job.
There's no money for that.
Much too political.
Impractical.
Too elementary.
A waste of time.
Yes, but . . .
No way.
Too fast.
Too slow.
Too structured.
Too loose.

QUALITY GOALS

Baldrige Award Categories

Problem: Companies can be guided by the Malcolm Baldrige National Quality Award criteria in their quality goal setting. However, when it comes to setting the stage for empowered and motivated workers to truly contribute their best, trainers and managers must think twice about the nature of people at work. Program designers and leaders must be careful not to create such a flurry of new projects, procedures, courses, and activities that objectives, transfer of concepts and skills, and results get lost in the shuffle of change for change's sake. It's easy to get caught up in the group approach of "get everybody on board at once" and try to do too much too fast. It's easy to be enticed by the public relations rewards of the prize, and go for maximum visibility for all employees.

Plan of Action: The Baldrige award criteria are in fact a useful guide for organizations bent upon change. For example, the 1994 categories are:

- Leadership
- Information and Analysis
- Strategic Quality Planning
- Human Resource Development and Management
- Management of Process Quality
- Quality and Operational Results
- Customer Focus and Satisfaction.

The secret in using these categories as a guide is to define an approach to each category that enhances the role of the individual. This should have the effect of narrowing the focus of quality goals in each category, and should head off the great pull towards doing too much too fast.

Baldrige categories change slightly from year to year, so anyone planning to use them as a guide to quality goal setting and ultimately to total quality management should send for the current guidelines. These are available either from the Department of Commerce who manages the award, or from the American Society for Quality Control who administers the award program. These addresses are:

United States Department of Commerce
Technology Administration

National Institute of Standards and Technology
Route 270 and Quince Orchard Road
Administration Building Room A537
Gaithersburg, MD 20899

American Society for Quality Control
P.O. Box 3005
Milwaukee, WI 53201-3005

Examples: An example of this change in award criteria is a new emphasis in category 4.0 on "effectiveness indicators" (1994 and 1993 criteria) rather than only on "extent indicators" (1992 criteria). The trend in the newer guidelines is to ask "why?" rather than simply "how much?" While seemingly a small thing, this distinction is indeed a profound reflection of dramatic change in the standards for success in the human resources area. It used to be that training's success was measured in terms of how many person-hours of training each employee received, how many hours of training an instructor delivered per month, or how many persons per class per week came through the training center. Asking "effectiveness" questions is totally different from asking these old "how many and how much" kinds of questions. Accounting and accountability for effectiveness measures is different from simple frequency counts of hours or bodies. Design of programs for human resources development for "effectiveness" is vastly different from design of programs that simply count numbers.

Another clue to change is apparent in the new title of category 4.0 of the list of award categories. In the 1992 guidelines, category 4.0 is "Human Resource Utilization." In 1994 and 1993, it is "Human Resource Development and Management." This subtle difference also reflects a larger issue in quality goal setting for human resources, and this is the distinction between the thinking that views human resources as resources to be "used up" as capital or supplies are used up, versus the newer thinking that recognizes the value of individual persons at work and recognizes the need for nurture and development of these human beings. The notion of resource "utilization" is quite different from the idea of management of developing persons.

Other examples of a more individualistic approach to defining value and quality in human resources are evident in other areas of strengthening in the 1994 and 1993 award criteria. These are: inclusion of a provision for linkages between processes and results that ultimately define "learning cycles." A Deming-like definition of stages in learning cycles is spelled out as a planning stage, a stage for execution of plans, a stage of assessment of progress, and a final revision stage. (Deming's rule of thumb is "plan, do, check, and act;" Shewhart's Cycle, before Deming, was "plan, do, study, and action" with "customer satisfaction" at the center.) The term "alignment" is scattered throughout the Baldrige Award Guidelines, emphasizing the focus of learning cycles and continuous improvement at all levels and in all parts of a company. Learning, of course, begins in individual persons; any organizational learning that results is a sum of the individual learnings upon which that organization is structured.

1992 guidelines contained a category titled, "Quality of Products and Services;" in the 1994 and 1993 guidelines, this category was changed to "Management of Process Quality." These words reflect a major change in criterion and suggest a stronger case for building quality into an organization instead of inspecting it out at the end. Statistical quality control (SQC) has finally been institutionalized in the guidelines as statistical process control (SPC). This, too, points toward a more personalized, dynamic, and interactive measurement system for operations of all sorts within organizations. A new section on employee well-being and satisfaction suggests a connection between employee well-being in the broadest sense and customer satisfaction. In the later guidelines, there are requirements for stronger relationships between customer requirements and the requirements spelled out for operational performance. The new guidelines present a tighter system for valuing all of the human elements that must work together for a company to achieve quality in all that they do.

Finally, the 1994 and 1993 guidelines encourage invention, innovation, and creativity in all aspects of company decisions throughout the workplace. How decisions are made, how problems are approached and solved, and how work is organized are all scrutinized under the creativity filter in the later guidelines. Imaginative approaches to developing and delivering product are seen as value-adders for customers. "Full participation and personal and organizational growth" are written into the 1994 guidelines.

PUBLIC LAW 100 - 107, THE MALCOLM BALDRIGE NATIONAL QUALITY IMPROVEMENT ACT OF 1987

Background of The Malcolm Baldrige National Quality Award. The award was created by Public Law 100 - 107, signed into law on August 20, 1987. It is based on the findings and purposes spelled out in this piece of legislation. The award is named for Malcolm Baldrige who served as Secretary of Commerce of the United States of America from 1981 to 1987.

The following sections from P.L. 100 - 107 provide the framework for much of the challenge in human resources development:

". . . American business and industry are beginning to understand that poor quality costs companies as much as 20 percent of sales revenues nationally and that improved quality of goods and services goes hand in hand with improved productivity, lower costs, and increased profitability. . . .

. . . improved management understanding of the factory floor, worker involvement in quality, and greater emphasis on statistical process control can lead to dramatic improvements in the cost and quality of manufactured products. . . .

. . . in order to be successful, quality improvement programs must be management-led and customer-oriented, and this may require fundamental changes in the way companies and agencies do business. . . .

. . . the concept of quality improvement is directly applicable to small companies as well as large, to service industries as well as manufacturing, and to the public sector as well as private enterprise. . . .

. . . and, that the award guidelines can be used by business, industrial, governmental, and other organizations in evaluating their own quality improvement efforts. . . ."[7]

WORKSHEET 1 - 9

BALDRIGE AWARD CATEGORY 4.3, EMPLOYEE EDUCATION AND TRAINING

Notes on Employee Education and Training: Point (a) of the award criteria in the Employee Education and Training section tells companies that they will be rated on how the company determines needs for the types and the amounts of "quality and related education and training" for all employees, taking into account their differing needs.

At face value, this seems like a reasonable and clear criterion. Alas, however, many competitors for the Baldrige have mis-read this to mean 'what courses do we have to send employees away to in order for the whole company to be covered with everything we need to know about quality?' Many companies have spent enormous amounts of time and money on training for everyone on everything about quality, and, unfortunately missed the point of the criterion for training needs assessment. The Wallace Company, 1990 winner of the Baldrige Award in the small business category, is illustrative. A company of just 280 persons, Wallace spent on average $235,000 per year for three years on quality training, and trained every employee.[8] In spite of enormous increases in profit, and of other successes, The Wallace Company went out of business within two years of having won the Baldrige. One of the reasons might have been a mis-interpretation of needs assessment that used a broadscale approach instead of an individual approach to training needs.

Early Baldrige guidelines (1988, 1989, 1990) have been improved upon in recent years with notes and explanations in the education and training areas. In 1993, the guidelines were changed to include a specific note that ". . . delivery may occur inside or outside the company and may involve classroom or on-the-job delivery." The 1994 guidelines repeat this and include the phrase "structured on-the-job training." Future guidelines in the human resources development area, and specifically in the education and training area, can be expected to continue to focus on more narrowly defined approaches to training needs assessment because more careful definition of individual need will result in savings in the cost of quality at this upfront process in the design phase of training. More narrowly focused individual needs assessment techniques will build quality into training at the earliest stages, and therefore form a quality foundation for the rest of the design process. This kind of needs assessment is process improvement at its best.

The corporate bias in training delivery for years has been the classroom because of its seemingly cost-effective presentation accounting of one instructor per twenty students and its administrative convenience. Unfortunately for the challenge of addressing student needs, this model has seldom served adult students well, and has caused many organizations to spend resources poorly. When it comes to behavior change or transfer of new skills, the classroom delivery of training falls short. The potential for failure in the classroom model is further compounded when the instructor chooses a lecture method of delivery, and the classroom is located miles away from the student's job. These elements of distance from a person's real work only make training transfer more unlikely; and, the more these elements are added together, the more quality training is likely to be seen as an enormous expense with questionable payoff.

BALDRIGE AWARD CATEGORY 4.3,
EMPLOYEE EDUCATION AND TRAINING

Obviously some changes must be made in helping people to see that there are other options besides classroom training. The new 1994 Baldrige guidelines have taken a step in this direction by providing readers with a note to section 4.3 on Employee Education and Training. This note says, in part, that "Quality and related education and training address the knowledge and skills employees need to meet their objectives as part of the company's quality and operational performance improvement plans"—the emphasis is on "their objectives."

The note goes on to spell out some of the kinds of education and training that are possible. Use this list to get your creativity going regarding who needs what kind of training:

- quality awareness
- leadership
- project management
- communications
- teamwork
- problem solving
- interpreting and using data
- meeting customer requirements
- process analysis
- process simplification
- waste reduction
- cycle time reduction
- error-proofing
- job enrichment skills
- basic skills such as reading, writing, language, arithmetic, and basic mathematics that are needed to meet quality and operational performance improvement objectives
- other training that affects employee effectiveness, efficiency, and safety.

Nowhere in the guidelines does it say that everyone must be sent away to a high cost quality program for a week or a month. Managers and trainers must be careful to not mis-read the intent of the guidelines, and see, instead of megadoses of classroom training, the wonderful possibilities and challenges of meeting the training needs of each employee in so specialized a way that employee effectiveness, efficiency, and performance are enhanced.

QUALITY GOALS

ISO 9000

Problem: ISO 9000 and its sub-titles (9001, 9002, 9003, 9004, etc.) is a set of quality standards established by the International Organization for Standardization, Geneva, Switzerland. Following the standards results in official certification by registered and approved certification agencies. Certification is expected to be required by all companies doing business in Europe by the year 1997.[9] Major U.S. companies who are ISO 9000 certified are expected to also require their suppliers to be ISO 9000 certified. For companies seeking global markets, ISO 9000 will soon become a daily part of their vocabulary. In the United Kingdom alone, there are more than 20,000 companies who are already ISO 9000 registered.[10] *Quality Digest* predicts that more than 500,000 companies in North America will seek certification "in the short term."[11]

The certification process is rigorous, time-consuming, and expensive. A recent report in the American Management Association's *Small Business Reports*[12] estimates that about 40 percent of companies who try for certification fail their first audit, that the audit process can take up to 18 months, and that third-party registrar and consultant fees can easily top $40,000. The major problem causing difficulty and resulting in lack of certification is that the procedures for doing quality work that have been described by companies themselves in the required certification documentation are not being followed by employees. When inspectors and auditors observe how work is actually done, the words in the quality manual don't match the reality of workers performing work. Even more than the Baldrige Award Criteria, ISO 9000 standards and the certification process point to the necessity for every worker to be the best that he or she is capable of being. ISO 9000 audits require that auditors certify quality in work processes by matching up the good words in the documentation with *individual* performance. If there is a mismatch, the company fails the audit. The onus is on individuals on the job. Companies generally show a preference for preparing for certification themselves, as opposed to hiring full time consultants to "take them through the paces." Certification often happens more quickly when consultant use is kept to a minimum and the full employee base is building quality in from the bottom up. Clearly, individuals whose companies are seeking registration under ISO 9000 must be fully informed, appropriately skilled in the tasks of the job, disciplined in the standards of the tasks that they do, and able to solve problems within the context of the other quality-based procedures detailed in the various documentation manuals. The setting of the ISO 9000 certification search is made for peer training.

Some proponents of the process, arduous though it is, welcome the discipline as a return to the comfort of the "good old days" prior to the 1980s rush to quality circles and self-directed work teams. Organizations that are used to procedure-driven ways of doing business seem to like the documentation aspects and internal focus of ISO 9000.

Plan of Action: Guidelines for preparing for registration/certification are available from the American National Standards Institute, New York, and the Registrar Accreditation Board, Milwaukee, Wisconsin.

Basically, the process toward certification involves several major phases:

- Choosing a third-party registrar from among those certified to conduct the audit,
- Preparing the quality documentation manuals and lists of procedures,
- Reviewing documentation and planning efforts with the registrar,
- Participating in the on-site audit,
- Participating in periodic (every 6 months) follow-up compliance visits, and
- Seeking a renewal audit every 2 - 3 years.

In all of these processes, employees at every level must be involved in design and verification that what is said on paper in fact happens in the shop or office.

Examples: An article in *Business Week* reports that press calibration workers at DuPont are much happier with their results since adopting ISO 9000 standards rather than depending on their self-managed work teams to perform reliably over time. The same article reports also that British Airways cargo handlers were able to reduce customer complaints by 65 percent and time spent fixing problems by 60 percent the first year after ISO 9000's training standards for needs assessment were implemented.[13] The CEO of Minco Technology Labs, a 130-person company in Texas who became certified in order to compete in the worldwide electronics market, perhaps best sums up the advantages of the standards and the certification process by stating, "There is absolutely no way you can pull the wool over auditors' eyes because they're not talking to your quality manager, they're talking to the people on the floor, so you better be sure you're living your quality system."[14]

ISO 9000 STRUCTURE

WHAT'S INCLUDED IN EACH SERIES

ISO 9000	Guidelines for application

ISO 9001	Standards for registration in:
	(in-depth standards for:)
	    Design
	    Development
	    Production
	    Installation
	    Servicing

ISO 9002	Standards for registration in:
	    Production
	    Installation

ISO 9003	Standards for registration in:
	    Final Inspection
	    Test

ISO 9004	Guidelines for application in a
	Quality Management System
	    including:
	    Product/service requirements
	    Organization and control
	    Customer satisfaction
	    Producer responsibility
	    System guidance

Note: Modifications to existing series and additions to the series as presently configured are continuously being made.

WORKSHEET 1 - 11

ISO 9000 AUDITED BUSINESS FUNCTIONS

Note to trainers: These are some of the typical business functions that are standardized in ISO 9000 guidelines. Trainers would be wise to consider design and delivery options to meet the needs of specific individuals who work in jobs within these functions. During ISO 9000 certification audits, third-party auditors evaluate the performance of individual workers according to standards in the guidelines and company documentation based on these standards.

> Design
> Documentation
> Purchasing
> Process control
> Inspection and test
> Failure analysis
> Failure correction
> Packing
> Shipping
> Internal audit
> Use of statistical methods
> Customer service
> Contract administration
> Training

An example of an ISO 9000 standard in the area of training is:

> "Specifies methods to identify training needs and keep records."

Organizational documentation must be developed to illustrate that the company does this. During the development of training, auditors must have demonstrated to them that persons doing needs assessment have specified appropriate methods for doing training needs assessment, choose appropriate methods, follow appropriate procedures during conduct of needs assessment, use valid forms for record-keeping regarding needs assessment, and keep accurate records.

Meeting just this one standard, obviously, can take a great deal of time in bottom-up deliberation, experimentation, testing, and validation. Individual competency is paramount.

QUALITY GOALS

Planning for Quality Goals

Problem: The problem in setting quality goals is that there are several key dimensions of goal setting, several key types of planning, and many dimensions of quality. These variables interact at both macro-levels and micro-levels, affecting the company as a whole as well as the individuals who work there. This brief overview of these variables will help you see the problem of planning for quality goals more clearly and help you choose an appropriate variable on which to work.

These are some of the key dimensions of goals:

1. A goal is driven by a realistic business reason.
2. A goal is both perceived to be attainable and is attainable.
3. A goal has a payoff for individual persons at work.

These are some of the key types of planning:

1. Strategic planning
2. Operational planning
3. Financial planning
4. Information planning
5. Market planning
6. Work planning
7. Project planning

These are some of the important dimensions of quality:

1. Process quality
2. Service quality
3. Product quality

also,

4. The customer's definition of quality
5. The measurement of quality
6. Skills for ensuring quality
7. Knowledge about quality
8. Communication about quality successes and failures
9. Rewards for achieving quality

Your task in establishing quality goals will be to assure that each goal statement is *complete* regarding all three dimensions of goals, is *clear* regarding the type of planning that forms the context for the goal, and is *specific* regarding the dimension(s) of quality that are involved in the company's reach toward the goal.

Plan of Action: Numerous total quality management consultants and "quality gurus" have their favorite approach to quality planning and goal setting. Most contain these features:

- Choosing a specific problem (error, complaint, shortfall, defect) on which to focus
- Defining the business reason driving this choice
- Identifying customers
- Having customers define what they need and want
- Describing the present product/service with its problems
- Defining causes of problems
- Describing product/service features that will satisfy customers' needs and wants
- Stating objectives for revised products/services
- Defining processes and methods for achieving objectives
- Testing, checking, verifying validity of processes and methods

The point in all this is that planning for quality goals is not a "blue sky" activity with lofty words and statements that make everyone feel good. Quality goal-setting must be related very directly and specifically to the business and its customers. Quality goals very often are best stated in terms of specific kinds of measurements that focus narrowly on correcting a small but nagging problem. Following the "small is beautiful" paradigm in goal-setting will help you make the tough transition into implementation of plans to meet the goals—this is when quality improvement begins, and it goes forward, one person at a time.

Examples: Motorola was one of the first winners of the Baldrige award. Some key characteristics of their quality goal-setting are instructive. First, they were driven by a burning business reason: loss of global markets to Japan, dropping from second to fifth in world-wide computer chip sales.

Motorola's now famous "Six Sigma Program" enunciated its corporation-wide quality goal to be "six sigma" in all its quality measures, that is, statistically speaking, to reduce errors and defects in products and processes to the nearly infinite tail of the normal curve, extending out six standard deviations to compute error rates (rather than the typical two standard deviations used by most statisticians). The statistical standard for six sigma calculation is 3.4 units per million, that is, less than three and one-half problems per million possibilities. Motorola adopted the Six Sigma standard as its new quality goal.

No doubt to the cries of naysayers who said 'You gotta be kidding!,' Motorola's leadership pressed forward, bringing department after department along gradually toward the Six Sigma goal. In the first few years of the effort, Motorola reduced defects from 3,000 per million to 200 per million[15]—not yet 3.4, but on its way. The Six Sigma concept fit within the corporate culture of manufacturing and statistical measures of progress. Basically, the goal made sense to persons trying to change. Employees obviously believed that the goal was attainable and worth working for.

In addition, Motorola employees have been trained to go beyond customer satisfaction and aim for the anticipation of customer needs. The Japanese have a name for this notion, the "Kano Model," which specifies what features employees think will surprise and delight customers, not simply satisfy them. Motorola employees have been rewarded for pressing on with this new thinking: their company is now the world's largest manufacturer of cellular phones, and has even taken market share of related products in Japan.[16] Motorola's quality goals have spurred employees on to reaping the rewards of seeing their company grow and prosper in new and exciting ways as a direct result of their efforts.

Quality goal-setting also paid off for Jiminy Peak Resort, a ski area and recreation center in New York. Jiminy Peak is a small operation compared to a Motorola. However, its approach to quality goals was similar. In this case, customer complaints about rooms not being ready on time prompted a quality investigation into causes of the problem and objectives for its solution.

Teams of employees who are involved in getting rooms ready for customers were set on the task of finding out exactly why rooms were not ready. They found that cleaning the rooms was often delayed because of a shortage of supplies or broken equipment; and because employees felt that those things were management's problem, they simply took the time they needed to compensate for those lacks, driving the waiting time for clean rooms up for the incoming vacationers.

When the specific problems were hunted down, identified, and solved, employees saw a 71 percent improvement over the year. Jiminy Peak's CEO set his corporate quality goal as "doing it right the first time, every time" noting that reworking something not done right the first time often has the effect of not only of unhappy customers, but also often doubles labor costs associated with a task.[17] The CEO's lofty quality goal came right down to earth when his employees counted containers of carpet shampoo, bars of soap, and types of vacuum cleaner repairs pending.

Another Baldrige award winner, Ritz-Carlton Hotels has a similar story. Like the CEO at Jiminy Peak with a maximum of about 800 employees, Ritz-Carlton's CEO with a headcount of about 12,000 employees operates in a customer service-intensive business known for nearly 100 percent turnover in staff. Ritz-Carlton already had a reputation for good service, and five years ago, posted a "customer satisfaction rate" of 91 percent. Last year, that rate increased to 97 percent with the adoption of the Ritz's "Gold Standards" which include a detailed set of steps to service and employment basics. Also during the same five year period, the number of defects in employee-customer transactions fell from 50,000 defects per million transactions to just four. Sounds a little like "Six Sigma," doesn't it? This could never have happened without ordinary people counting ordinary business tasks in day-to-day operations. There's no magic in achieving quality; it happens when individuals at work have the will to measure what's important and the tools with which to do the counting.

In addition to the specificity of targets and quantitative measures, Ritz-Carlton's quality goals are backed up with a passionate CEO who tells the world that the company exists not just for shareholders' return on investment, but also for the "fulfillment of employees." Ritz-Carlton believes that training has a big payoff because it gives workers the knowledge and opportunities they need to remain employable in such a business. Ritz-Carlton has been richly rewarded by its employees who in 1993 posted only a 30 percent turnover rate within an industry standard of 100 percent. The Ritz had retained 70 percent of its investment in employee empowerment and training, definitely a value-added edge over its competitors in the human resources development arena. In the words of the Ritz's CEO, "by 1996, the company aims to achieve zero defects and 100 percent customer satisfaction." And, he believes, committed leaders, and involved and educated employees will make it all happen.[18]

You don't have to be a Fortune 500 company or a high profile business to "do quality." These final two examples are from small companies whose employees also had the will and tenacity to set quality goals and make quality improvements based on them. These companies illustrate the important principles of identifying the cost of poor quality and removing the reasons for it. The clue to success in both these examples is that individuals, empowered and emboldened by quality goals, spoke up about how they did their jobs and what they needed to do them better.

A busy three-shift warehouse operation routinely found that about 3 percent of its shipments required re-packing by the air express carrier it used. Obviously, the carrier was not happy about this, and the supplier relationship suffered. There was a process quality error in the pipeline from warehouse to end customer.

When warehouse employees and supervisors began to check into the problem, they discovered to their surprise that the warehouse picking operation on the "graveyard" (midnight to 8:00 a.m.) shift was producing all of the errors. Upon further investigation into causes, employees revealed that the computers that helped them track accuracy in picking stock were turned off at the end of second shift and were simply not available to help them do their jobs. Mistakes resulted. The simple solution to the quality problem was to turn the computers back on for the third shift. In a business-as-usual company, demoralized employees would have just continued to do their jobs the best they could and take the error hit as an acceptable price for doing business. In an organization with quality goals, employees with something to say about how they work best speak up and are heard. Specific plans are made to improve the process—at the individual employee level.

INC. Magazine[19] ran an article about a "meek, rather mild-mannered process engineer" at Spectrum Control in Pennsylvania who got all fired up about his company's new commitment to quality and specifically to its goal of "zero defects." To him, this meant that the ceramic capacitors that came into his organization to be soldered were in fact capable of holding solder, 100 percent of the time. That is, the weekly dump of 75,000 capacitors could be expected to go immediately to the next step of assembly, which was his responsibility.

Unfortunately, the business-as-usual approach at Spectrum was a reject rate for the incoming capacitors of about 30 percent, resulting in close to 75 percent of engineering time diverted to dealing with the rejects. The mild-mannered engineer wrote a torrid memo to the VP of Engineering, copying everyone who was part of the problem, calling the reject rate "an albatross" and calling for corrective action in the inbound materials.

Spectrum employees were reported to have said that the new quality initiative was like quitting smoking, giving up drinking, and going on a diet all at once. What they were grappling with was a culture shift from the notion of AQLs, or Acceptable Quality Levels to the notion of zero defects, and from the measurements of end-of-process inspection to the measurements of in-process inspection. In the process of working towards the quality goal, the 'mild-mannered engineer' who blew the whistle and took the company to task "became a minor celebrity."[20]

The section of worksheets that follows these examples gives you guidelines for your own quality goal setting as you wrestle with issues of process, service, and product quality like these employees in the above examples.

PLANNING TEMPLATE FOR QUALITY GOALS

Simple statement of the quality goal:

True facts of the current problem situation:

Who must be involved in standard-setting:
  name   *telephone number*

Desired characteristics for revised processes/services/products:

PLANNING TEMPLATE FOR QUALITY GOALS

Measurement and improvement timeline:

item for action	1Q	2Q	3Q	4Q
1.				
2.				
3.				
4.				
5.				
6.				
7.				
8.				
9.				
10.				
11.				
12.				
13.				
14.				
15.				
16.				
17.				
18.				

WORKSHEET 1 - 12 (SAMPLE)
PLANNING TEMPLATE FOR QUALITY GOALS

Simple statement of the quality goal:

We will work to continuously improve our services, processes, products, and ourselves.

True facts of the current problem situation:

— *We operate under acceptable quality levels (AQLs) that vary from department to department—range of 30% - 95% AQLs*
— *There are no quality standards for services; a few inconsistent ones for processes*
— *No one has ever paid attention to self-improvement*

Who must be involved in standard-setting:
    name   *telephone number*

(all salary grades must be represented; draw a sample of about 15 people representative of the numbers of employees in each salary grade; use the blue edition of the company phone book)

Desired characteristics for revised processes/services/products:

— *simple, unambiguous measures for everything*
— *visible progress charts on walls everywhere*
— *process usefulness, lack of redundancy*
— *need service standards in small increments*

PLANNING TEMPLATE FOR QUALITY GOALS

Measurement and improvement timeline:

	item for action	*1Q*	*2Q*	*3Q*	*4Q*
1.	*brainstorm the concept of promotion*	___			
2.	*look at print and electronic communication differently*	_____			
3.	*select employee sample before summer vacation*			___	
4.	*build customer-base scenarios for 5 years from now*	_____			
5.	*ask employees what they need to know in each scenario*			_____	
6.	*prioritize knowledge/skills for each of five years*				_____
7.	*etc.*				
8.					
9.					
10.					
11.					
12.					
13.					
14.					
15.					
16.					
17.					
18.					

THIS TO THAT WORD LISTS

Note to trainer or supervisor: Use these thought provoker lists as a handout at a meeting, as an overhead transparency at a training session, or as a piece of mail when your organization or group begins the planning for setting quality goals.

Quality begins with a shift in attitude from this . . . to that!

from this .... to that

from this	to that
hiding errors	exposing errors
keeping quiet	speaking up
management-designed work	employee-designed work
dictate	collaborate
suspicion	trust
classroom training	continuous learning
top-down	bottom-up
vertical	horizontal
wait	initiate
play it safe	take risks
shareholder return	quality
wait	do
do it yourself	ask for help
giant steps	baby steps
broadscale	narrow
accept errors	fix errors

GOALS FOR PROCESS QUALITY

Note to participant: A good place to start setting process quality goals is your organization chart or company telephone book to see how your company is organized. List the names of major organizations such as finance, human resources, sales, marketing, customer service, information processing, public relations, technical writing, engineering, research and development, assembly, drafting, etc. Then, give a try at listing under each organization name the major **"things that they do,"** that is, how they do work, not things that they produce. The idea is to make a list of the major *processes* that go on in your company. As you complete this task, you'll see some redundant processes, and this is where you'll focus your attention regarding goal setting.

Two examples might be: "process forms" and "write." Your next step is to find out how these things are done in these departments and see if there are consistencies or inconsistencies in the way these processes are done. Determine if these processes need fixing or could be made better. Write down what you think. Relate your suggested corrective actions to a specific process in a specific department. Try to take a look at the whole business; you'll be surprised at how your job is related to other jobs, and how what you do at work makes a difference.

SAMPLE

Example:

Sales Department (what they do)	Corrective Actions/Comments
learn product features	need more accuracy in describing features
make phone calls	should do more of this; excellent payoff
write letters	writing is too stilted/formal; make more personal
talk to clients face to face	should make notes and send notes around "F.Y.I."
use reference materials	poorly catalogued and out of date; wasting time
negotiate with clients	good success; can Sales teach us how to do it?
close deals	reps. are good at this; can we help them do more?
process orders	they never do it on time; why?
deliver products	is warehouse interface as efficient as it could be?

GOALS FOR PROCESS QUALITY

Note to participant: Use this form to record process operations and your own corrective actions and comments. Add other forms and customize to your own company.

Organization name: _____

Process operations (what they do)   *Corrective actions/Comments*

Organization name: _____

Process operations (what they do)   *Corrective actions/Comments*

Organization name:_____

Process operations (what they do)   *Corrective actions/Comments*

WORKSHEET 1 - 15

GOALS FOR SERVICE QUALITY

Note to participant: Building quality into service is not always as apparent an activity as building quality into a product or a process. This effort requires a three-prong approach: first, you must define what employees do when they deliver service; second, you must define the kinds of standards against which you intend to measure success, and third, you must set quantitative goals within those processes and standards. Service deliverers often have a hard time thinking in terms of quantitative measurement and incremental improvement. It's your job as a trainer to help individuals at work see how they can make a difference in service delivery.

As in process measurement, measurement in services is aimed at pinpointing things that individuals can do to make the end result one of higher quality. All of your efforts at definition should be directed at what the individual does and can do to make a positive change. Be careful not to set goals that are too global or to define measures that are too broad and inclusive. Thinking small is thinking smarter when it comes to quality.

Some options in standards for service quality:

1. **Effectiveness:** automating high volume or routine operations, that is, tackling the effectiveness issue in the key processes of delivering service; often focusing on the systems that support service delivery

2. **Efficiency:** consolidating steps or functions that seem redundant, addressing the efficiency and time management issues often involving accountability and "sign off" procedures

3. **Job enhancement:** examining the way jobs are performed, the steps or procedures in each job, to see if each job is as interesting and challenging as it can be in delivery of service; the value added could be found in design of jobs

4. **Competitive advantage:** analyzing market forces, supply and demand, price, packaging, consumer product feature preference, consumer expectation regarding level of service, in order to adjust the delivery of service to meet or exceed customer requirements for service

5. **Communication:** fine-tuning the various communication systems and channels that have an impact on service, including use of various technologies and the use of feedback

GOALS FOR SERVICE QUALITY

Definition of the service: _____

      standards checklist   (check all categories of standards that apply to this service)

_____ 1. effectiveness

_____ 2. efficiency

_____ 3. job enhancement

_____ 4. competitive advantage

_____ 5. communication

Quantitative goals for achieving quality in this service: _____

_____

_____

_____

- -

Definition of the service: _____

      standards checklist   (check all categories of standards that apply to this service)

_____ 1. effectiveness

_____ 2. efficiency

_____ 3. job enhancement

_____ 4. competitive advantage

_____ 5. communication

Quantitative goals for achieving quality in this service: _____

_____

_____

_____

_____

- -

(Note: Add more sheets as needed)

WORKSHEET 1 - 15 (SAMPLE)

GOALS FOR SERVICE QUALITY

Definition of the service: _____*delivering mail*_____

       standards checklist (check all categories of standards that apply to this service)

_____ 1. effectiveness

_√_ 2. efficiency

_√_ 3. job enhancement

_____ 4. competitive advantage

_____ 5. communication

Quantitative goals for achieving quality in this service:

2. *efficiency - begin delivery 1/2 hour later, after employees have come off break so they're less likely to want to waste time talking*

3. *job enhancement - institute procedures for each delivery person to seek feedback from customers at 3 month intervals*

WORKSHEET 1 - 16

GOALS FOR PRODUCT QUALITY

Note to participant: Companies who make products have long been used to measuring and counting. In most instances, these companies have a head start on quality goal-setting because they are accustomed to using statistical analysis to measure and report their progress toward production quotas and objectives.

If you are an employee in a company like this, and have been doing your part to measure and count, your task as you think about continuous improvement in your product is to challenge yourself to think creatively about the appropriateness of what you count. Perhaps what you are counting doesn't really matter in terms of product quality. The list below will help you think beyond the typical measurements of production. Ask yourself these questions as they relate to your part in product creation. Practice asking "who" and "why" instead of the usual "what" and "how much."

1. **Forecasting:** Are the numbers upon which the forecast was made truthful, good numbers? Who developed them, and was that person fully informed?

2. **Engineering/Design:** Was design work done in a vacuum? Who is the user of this product or this design, and was that person consulted about application issues? Were designers aware of market concerns and trends? If not, why not, and can we do it better the next time?

3. **Features:** Look beyond error and defect rates and standard control charts. Look for fitness for use characteristics such as consistency, completeness, uniformity, ease of use. Do we measure the right things regarding product features?

4. **Systems:** Look into the systems that support product development—information systems and data processing, training, purchasing, accounting, testing, material handling, packaging, shipping, inventory management, etc. Look at what's measured and counted in these systems and ask yourself if each system that you need to support your part in the product is working for you or against you.

5. **Measures:** Are the measures that you are being asked to use doing the job for your customers? Is there a better way to measure what's really important to the customer through your particular job?

GOALS FOR PRODUCT QUALITY

ANALYSIS CHECKSHEET

Directions:

1) Write the name of the product you are working on, or specify your particular job in making this product on the line below.

2) Using the five points explained previously, analyze your job in terms of each point. Then place a check mark in any cell on the matrix that applies to your job.

3) Finally, make notes in the left column of boxes regarding better, more accurate, or more appropriate measures for each matrix cell you have checked.

PRODUCT/JOB: _____

	Forecasting	Engineering/Design	Features	Systems	Measures
suggestions for better measures					

WORKSHEET 1 - 16 (SAMPLE)

GOALS FOR PRODUCT QUALITY

ANALYSIS CHECKSHEET

	Forecasting	Engineering/Design	Features	Systems	Measures
PRODUCT/JOB: _____					
suggestions for better measures					
	✓				
			✓		

PRODUCT/JOB: _make fabric lining for picnic baskets_

---

suggestions for better measures

---

1. Forecasting - *I made 15 percent more liners than I needed to make, resulting in my time and materials wasted. The forecast was made by marketing people who always assume the market will grow—they automatically multiply last year's figure by 15 percent. Instead they should consider other factors too such as park closings, higher tax on imported wicker, the switch to a new fabric supplier, etc. that will affect next year's needs. They should always talk to us operators before setting the percent.*

---

2. Features - *We typically rate color quality, straightness of seams, and pattern matching at corners. We should also measure quality of the installation of the velcro strip around the top—some are not attached well and cause problems in ease of use later. The things we measure are the right things, but we missed this additional measure because it wasn't done in our department, but it's important because it affects our customer satisfaction.*

WORKSHEET 1 - 17

GLOSSARY OF QUALITY MEASUREMENT TOOLS

This glossary of tools[21] describes the major quantitative tools for measuring quality progress. When individuals are sent off to "quality seminars" these are the tools that they most often learn to use. It's good to have a working knowledge of at least these six as you follow your progress toward continuous improvement. Use these tools either for analysis or for tracking results of improvement efforts.

1. **Cause and Effect Diagram** (Fishbone Diagram)
   The cause and effect (fishbone) diagram helps you to identify the probable causes of a problem. Graphically it resembles a fish skeleton, with the quality problem (the effect) represented by the spine and various causes of the problem represented by the ribs or bones on either side of the spine. To identify causes, work either from a frequency checksheet or a brainstorming group. Show relationships within major causes, resulting in a dispersion type fishbone diagram.

2. **Control Chart**
   The control chart shows departures from a standard in the continuing performance of a process. Its most common form is the X-bar and R chart which monitors the mean value and the range between minimum and maximum values. The control chart is based on the idea that fixable problems can be identified because they will cross the upper or lower control limits established for a process when that process becomes unstable.

3. **Flowchart**
   A flowchart is a representation of all of the steps in a process. Two flowcharts, an ideal process and an actual process, can be effectively contrasted to analyze the source of a problem. Obviously, an expert in dealing with the process in question must design the control charts for comparison. The flowchart uses simple symbols to represent actions: ovals start and stop actions; boxes are steps in the process; diamonds are decisions; and arrows are the direction of the action. All feedback loops must have an escape, and the entire chart must be connected.

4. **Histogram**
   A histogram is a bar graph of measurements. Typically, the measurements or categories of measurements are across the horizontal axis and the frequency of occurrence is on the vertical axis. A histogram is usually constructed from a frequency table of occurrences within the boundaries of categories. From a histogram, you can see a quick overview of variation in your data, as normal processes can be expected to produce a histogram resembling the shape of the normal curve.

5. **Pareto Diagram**
   The Pareto Diagram is a vertical bar graph and line plot indicating the cumulative incidence of error found in various parts of processes. It is based on the principle that it is better to concentrate corrective action on the vital few 20 percent of problem areas which generate 80 percent of the problems, than on the trivial many where numerous errors, but unimportant ones, are present. It is generally derived from a frequency of error checksheet of data collected over time.

6. Scatter Diagram

A scatter diagram is a plot of points representing the relationships between variables. Scatter diagrams are derived from data collected in pairs that are suspected of having a relationship to each other. One variable is represented by the horizontal axis and the other variable is represented by the vertical axis. A point is placed on the graph for each item in the sample, indicating the measure of both variables. If the picture of all the points resembles a straight line, diagonally from lower left to upper right, the relationship between the variables is assumed to be strong, that is, as the variable on one axis changes, the variable on the other axis changes also.

Other basic analysis and measurement tools

Other basic measurement tools can be helpful in analysis and diagnosis of quality problems and can be used effectively in tracking and reporting progress toward continuous improvement. Don't forget to take a look at the "qualitative" measurements also—those indicators of defects or problems that can be counted, ticked off, logged, and followed over time. Such things might include internal complaints, customer complaints, employee suggestions, progress made on performance reviews, profit and loss statements, stock performance. These are some of the measurement tools that are frequently used by individuals and that can be used effectively in a quality measurement effort:

- measures of central tendency: mean, median, mode
- measures of dispersion: range, standard deviation
- the normal curve
- percents and percentiles
- frequency counts
- reliability calculations
- regression lines
- pie charts

Endnotes for Chapter 1
Notes 1 through 21

1. Robin Schatz, "Survey shows workers look for job satisfaction," *Newsday*, reprinted in *The Berkshire Eagle*, September 5, 1993, p. 2E.

2. Robert B. Reich, "A 'We' Company," *The Washington Post*, reprinted in *The Berkshire Eagle*, August 2, 1993, p. A7.

3. Richard Y. Chang, in a workshop, "Curing the 'Excessive Activity Syndrome' Epidemic Spreading Through Quality Improvement Initiatives" at the ASTD 1993 National Conference, Atlanta, GA. A related article by Chang is, "When TQM Goes Nowhere," in *Training & Development*, January 1993, pp. 22-29.

4. Paul H. Billings, "Project T.E.A.M. Introduction to Statistical Process Control. ERIC document ED 328 693, 1990. Classes of SPC use are described on p. 4.

5. Shirley K. Whitten, "Award-Winning Total Quality at the Naval Publications and Forms Center," in *National Productivity Review*/Vol.8, No.3, summer 1989, pp. 273-286.

6. Abraham H. Maslow, *Motivation and Personality*, 3rd ed., New York, Harper, 1987.

7. Public Law 100 - 107, section on Findings and Purposes, Washington, D.C., August 20, 1987.

8. Numbers on training are taken from the promotional and informational materials furnished by law by The Wallace Company after having won the Malcolm Baldrige National Quality Award in 1990.

9. John Sprague, *Revitalizing U.S. Electronics: Lessons from Japan*, Boston, Butterworth-Heinemann, 1993, p. 121.

10. Osman Kent, "ISO 9000: A Quality Opportunity," in *BYTE*, July 1993, p. 36.

11. Mark Morrow, "U.S. ISO 9000 registrations double," in *Quality Digest*, November 1992, p. 18.

12. Don Nichols, "The Seal of Approval," in *Small Business Reports*, September 1993, pp. 57-61.

13. Jonathan B. Levine, "Want EC Business? You Have Two Choices," in Science & Technology column, *Business Week*, October 19, 1992.

14. Reported by Don Nichols in the article, "The Seal of Approval," in *Small Business Reports*, September 1993, p. 61.

15. *INFO-LINE, Fundamentals of Quality*, American Society for Training and Development, Alexandria, VA, 1992, p. 8.

16. *Ibid.*

17. Gae Elfenbein, "Quality pays dividends, Fairbank tells suppliers," in *The Berkshire Eagle*, November 22, 1991, p. D1.

18. Keynote speech by Horst Schulze, president and CEO of Ritz-Carlton Hotel Company, at the 1993 Annual Conference of the American Society for Training and Development in Atlanta, May 11, 1993. Audiotape of the speech is available from ASTD, King Street, Alexandria, VA.

19. Craig R. Waters, "Quality Begins at Home," *INC.*, August 1985, pp. 68-71.

20. *Op. cit.*, p. 71.

21. Adapted from "Glossary of Quality Tools" from *Trainer's Complete Guide to Management and Supervisory Development* by Carolyn Nilson, Englewood Cliffs, NJ: Prentice Hall, a Division of Simon & Schuster, 1992, pp. 30-31. An excellent guide to the use of quality tools is available from AT&T Bell Laboratories for $29.95. Order select code 500-049, *Process Quality Management & Improvement Guidelines*, Issue 1.1, by the AT&T Quality Steering Committee, October 1988. Telephone 1-800-432-6600, or write to AT&T Customer Information Center, Order Entry Department, PO Box 19901, Indianapolis, IN 46219.

CHAPTER **2**

OVERVIEW OF PLANNING AND GOAL-SETTING: BUSINESS OBJECTIVES

Quality goal-setting, the subject of the initial pages of this book, has its own characteristics which incorporate many good ideas that can form the foundation for business planning that supports an individualistic approach to training. Some of these key "quality" characteristics are:

- customers are at the center
- top management leads
- facts and data are in abundance
- employees are involved and empowered to various degrees
- continuous improvement is the approach to work.

These key characteristics are being embraced in the name of "Total Quality Management" (TQM), tried in a wide variety of companies, and have been marked by a range of success across the field of implementation.

The numbers are instructive: *Training* magazine recently[1] ran an article containing an estimate that for each 40 hours of labor, four to six hours will be taken up in activities related to employee empowerment and team development. The author noted that about 15 percent of a typical operations budget generally gets siphoned off to the work of self-managed work teams that usually are part of a TQM effort. The advice to readers was that if you don't have the stomach to tolerate these numbers, forget about TQM. Articles similar to this are cropping up in the business press with increasing frequency.

Florida Power and Light's (Baldrige winner) CEO cautions, in an article[2] in *Harvard Business Review,* that companies need to allow employees freedom and creativity to interpret some seemingly strict "quality" rules and measurements, and to encourage them to get out of the developmental stages of TQM so often marked by a seemingly unending emphasis on structured reporting. Others warn against thinking of TQM as a "religion," a "program of the month," or a "fashion statement." Quality efforts should be seen as the way to get work done, how to do business—the means, not the end itself. The issue becomes a company's ability to put quality goals and methods in their rightful place, a place that is complemented, to be sure, by organizational structures and corporate goals for the business.

Re-thinking the way business is organized. Re-engineering guru, Mike Hammer, in an interview[3] with a *Forbes ASAP* staffer, advocates "horizontal" organization "by process" which leads to "congruent goals, flexibility, customer orientation, and speed." Hammer's approach is echoed by many others, such as corporations all over America who are re-engineering themselves to be more flexible and more customer-focused. A manager at Eastman Kodak, for example, suggests literally turning your organization chart upside down to put those closest to the real action of a company on top.[4] The Mead Paper Company, a specialty paper company in Massachusetts employing about 350 persons, also re-thought its way into a more "process oriented" business structure, re-drawing its hierarchical, pyramidal organization chart into concentric circles, the center of which is "customer." Mead's CEO, featured speaker at his Chamber of Commerce meeting, defines his company's "critical success factors" as the processes that guide decision-making and lead to success. He defines these as: communication, service, quality, people, innovation, and effectiveness. He has recast departments into project teams, and created various cross-functional committees to plan and guide work. He has introduced a new term, "stakeholder," into Mead's vocabulary, and by this, he means customers, employees, financial backers, and the community—all in business together. He has promised a new involvement with local schools.[5] Mike Hammer says that executive titles should be thrown out and replaced by appellations such as "Process Owner of Finding and Keeping Customers" instead of "VP, Marketing." Hammer defines re-engineering as "radically re-thinking and re-designing those processes by which we create value and do work."[6] Mead paper is embracing this approach.

Strategic thinking by leaders at the top of organizations who are courageous enough to be "radical" in their views of organization structure is what's needed in order for individuals at work to become truly empowered in a lasting sense. *The New York Times* recently ran an article featuring several companies who were not afraid to get tough with their corporate underpinnings. One of the cases presented in this article is that of the Shelby Die Casting Company in Mississippi who, after experiencing some early failures with the way they organized their self-directed teams, re-thought the process and actually fired all their supervisors, wiping out an entire—formerly 'sacred'—structure so that the processes of communication and trust could be fostered in ways never dreamed of before.[7] President and Mrs. Clinton's proposals on health care reform, made public during the early fall of 1993, are based on this kind of 'radical thinking,' or re-engineering principles. The burden of all leadership is to think creatively. Academics call it "the paradigm shift," and it's what has to happen for individual people at work to become free to contribute their best to the economy. The indisputable and joyous fact is that more and more companies of all sizes and types are moving in this direction of strategic thinking, preparing the way for a parallel new kind of thinking in the nurture and use of human resources.

Critical and core—the real challenge for planners.   More than a decade ago, Tom Peters, the wild man of management reform, called corporate America to task in his best selling book collaboration with Robert Waterman, *In Search of Excellence* (Harper & Row, 1982), for being complacent and getting sidetracked from what business was all about. Among his exortations that have stuck as important business wisdom over the years is his plea that companies "stick to the knitting." His voice was among the loudest and most consistent over the decade since this book was published in calling for business to refocus its central mission on "the customer." Organizations from the barber shop to the federal government have gotten the message that they'd better take a fresh look at who their customer is, exactly what it is that the business delivers, and that the service receiver, not the service provider, is the one who should be dictating the direction of the business. Defining the critical processes and the core business is the major challenge for organizational planners.

At about the same time Peters and Waterman were doing their research for that landmark book, other movements were happening around the world that were pointing toward new ways of thinking about work value and output. Notably among these were the groundbreaking work at Volvo, specifically at its Kalmar auto assembly plant in Sweden in the late 1970s, and the quality circles work in Japan throughout that decade.

Volvo's president, writing in 1977, said "We are still in the era that Adam Smith described so many years ago, where 'a worker gives up his ease, his liberty, and his happiness when he goes into industry.' If we can give him back his ease, his liberty, and his happiness, or at least give him conditions under which he can find them for himself, I believe we will come closer to a 'post-industrial' society." At the Kalmar plant, Volvo's top management leadership recognized that the traditional assembly line organization of work might just not be the best way to organize work; that people at work might just work better, more happily, and more innovatively in groups. Volvo was among the first Western businesses that focused on creating a work environment designed to encourage individualism within a group context. Volvo's core business was very clear and very traditional; the Kalmar experience, however, was a revolution in thinking about the way in which critical processes were accomplished.[8]

Meanwhile, halfway around the world, Japanese workers were grouping together in quality circles for the purpose of thinking about and doing work collaboratively. A host of political, economic, and cultural influences combined to support this way of organizing business and doing work, and the successes of Japanese quality circles are many and well-publicized. Replicating or at least adapting the quality circles' format was tried in many U.S. organizations during the late '70s and the 1980s. The 1990s move toward self-directed teams and empowered employees grew directly from the lessons learned from these 'revolutionary' ways of thinking about and organizing work and workers.

General organization development wisdom suggests that some of the major changes during the decade of the 1980s were that employees were less accepting of authority, less trustful and confident that the traditional top-down institutions could continue to have their well-being in mind, and more insistent that they be given their legitimate voice in how work should be done at their individual work stations. The '90s have taken all this at least one step further—now, employees want not only to define their own jobs but also to understand how their particular job meets or exceeds customer demand and fits within the entire system of work—how their work is aligned with the company's reason for being. Tom Peters presents a powerful parable for this in the opening of the first chapter in his 1987 book, *Thriving on Chaos* (Knopf), where he says that the old saw, "if it ain't broke, don't fix it" should be revised to say "If it ain't broke, you just haven't looked hard enough. Fix it anyway." Looking hard is the job of today's business planners. Zeroing in on exactly who the customer is, and defining how the critical processes of the business are working to produce that core product or service for that customer are the analysis challenges of our time.

Several examples are illustrative: network television in my viewing area has been airing an advertisement by Home Depot, the one-stop shopping center for home repair supplies and do-it-yourself building materials. This ad begins and ends with a smiling, friendly young woman who says "We're in the customer service business." Rapid images in the background leave the viewer with a sense of all kinds of customers being served as they rush around the aisles stacked high with everything one could ever need for a weekend project. Intellectually, a person driving past a Home Depot store might describe it as a hardware supermarket, and might even be tempted to say its business was home improvement. But, listen to the happy face on the 30-second TV spot: "We're in the customer service business." That's it, pure and simple—critical and core: customer service. No doubt, some organization development specialists looked at Home Depot and thought, "this ain't broke;" but they fixed it anyway and launched one of the most successful customer service businesses of the '90s. Ask anyone who shops there. Consistently, across the country, Home Depot is in the customer service business; and because they are, they sell plenty of hardware too.

How about the weight loss programs that are really in the business of selling self-confidence, or the fragrance and cosmetic companies who are really in the business of selling sex appeal? Marketers and ad copy writers have known for a long time that products are often just a means to an end, and that consumer acceptance always depends on the product's ability to sell its ultimate benefit or value. Those business leaders who must be planners and set business goals should always be aware of just exactly what business they are in and what the consumer really wants. AT&T's stockholders and retirees breathed a collective sigh of relief and jubilation when the telephone giant announced in autumn of 1993 its intent to acquire McCaw Cellular Communications, a cellular telephone company, after having watched with incredulity over the years since divestiture as AT&T dabbled in one business after the other, like typewriters and home security systems. AT&T watchers cheered when AT&T at last took a strong stand regarding just exactly what its core business was—and, lo and behold, it was telephones! AT&T stakeholders had been through a decade of wandering around the edges; it seemed like finally the company re-focused appropriately on its core business. AT&T's large expanded stakeholder community applauded, its competitors shivered, the business press and media gave favorable coverage, and securities analysts and Standard and Poor's responded with excellent ratings to this bold, strategic step that had been a long time a-coming.

"A Company of Businesspeople." This was the title of *INC.* magazine's cover story in April 1993. In this article, *INC.* profiled a number of small and mid-size companies who had defined their businesses in new ways without succumbing to the latest fads of organization development. One of the featured companies was Southwest Airlines who now circulates all financial information to all employees. No longer is the profit-and-loss statement for executive eyes only. Employees now see regular reports on revenue, passenger miles, and fuel usage. Southwest also developed the first profit-sharing program in its industry, and requires employees to reinvest a portion of their profit-sharing funds in company stock. Southwest truly makes employees part of the company's success, defining them as businesspeople and giving them the business tools to make business decisions that are good for the company and good for themselves. They operate on the principle that with authority comes responsibility, not to a supervisor or a set of directives, but to the marketplace.

INC. suggests that creating a company of businesspeople is a whole new way of thinking, very different from the old "wage-labor" idea of management wherein employees just did their jobs and management supervised them. The movement towards creating a company of businesspeople was begun so that those who thought of themselves as just employees as well as those who thought of themselves as bosses would both think of themselves as colleagues—peers—working together in the business. This, of course, means that the traditional narrow definition of jobs must change, and that workers must have the freedom and skills to do the company's work in a way that each deems is the best way. It means that the company must be structured so that employees are supported in their growth as business people, and it also means that information, communication, and reward systems within a company must change.[9]

Just-in-time thinking, a boon to planners of the '90s. "Design big and implement small" is an exhortation attributed to re-engineering's Mike Hammer.[10] Revolutionary thinking, the stuff of paradigm shifts, is a big design order. However, when it comes to finding and fixing problems in critical processes, the focus must be on small elements and precisely defined variables. "Just-in-time" made its debut and its fine reputation in inventory management, claiming credit for building value for both the company and its customer into the critical process of filling customer orders. As a concept, doing things "just in time" plays well on any stage. It must be based on real numbers, tied tightly to a valid business objective, set up for immediate turnaround or use, and in general saves time, resources, and money. Planning for "just-in-time" action works very well with the "continuous improvement" focus of the quality movement. It should be a key part of any strategic planning.

Re-focusing one's thinking about organizational life so that "just-in-time" can thrive takes some doing. The first shift in thinking must be in looking at all processes in terms of their outcomes, actual and projected. Needs assessment guru Allison Rossett talks about the "Actuals and the Optimals";[11] Bob Mager, the "objectives" man of the past two-plus decades in instructional design, talks about "discrepancy analysis, or what is versus what should be."[12] Vision and a mission within sight of accomplishment must take into account both the actual and the optimal. When it comes to making the vision appear within grasp and the mission do-able, corporate planners and goal-setters must begin with current reality. Then, increment by increment, small step by small step, establish objectives that can be met—measured and met.

Ah, there's the rub. Before proclaiming in lofty terms the vision or mission of an organization, you must know what the unit of measurement is, and you must know where on some continuum of success you currently stand. You must know the standards for quality, for cost-effectiveness, for process and product viability in your own market. You must accept the fact of where you are now, and agree with other stakeholders in your organization where you want to be some time from now. Employees can be expected to make a commitment to a goal that's real, but they cannot be expected to declare "loyalty" to some lofty but foggy slogan.

Working hard and smart for clear, present, achievable objectives—the just-in-time notion applied to motivation for work is certainly worth pursuing. Workers at all levels in a company like to know that what they're doing makes sense in the narrow conduct of their work, and want to feel that they have an unequivocal idea of what constitutes good performance. Most employees want to know that they are doing a good day's work for a day's pay, and that what they do is aligned with a larger corporate mission. Just-in-time thinking can be applied to the wide range of work processes, including human resources development processes. It is not a concept reserved only for production-related work. To be sure, "just-in-time" applied to a wide range of work efforts can significantly help reduce the input resources required in the traditional productivity formula, *Productivity = Output divided by Input.* Input resources are things such as time, person-hours, dollars, raw materials, information, r&d costs, travel, and many other specific kinds of resources that can be counted. Knowing where you're going, knowing how to get there, and knowing when is enough are all just-in-time prerequisites. It just takes clear corporate and individual goals and an attitude of "we're all in this together" to make it work.

Organizational "Big Pictures." Much has been said about the goal of creating "high-performance workplaces" by President Clinton, Commerce Secretary Brown, and Labor Secretary Reich. Observers to this economic development thrust of a new administration, particularly as it was enunciated in July 1993 at the high-level conference on "The Future of the American Worker," noted that the Clinton team is tying its economic development agenda to what happens to the human resources inside businesses. This, according to ASTD's chief economist, Anthony Carnevale, is something entirely new for a Federal administration which usually focuses on tweaking factors in the external climate of business, such as lowering interest rates or investing in infrastructure.[13]

Organization development practitioners and performance technologists have been at work over the years refining their analysis and diagnosis approaches and systems. Both fields are full of models for dissecting companies, groups, and work. Literature searches in either of these fields will turn out pages of ways to envision organizations. Among the commonalities are that strategies, structures, and systems are all targeted for analysis in addition to the people and the work itself. In productivity calculations and effectiveness indicators, inputs, throughputs, and outputs are all spotlighted. The culture, value systems, rewards, and motivations for work are also usually part of the big picture. In today's analysis, particular emphasis generally is put on technology's role in production or services, on information movement and management, and on communication patterns within the stakeholder community. Flexibility in the way people work (i.e., part-time, at home, bartered, flex-time, consultants, etc.) gets a discriminating eye from today's organizational and business analysts. Goals and objectives, visions and missions, standards for good work, measures of progress and success—all are part of the organizational big picture when it comes to planning for being in business and for staying in business today. The key change today from organization development efforts of the recent past is that today, the unmistakable message is that it's the investment in the human resources of an enterprise that will make it competitive in the future. How best to do this is job number one for all those who believe in the power of just one person at work.

BUSINESS OBJECTIVES

Corporate Mission

Problem: One major problem in defining a corporate mission is the broad issue of "transference," or, more simply said, the problem of being grounded in reality. The corporate mission statement should be seen as the reality-based statement of possibilities, given a skilled and motivated work-force.

Developing a corporate mission statement should not be viewed as an exercise in choosing the best and loftiest-sounding words to describe an ideal state. Rather, it should be an exercise in which persons who are in touch with the "warts" of an organization—the obstacles, the constraints, the shortcomings—can describe the possible future of the company as it exists in its own unique situation. The corporate mission statement should not be a description of the "impossible dream."

It should, however, describe a challenge or a "reach" for the company and for the individuals in it. The reality-based orientation of the corporate mission statement is necessary because it should become a focus for commitments of time, personnel, and material resources as the organizations, teams, and individuals within a company try to accomplish that corporate mission. *Reality with a reach* should be the guideline to enable employees to know where to begin and what to do first as they try to change their ways of doing things to accomplish the mission.

Plan of Action: Transferring the challenge from the piece of paper to the business of improvement should be the clear mandate of each employee reading a corporate mission statement. In order for this to happen, the corporate mission statement must include clear statements of challenges directed to employees as well as clear statements of responsibilities for organizations within the company. Statements of commitment, philosophy, beliefs, or intents should also, obviously, be included.

This is one possible plan of action for developing a corporate mission statement:

1. State the corporate commitment to "goodness" in some recognizable company product or service.
2. Tell what values you believe in; that is, say, "We believe that . . ." and expand on that belief with a focus on action by a statement such as, ". . . and therefore, we will do. . ."

3. Write a simple sentence clearly stating your mission.
4. List the challenges to employees.
5. List the responsibilities of groups or organizations. Consider all stakeholders: suppliers, directors, workforce, customers, stockholders.

This graphic will give you a quick-reference summary of the above steps:

> 1. Commitment to "goodness"
> 2. Belief
> 3. Simple mission statement
> 4. Employee challenges
> 5. Organizational responsibilities

Examples: This group of five examples represents one example in each of the categories of the five points in the box above. Each is from a different business. Some examples are from the corporation as a whole; others are from organizations within corporations.

1. *Commitment to "goodness":* This is a commitment statement from the human resources organization of a large, multi-national banking conglomerate:
   "We are committed to supporting the business goals of the Bank by serving, influencing, and leading it in developing its employees."

2. *Belief:* This is a belief statement from a public utility:
   "Because our functional assignments are defined by customer category, we believe that development of individual competencies will result in more successful customer contacts."

3. *Simple mission statement:* This is from a foundation set up to alleviate poverty in a certain target population:
   "Through charitable acts, we hope to restore dignity and self-reliance among those we are trying to serve."

4. *Employee (member) challenges:* This is from a professional association:
   "We challenge members to provide a warm, sharing atmosphere that encourages synergy and makes each person feel welcome."

5. *Organizational responsibilities:* This is from a food packaging company:
   "We will have a well-designed plan—a routine, one step at a time—that we follow as we do things right routinely every business day."

WORKSHEET 1 - 18

CORPORATE MISSION STATEMENT

Corporate or organization name: _____

Commitment to "goodness" in process, service, or product: _____

_____

_____

_____

Belief: _____

_____

_____

Mission: _____

_____

Employee challenges: _____

- •   •
- •   •
- •   •

Organizational responsibilities: _____

- •
- •
- •
- •
- •

CORPORATE MISSION STATEMENT

Corporate or organization name: *Kindly and True, Attorneys at Law*

Commitment to "goodness" in process, service, or product: *We are committed to maintaining the highest degree of professionalism and excellence in the practice of law as we enter this period of unprecedented rapid expansion of the firm.*

Belief: *We believe that building a strong internal structure within the firm through continuing education and community outreach is the best way to assure that professionalism and excellence during this period of growth.*

Mission: *Our mission is to gain a community-wide reputation for service of excellence.*

Employee challenges: *We challenge each professional and support employee to:*

- seek specific educational opportunities tied to individual needs
- volunteer in the community
- demonstrate personal commitment to the firm

Organizational responsibilities: *The firm will provide to employees:*

- tools (equipment, supplies, training, research documents, etc.)
- a good place to work (collegial, open, friendly, supportive, facilitative)
- leads for potential excellence in service
- monitoring, evaluation, and feedback regarding each person's progress in accomplishing this mission during this period of growth

BUSINESS OBJECTIVES

Personal Mission

Problem: Organizational analysis consultants, either internal staff members or external consultants, like to use the term "alignment," by which they mean that state where individual efforts and organizational efforts work together to achieve business goals. One of the major tasks of human resources professionals is to help individuals identify their own unique roles in the move towards alignment.

Productive employment in our modern economy will undoubtedly depend on workers' abilities to use their minds well, to work smarter. A shrinking labor force in terms of numbers of workers will be replaced at the turn of the century by an expansion of individual capabilities. As the editor-in-chief of *U.S. News & World Report* said, "We may be moving toward an economy whose growth depends, paradoxically, not on the expansion of its labor force but on its contraction."[14] "Learning to learn," "continuing education," and "learning organization" are all terms cropping up in the business literature with greater frequency as the 1990s speed onward. Even the US Congress's National Education Goals (Educate America Act of 1993) includes the term "further learning" and the clause, "all students learn to use their minds well" as goals for school children by the year 2000. American public opinion is being shaped by leaders and reflected by the business press in a curious way that suggests a kind of alignment of political goals and economic goals that unmistakably includes the individual's ability to learn as a key basis for such alignment. How this merger of individual and societal, personal and corporate can be made to happen is the challenge of developing a "personal mission" for employees.

Ways of knowing, and not necessarily only ways of behaving, should be the goal in developing a personal mission to align with a business mission. Thinking about thinking, and expanding on one's models for problem solving are important practical, business considerations in the new economy of more brain and less brawn. High performance workplaces will prosper by relying heavily on workers' abilities to recognize, analyze, and solve a host of business problems. The individual worker's cognitive *development* is seen as an economic resource. The old days of hiring exactly the right talent you need are gone. Business now must be prepared to invest in the individual development of its employees—all of its employees, in new ways that result in creative approaches to work and, ultimately, to corporate contributions to the world at large. Helping employees see how to align their creative selves with the company's business goals is one of the major human resources challenges of the next decade.

Plan of action: Fortunately, there is some guidance for this formidable task. There are three approaches to developing a sense of personal mission. The first takes its inspiration from the work of Stephen Covey in his best selling book, *The 7 Habits of Highly Effective People* (Fireside/Simon & Schuster, 1989). The second is suggested by Peter Senge in his chapter on "personal mastery" in his best selling book, *The Fifth Discipline* (Doubleday Currency, 1990). Covey's approach is spiritual; Senge's systemic. Covey starts with building character, from the inside out; Senge spends more time relating one's personal discoveries and mandates to the forces and structures within one's working environment.[15] The third is an educational psychology approach centered around refinement of the cognitive task of problem solving.

Business literature in the area of career development and educational literature in the area of problem solving provide further clues to defining a workable foundation for personal goal setting. Several decades of investigation, particularly in the educational psychology area of vocational-technical education, provide us with many studies and case examples of the psychological bases of problem solving as it relates to personal development in one's career. The large body of information in vocational-technical education is available to the public through the national ERIC system, accessible through school, college, corporate, and public libraries. The ERIC Clearinghouse on Adult, Career, and Vocational Education is located at Ohio State University, Columbus, Ohio.[16] The National Occupational Competency Testing Institute (NOCTI), located at Ferris State University in Big Rapids, Michigan, can also provide information about the educational and psychological bases of personal occupational competency.[17]

Examples: With these three approaches in mind, and references for further investigation in each, the following section of worksheets provides specific examples of how to help employees develop a personal mission aligned with the business mission. Use these worksheets as idea-generators, mixing items from each worksheet in any way that suits your own situation. Remember that self-awareness and focus are the first steps to alignment. Flexibility, an important foundation for continuous learning, comes later, as individuals develop an understanding of and appreciation for their peers' journeys towards alignment.

Managers, supervisors, trainers, outside consultants, or fellow workers can function in a facilitative leadership role to accomplish this task of defining personal missions.

WORKSHEET 1 - 19

PERSONAL MISSION STATEMENT, SPIRITUAL APPROACH

Name: _____ Date: _____

Directions: Use the checklist below to identify the spiritual bases of your daily living. Begin by simply checking all values that you think apply to yourself. Add any others to the list and check them. Then prioritize those which you checked, giving a number one to that value which you consider most important. Finally, take the top five values you've checked and tell how each value can be used at (transfers to) work. This transfer could be either in your present job or in some other job you see yourself holding in the future. Add more pages as necessary.

Values Checklist, or Who I Am

check	priority	
_____	_____	honesty
_____	_____	acceptance of diversity
_____	_____	fairness
_____	_____	sharing
_____	_____	patience
_____	_____	excellence
_____	_____	protection
_____	_____	generosity
_____	_____	faith in others
_____	_____	
_____	_____	

How these priority values of mine transfer to the job

1.   : _____

2.   : _____

3.   : _____

4.   : _____

5.   : _____

PERSONAL MISSION STATEMENT, SPIRITUAL APPROACH

Name: _K. Eriksen_   Date: _12/19_

Values Checklist, or Who I Am

check	priority	
✓	2	honesty
		acceptance of diversity
✓	3	fairness
✓	5	sharing
		patience
✓	1	excellence
		protection
		generosity
✓	4	faith in others

How these priority values of mine transfer to the job

1. excellence: *I like to do good work and expect everyone else to also.*

2. honesty: *I am forthright and tell the truth even if it means it highlights a problem.*

3. fairness: *I believe I am fair regarding what I need and want on the job. I respect others and help others to be treated fairly when I see injustice.*

4. faith in others: *I believe most people at work want to do a good job. I try to facilitate rather than control.*

5. sharing: *I am by nature a teacher and learner. I feel good when I share my knowledge and skills with others.*

PERSONAL MISSION STATEMENT, SYSTEMS APPROACH

Name: _____ Date: _____

Directions: Finding your own personal relationship to "the system" in which you work requires that you think about your work environment as a whole, that is, a synthesis of all of its parts. Complex systems, of course, resist being changed; attacking symptoms of trouble or effects of malfunctions seldom really change the system. Individuals are encouraged, in this age of speed and information overload, to look for the interconnectedness of the work system's many parts and to identify precise points of leverage at which one person can make a small change that has the potential for great effect. Use this classic "brainstorm" metaphor to help identify the major parts of your work system. Fill in the ovals, so that the one farthest from the hub contains your own personal leverage point. Add other ovals of various sizes; connect them; think of them as neural networks in your brain. Forget boxes and charts; think in terms of a network of influence. After your personal brainstorm exercise, take the idea from each farthest oval (smallest ones) and expand that idea into an action that you can do to leverage the system. Use the lines at the bottom of this page to do this. Make this your personal mission statement from a systems perspective.

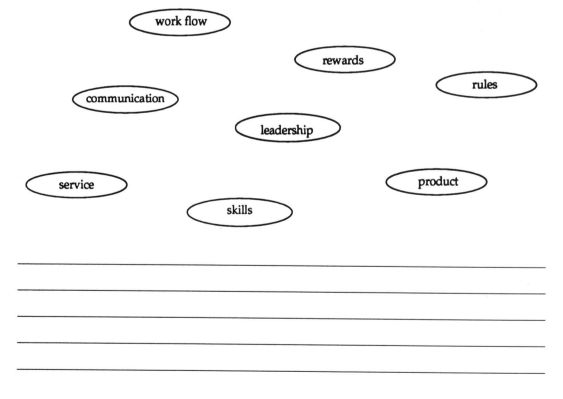

_____

_____

_____

_____

_____

WORKSHEET 1 - 20 (SAMPLE)

PERSONAL MISSION STATEMENT, SYSTEMS APPROACH

Name: ___K. Eriksen_____   Date : ____1/30____

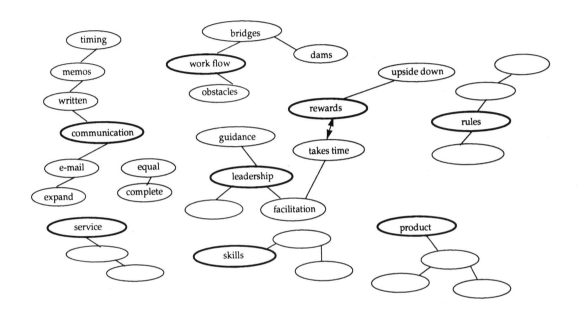

I will work to improve communications in my organization by establishing standards of completeness for all types of communication, setting closer timing intervals for written communications, and taking steps to expand e-mail accessibility. I will also restructure the reward system in my organization by first pledging to value time differently, recognizing that facilitative leadership must allow, encourage, and reward employees for doing the job right even when that takes more time.

71

WORKSHEET 1 - 21

PERSONAL MISSION STATEMENT, PROBLEM SOLVING APPROACH

Name: _____   Date: _____

Directions: Use this problem solving checklist as a self-analysis tool to refresh your memory about the many different ways there are to attack a problem. Remember, too, that work consists mostly of processes, and not just content. Knowing *how to do* the job, not only knowing about the job, is what really counts. New hires and college recruits know about the job; but it's those on the job already that know how to do it.

As you fit your job into the company's mission, think about how you do your job and how the processes and procedures of work as you do it can be done better. Think of what "high performance" means to you. Think of the range of problem solving techniques and then dare to experiment by expanding or enhancing the way you work by trying a new or forgotten problem solving technique in some of the tasks of your job. Check all techniques that you either do or think you'd like to try in order to do your job better. Make this list work for you; be radical or conventional, but be yourself. Make choices that will support your personality and your job for the good of the company. Summarize your problem solving choices in a personal mission statement.

Problem Solving Checklist

do now		*would like to try*
_____	use analogies	_____
_____	map or flowchart	_____
_____	infer and suppose	_____
_____	trial and error/experiment	_____
_____	separate means and ends	_____
_____	prioritize	_____
_____	categorize/organize	_____
_____	strategize	_____
_____	build scenarios	_____
_____	project/hypothesize futures	_____
_____	work backwards	_____
_____	monitor my own work	_____
_____	evaluate my own work	_____
_____	ask for help	_____
_____	reflect	_____
_____	compare and contrast	_____
_____	get new information	_____
_____	get new skills	_____
_____	truncate/reject	_____
_____	sample	_____

_____

_____

_____

PERSONAL MISSION STATEMENT, PROBLEM SOLVING APPROACH

Name: _____K. Eriksen_____   Date: _____3/31_____

Problem Solving Checklist

do now		would like to try
_____	use analogies	_✓_
_____	map or flowchart	_____
_✓_	infer and suppose	_____
_✓_	trial and error/experiment	_____
_____	separate means and ends	_____
_____	prioritize	_✓_
_✓_	categorize/organize	_____
_____	strategize	_✓_
_____	build scenarios	_✓_
_____	project/hypothesize futures	_____
_✓_	work backwards	_____
_✓_	monitor my own work	_____
_✓_	evaluate my own work	_____
_____	ask for help	_✓_
_____	reflect	_✓_
_✓_	compare and contrast	_____
_____	get new information	_____
_____	get new skills	_____
_____	truncate/reject	_✓_
_____	sample	_____

I will approach my work in such a way as to imagine its strategic effects, employing more creative techniques like scenario-building, prioritizing behaviors of value, being firm in rejection of inappropriate actions and ideas, taking the time to ask for and use information from others, and making time for more reflection upon my own actions.

WORKSHEET 1 - 22

COMPOSITE PERSONAL MISSION STATEMENT

Directions: Create this composite personal mission statement, an expression of your own alignment with your company's mission by combining the company's mission statement (Worksheet 1 - 18) with your self-analysis as reported on Worksheets 1 - 19, 1 - 20, and 1 - 21. Add connecting phrases or synthesizing ideas so that your composite personal mission statement truly reflects an integrated and "uniquely yours" point of view. Transfer the words from the previous worksheets to this worksheet as a start.

Corporate mission: (from Worksheet 1 - 18) _____

_____

_____

* *

Name _____   Date: _____

My personal mission, spiritual approach: _____

_____

_____

_____

_____

_____

My personal mission, systems approach: _____

_____

_____

_____

_____

_____

My personal mission, problem solving approach: _____

_____

_____

_____

_____

WORKSHEET 1 - 22 (SAMPLE)

COMPOSITE PERSONAL MISSION STATEMENT

Corporate mission: (from Worksheet 1 - 18) *It is the mission of this Residential Center to promote and protect residents' human rights in health care and community life. We believe that self-esteem is the foundation of a healthy outlook on life and one's ability to make a contribution to community living. To accomplish our mission, we dedicate ourselves to providing a competent and skilled staff who treat individuals with respect and who encourage their active participation in the life of the community.*

* *

Name: Kris Eriksen, Personnel Coordinator   Date: 4/15

My personal mission, spiritual approach: *I will strive for excellence in my own work and facilitate excellence in the work of others whose work affects my work. I will do this through demonstrating honesty in all my dealings on the job with suppliers, colleagues, and clients. I will depend for excellence on being fair, believing in the worth of individuals, and sharing information and skills with others.*

My personal mission, systems approach : *I will take steps to improve all forms of communication between and within organizations here, and I will initiate discussions regarding a renewing, challenging, and supportive reward system that revalues the resource of time within a model of facilitative leadership in service.*

My personal mission, problem solving approach: *I will be more creative and strategic in the work that I do, embracing a range of behaviors with a heightened sense of decision about what is good and what is not good. I will ask for help when I need it, take a stand on matters of importance to my work, and make time for reflection on my actions.*

BUSINESS OBJECTIVES

Planning with People in Mind

Problem: The problem in most business plans is that they look more like accounting documents than like planning with people in mind. The challenge most planners have is to structure the corporate identity and chart its operational path so that the people who comprise the company can envision themselves and their individual missions within it.

There are lots of good words here that should be highlighted and elaborated: "Structure the corporate identity" is a challenge to planners to make the corporate mission an integral part of each element of the company structure—the issues, the decisions, the competition, the tangible and human resources. The "reach" articulated in mission statements has to be given form in the business plan, and that's what structuring the corporate identity is all about.

"Charting its operational path" is the main function of the business plan. The business plan has to turn the commitments, beliefs, employee challenges, and organizational responsibilities into procedures, resource allocations, and timelines.

"Envision themselves" means that business planners develop their plans so that people can imagine themselves working within the framework of a plan that makes good business sense and sparks their creativity. It cannot just be a document of attractive numbers.

Plan of action: The classic format for a business plan includes these elements:

Executive summary
Introduction
Mission statement
Motivation or reasons for the plan
Market analysis
Business analysis
Operational plan: issues and decision dates
Controls and measurements
Resource requirements

The finished document must give anyone who reads it a very clear idea of what should be happening when. Planning with people in mind must also give the reader the impression that there's a vital role for each employee to play in executing this plan. It should not be a document that only the CEO can talk about with the board of directors.

Those who write business plans should take the time to understand the corporate mission statement and interview a representative number of individuals to discuss their personal mission statements before any writing on the business plan is done. As each element of the plan is addressed, keep foremost in mind the notion that people at work are behind any good number that appears in a planning document. Make yourself fully knowledgeable about the interactive people-intensive processes behind the deadlines, the dollars, the percentages, the targets, the headcounts, and the bottom line.

Example: This is the story of a small company in Indiana that manufactures ceiling tiles, insulation, and other fiber-based building materials. There are forty employees; the company grosses about $5 billion in sales annually. The company culture is old style: top-down, command and control, boss thinks and workers act. Four supervisors "ride herd" on approximately equal-number groups of hourly workers. One-way communication, favoritism, mistrust, and keep-your-mouth-shut are the obvious human resources environment. Three levels of management stand between the hourly worker and the man at the top of the organization chart. This description is the description of hundreds of small manufacturing, assembly, or packaging companies across the United States.

Then one day, things changed at this particular plant. A man with a mission replaced one of the old timer managers and began to talk about employee involvement. He looked at turnover rate, for one measure, and found that it was very low; that over the years, people stayed and believed in the company. It seemed obvious that there was a great deal of job know-how resident in this particular workforce, and, just maybe, the business could benefit from workers having more of a say in how things were done. The new plant manager's mission propelled him into structuring a new corporate identity that enlivened the workforce.

In addition, a new operational path needed to be charted. Key among the processes that demanded a new operational path was the decision-making process. It's hard for newly-empowered persons to suddenly want the responsibility for decision outcomes. It's especially hard to monitor, evaluate, and discipline fellow workers; it's even hard to develop vacation schedules when, as a developer, you have no "big stick" to carry when folks find it hard to come to agreement.

And finally, the business plan had to be created so that folks could make a transition from the old ways of working to the new ways of working. This particular plan, in fact, was developed as a "transition plan" that featured committees whose main tasks were to experiment, assess, and make recommendations. With this fluid approach to planning, the forty employees could envision themselves as involved employees with unique and valuable contributions to make. What a difference this was from the old way of doing things and the old ways of thinking. This was planning with people in mind.

WORKSHEET 1 - 23

BUSINESS PLANNING TEMPLATE

Directions: Use this planning template to make notes to yourself as you begin organizing your thoughts in preparation for writing a business plan. Begin by identifying the span of time for which this plan is to be implemented, e.g., 6 months, 1 year, 5 years, etc., and note the date on which you made the notes. Add more pages and expand the boxes as necessary.

Time span for this plan: _____   **Today's date:** _____

Introduction

Mission statement

Motivation or reasons for the plan

Market analysis

Business analysis

Operational plan: issues and decision dates

Controls and measurements

Resource requirements

WORKSHEET 1 - 23 (SAMPLE)

BUSINESS PLANNING TEMPLATE

Time span for this plan: _____ *10/1 - 3/31* _____ **Today's date:** ___ *8/10* ___

Introduction
(Preface this with 1/2 page summary of the entire plan.)
Talk about challenges of information dissemination and personal mastery

Mission statement
focus on maximizing the individual's capacity to learn

Motivation or reasons for the plan
- *downsizing*
- *elimination of middle management*

Market analysis
*find out what information networks (client/servers??) competitors XYZ, Inc.
and Zenith Productions use*

Business analysis
- *estimate savings in classroom-centered travel and time off work*
- *be sure numbers are accurate on planned RIFs for first quarter*
- *focus on current design staff's credentials and experience*

Operational plan: issues and decision dates
- *check vacation schedules for Jeff, Bob, Aggie and Fritz—be sure
to interview them by 9/15*
- *do a comprehensive flow chart for individualized training*

Controls and measurements
- *assign a person to be in charge of content quality*
- *assign another person to be in charge of process quality*
- *have design reviews by 10/30; run it like a 6-month project*

Resource requirements
- *build in 2 or 3 client/server systems*
- *write in renovations to library at about $45,000 (?)*
- *suggest better use of existing PCs*
- *fund several new pieces of software for each workstation*

Endnotes for Chapter 2
Notes 1 through 17

1. "Ways to Sink Self-Managed Teams" by Lawrence Holpp, in *Training*, September 1993, p. 42.

2. "When Times Get Tough, What Happens to TQM?" by Daniel Niven, *Harvard Business Review*, May-June 1993, pp. 20-34.

3. Interview conducted by Rich Karlgaard for *Forbes ASAP*, September 13, 1993, p. 75.

4. "Is Your Organization Poised for the Twenty-First Century?" by Stephen J. Frangos, *TQO* newsletter, December 1992, p. 9.

5. "Mead Quality Program Spreads Throughout 3 Plants in Lee," by Lewis C. Cuyler, *The Berkshire Eagle*, October 2, 1993, p. D1.

6. *Forbes ASAP*, op. cit., p. 70.

7. "Managing by Team Is Not Always as Easy as it Looks," by Aimee L. Stern, *The New York Times*, July 18, 1993, p. F5.

8. Pehr G. Gyllenhammar, *People at Work*, Reading, MA: Addison Wesley, 1977.

9. "A Company of Businesspeople," *INC.*, April 1993, pp. 79-93.

10. "The Reengineer's Manifesto" interview with Hammer and Champy, in *Information Week*, May 10, 1993, p. 9.

11. Allison Rossett, in the book, *Training Needs Assessment*, Englewood Cliffs, NJ: Educational Technology Publications, 1987, and in numerous articles and speeches.

12. Robert F. Mager and Peter Pipe, *Analyzing Performance Problems*, Belmont, CA: Lake Publishing Company, 1984; first published in 1970 by Fearon.

13. "Administration Prods Industry to Reshape Workplaces" in *National Report on Human Resources*, ASTD, September/October 1993, pp. 1 and 3.

14. Editorial, "Honey, I Shrunk the Payroll" by Mortimer B. Zuckerman, editor-in-chief, *U.S. News & World Report*, May 17, 1993, p. 76.

15. Both the Covey book and the Senge book are available from ASTD, Arlington, VA by writing the ASTD Book Publishing Service, PO Box 4856, Hampden Station, Baltimore, MD, 21211 or phoning ASTD headquarters at (703) 683-8129.

16. ERIC Clearinghouse on Adult, Career, and Vocational Education, Ohio State University, Center for Vocational Education, 1960 Kenny Road, Columbus, OH 43210, telephone: (614) 486-3655.

17. National Occupational Competency Testing Institute, 409 Bishop Hall, Ferris State University, 1349 Cramer Circle, Big Rapids, MI 49307, telephone: (616) 796-4695.

HUMAN RESOURCES CONSIDERATIONS

If you believe, with the Baldrige folks, that "employee development" is an important business practice, then you'll need to take a good, fresh look at the systems and supports for it throughout your company. The next section of this chapter will give you some ideas and tools for organizational analysis in the following general areas:

- personnel management, including training, motivation, rewards, and equal opportunity within a diverse workforce,
- facilities, information, and clerical support,
- management leadership, and
- learning organization requirements.

An overview of the new human resources considerations is instructive. In October 1988, an important study, *Workplace Basics*[1], commissioned by the U.S. Department of Labor and conducted by the American Society for Training and Development (ASTD) defined seven skill groups that employers said they required of their workforces. As the foundation requirement is "knowing how to learn," according to the report, employer complaints focused on "serious deficiencies" in problem solving, personal management, interpersonal skills, ability to conceptualize, organize, verbalize thoughts, resolve conflicts, and work in teams. Employers said that competitive challenges were forcing them to ensure that they had an "innovative and flexible" workforce.[2] Accumulation of knowledge—the piling up of subjects and skills—is no longer enough for economic strength; we need to know how to internalize, absorb, translate, and apply information effectively—and with greater speed than in the past. *Learning* to learn becomes the fundamental new human resources development challenge. The list of seven skill groups reported in this study is:

1. learning to learn
2. basic skills of reading, writing, computation
3. listening and oral communication
4. creative thinking and problem solving
5. personal goal-setting, self-esteem, career development
6. getting along with people, negotiation, teamwork
7. organizational effectiveness, leadership

Learning to learn is a highly individual, personal matter. It happens best when it's in the context of a problem or knotty issue on the job. It doesn't require a plane trip, a hotel room, an expensive seminar fee, a corporate training center, and time off the job. It does require commitment to work, personal competency, a strong sense of self, integrity, and trust in others at work. Programs that are designed to create awareness, "cover topics," or promote understanding without building personal competence fail to add value for customers, and in the long run, fail to compete.

CEOs reporting in the DOL/ASTD *Workplace Basics* study noted that competitive pressures often compel employers to move employees between jobs, putting a premium on the individual's ability to absorb, process, and apply new information. The complexity, quantity, and accessibility of information makes matters worse. The Aetna Life and Casualty Company president has been known to say, "Be quick, or be dead."[3] One of Chevron's mission statements for human resources development includes the guiding principle that ". . . we will foster an environment that inspires personal and organizational integrity . . ." These two corporate points of view encompass the range of challenge—the challenge to the employee, and the responsibility of the organization. It's economics at stake here—business viability and longevity—not the "nice to knows" of some well-meaning but off target course catalog or corporate curriculum developer.

So, the stage is set for more individualized training, for response to motivations of a different sort, for updated standards for workplace rewards, and for new searches for opportunities to learn. Employers are being prodded to think of and budget for training as a continuous learning process, with a direct business payoff.

THE PERSONNEL SYSTEM

Training Standards

Problem: A major problem in defining the new human resources system is the problem of defining the right things to measure. Said a different way, a key issue in human resources development is that of setting training standards. Doing the right thing right is the challenge, not just "doing it right the first time."

Measures of training "goodness" have varied widely over the decades of training as a profession. Human resources professionals are accustomed to measuring numbers of trainees per classroom, number of classrooms per semester or per month, amount of dollars paid into the training center or transferred into the human resources budget through internal accounting processes. Goodness, quality, and success in training have often been equated with growing numbers in any of these categories. Many a training manager got promoted or moved out based on these measures and the standard of higher numbers in headcount or dollars channeled into the budget. In this scenario, the dollars generated by the human resource of training were measured according to a similar standard of dollars generated by any other resource of the business.

A different approach to defining what "good" training is can be found in many large corporations and consulting organizations where instructional designers and instructional technologists are employed. Here, training goodness or the right training might be defined according to the time it took to create a course, or to the mathematical relationship between person-hours in development time to dollars brought in as a result of offering that particular course over a specified period of time (3 months, 2 years, 5 years). In this scenario, time equals money.

In addition, there have been organizations dedicated to competency-based or criterion-referenced measurement, in which specific "goodness" levels of performance have been identified and measures for each of these levels or tasks are specified. Trainees and trainers complete a checklist or tally sheet when they've demonstrated that each criterion has been met and each competency has been learned. In this scenario, goodness equals behavior.

The problem, therefore, becomes how to define the right standards for good training as individuals at work learn how to learn and increase their abilities to contribute their know-how to the company's work. The traditional standards of dollars into the budget, time expended, and demonstrated behavior each might have to be re-examined in light of the kinds of human resources *development* challenges currently being defined in American society.

Plan of Action: One approach is suggested by the field of performance technology, embodied in the current work of the National Society for Performance and Instruction (NSPI). Major directions for this field were set in the late 1970s by Tom Gilbert and "behavior engineering" work.[4] Current publications of NSPI include *Performance and Instruction* journal and the research publication, *Performance Improvement Quarterly*.[5] The basic ideas in this analytical approach to human resources is the categorization of human performance into six fundamental areas that affect a person at work. Gilbert's point, especially, is that "a course" directed at a person's performance very often is the wrong solution to the wrong problem. He and his followers advocate looking for performance problems in the wider business environment that influences a person's ability to do a job, and into the aptitudes, motivations, and psychological needs of individuals at work. Performance technology broadens the inquiry into performance problems, and thus is a helpful orientation for assessing training needs of today's highly individualized workforce performance demands.

One's ability to do good work in today's work environment indeed depends upon a close and comprehensive scrutiny of the nature of job tasks that need to be done. Redirecting one's thinking to the performance-technologists' broader scope is one way to begin defining just exactly what the appropriate standards are for today's training operation.

Examples: All of this can sound like such good logic and sound assessment of the current scene in American business. It's harder to find evidence that business is beginning to actually think this way. One case in point is General Electric.

Some background information is instructive: A recent survey by the National Society of Professional Engineers (NSPE)[6] looked at how well engineering schools prepare students for the real world of work. One thousand employers participated in the study conducted over two years. General Electric's program manager of university recruiting is quoted in *Technology Review* as saying that GE's new approach to interviewing college recruits is not to focus on their technical skills because GE assumes that those subject-focused skills have been learned and can be verified by a student's transcript and other academic documents. Rather, GE's college recruiters now focus on five other qualifications to assess students' readiness for engineering employment:

- communication and interpersonal skills
- analytical abilities
- self-confidence

- personal initiative, and
- willingness to adapt to change.

Engineering employment, of course, has a strong requirement of problem solving ability both in the new hires and in the workforce already in place. Communication, flexibility, and initiative all turn the focus back to the individual worker, as that person interacts with others on the job. The task of finding the right things to measure, or the right standards upon which to base a hiring decision in GE's case, is the human resources challenge. Creating training that is based on these standards is the next step after hiring. This will be a very different kind of training from the technical content-specific training that one typically found in corporate course catalogs of past years.

GE's recruiters report, unfortunately, in the MIT magazine, that engineering schools "are not covering any of those areas," resulting in GE's having to create a special training program (some call this an "educational" program, as differentiated from a training program which typically connotes a specific skill focus) to bring the new hires up to speed regarding these five critical qualification areas before they can even start their jobs.

The report goes on to say that 8 out of 10 employers placed a high value on teamwork, but only 1 in 4 college students was well prepared in this area; and more than 60 percent of the employers said the students' communications skills needed to be improved. The article concludes with comments from several different university administrators who talk in terms of "integrating" the practical and theoretical, and of teaching the budding engineers ways of thinking associated with the humanities and with the field of ethics.

That a major corporation, General Electric, has taken steps to suggest new standards of "goodness" is commendable. On a smaller scale, a technical proprietary school in Connecticut has recently begun teaching its electronics courses through the problem solving approach of creating the circuitry needed to operate artificial limbs and other life-enhancing electrical and electronic devices. The school's director of education reports that students and instructors alike respond well to the broader analytical challenges presented by a complex problem such as prosthesis operation. This school is trying to create standards of excellence in learning to deal with outcomes of technology that contribute to the quality of life. Other vocational-technical school programs at the high school and post-high school levels are building electrical cars as a way to teach electronics content within a context of environmental concerns as an outcome.[7] Figuring out the right things to measure in this kind of learning is the new task for businesses and schools alike. Fortunately, there are beginning to be some working models out there.

WORKSHEET 1 - 24

CONTEXT-SPECIFIC TRAINING STANDARDS CHECKLIST

Directions: Use this checklist as a reminder to yourself to look in many various places for new training standards. The secret of success in this endeavor is to uncover a need for knowledge or skill enhancement in the context of a specific job or job task. Think more in terms of the intellectual, procedural, or manual requirements of a specific person's job rather than in terms of the "topics in a three-day course." Check off any source that you intend to pursue. Follow this checklist with a plan for assessing training needs and setting training standards. Include timeline and contact persons' phone numbers.

Name of employee _____ Job or job task: _____

Look in these places to uncover the need for better training standards:

customer service
- _____ verifying customer needs
- _____ communication
- _____ organization of service
- _____ paperwork
- _____ quality of delivered service
- _____ repeat business
- _____ feedback and followup

sales
- _____ product knowledge
- _____ sales cost per unit
- _____ returns/rejects
- _____ selling techniques
- _____ managing time
- _____ prospecting
- _____ followup

information systems
- _____ hardware
- _____ software
- _____ network
- _____ system support
- _____ operating system
- _____ accessibility
- _____ accuracy
- _____ documentation
- _____ help system/hot line
- _____ downtime

production
- _____ quantity of output
- _____ quality measures/results
- _____ engineering/design
- _____ testing
- _____ inventory
- _____ waste/scrap/rejects
- _____ forecasting
- _____ shipping
- _____ wages, overtime
- _____ labor issues

management
- _____ job design and work flow
- _____ monitoring and feedback
- _____ accountability
- _____ schedules and deadlines
- _____ budget support
- _____ communication
- _____ turnover and workforce stability

(add any other job context areas that are specific to your company)

WORKSHEET 1 - 24 (SAMPLE)

CONTEXT-SPECIFIC TRAINING STANDARDS CHECKLIST

Name of employee: *M. Alexander* Job or job task: *Director, Language Institute*

Look in these places to uncover the need for better training standards:

customer service
- _√_ verifying customer needs
- _____ communication
- _____ organization of service
- _√_ paperwork
- _____ quality of delivered service
- _____ repeat business
- _√_ feedback and followup

information systems
- _____ hardware
- _____ software
- _____ network
- _____ system support
- _____ operating system
- _____ accessibility
- _____ accuracy
- _____ documentation
- _____ help system/hot line
- _____ downtime

management
- _____ job design and work flow
- _____ monitoring and feedback
- _√_ accountability
- _____ schedules and deadlines
- _____ budget support
- _____ communication
- _√_ turnover and workforce stability

sales
- _√_ product knowledge
- _____ sales cost per unit
- _____ returns/rejects
- _√_ selling techniques
- _____ managing time
- _____ prospecting
- _____ followup

production
- _____ quantity of output
- _√_ quality measures/results
- _____ engineering/design
- _____ testing
- _____ inventory
- _____ waste/scrap/rejects
- _√_ forecasting
- _____ shipping
- _____ wages, overtime
- _____ labor issues

graphics support
- _√_ *timing*
- _____ *creativity*
- _____ *quality*
- _√_ *availability*
- _____ *relevance*
- _√_ *cost*

WORKSHEET 1 - 25

PLANNING OVERVIEW FOR TRAINING STANDARDS

Directions: Transfer the checked items from Worksheet 1 - 24 to this worksheet in the first third of the form, noting any elaboration regarding the ultimate definition of a training standard for each item. In the next third of the form, draw a broad timeline during which you intend to accomplish the assessment activities associated with setting a training standard in each item. In the last third of the form, list contact persons who can be helpful during the standards development process.

Items from Worksheet 1 - 24: context areas in which to define new training standards:

Timeline for assessment associated with defining new training standards:

Contact persons:

WORKSHEET 1 - 25 (SAMPLE)

PLANNING OVERVIEW FOR TRAINING STANDARDS

Items from Worksheet 1 - 24: context areas in which to define new training standards:

1- *verifying customer needs—we should have more accurate individual needs assessment procedures*
2- *paperwork—should be more learning/competency based*
3- *feedback and followup—should do more in definite intervals*
4- *accountability—without it how do we know if teachers are doing their jobs?*
5- *turnover—teaching staff needs positive feedback to know they're doing a good job*
etc.

Timeline for assessment associated with defining new training standards:

1- *design and test individ-*   *xxxxx*
    ual assessment proce-
    dures
2- *get standards for various*   *xxxxxxx*
    language competencies
3- *establish intervals*   *xx*
4- *re-do all registration and*   *xxxxxxxxx*
    accountability forms
etc.

	October	November	December	January

Contact persons:

1- *individual needs assessment—Nico in Berlin has expertise*
2- *paperwork/competency—"benchmark" this with a visit to Ursula's Institute*
3- *feedback and followup—check with AT&T—see Maggie from the May conference*
4- *accountability—see if state department consultant C. Matthews can meet in October*
5- *turnover—talk to Prof. Schein in Psych Dept. about her model and pilot test*
etc.

WORKSHEET 1 - 26

CHECKLIST OF TRAINING STANDARDS ASSESSMENT METHODS

Directions: Use this checklist as a reminder that information about the need for new, more appropriate standards for training can be discovered through a variety of methodologies. Check off all that could apply to your situation and use them in creative ways to get at performance problems that can be fixed by starting with good standards.

_____ 1. structured observation

_____ 2. structured interview

_____ 3. pencil and paper survey

_____ 4. e-mail survey

_____ 5. work sample

_____ 6. performance assessment by the performer

_____ 7. videotaping/audiotaping

_____ 8. peer evaluation

_____ 9. customer evaluation

_____ 10. performance review documentation

_____ 11. job analysis

_____ 12. task analysis

_____ 13. force field analysis

_____ 14. brainstorming

_____ 15. team assessment

_____ 16. corporate mission statements

_____ 17. personal mission statements

_____ 18. benchmarking

_____ 19. use of advisory committee

_____ 20. analysis of legislation

_____ 21. focus group

_____ 22. statistical analysis

_____ 23. graphical representation

_____ 24. consensus

THE PERSONNEL SYSTEM

Motivation and Rewards

Problem: One of the problems giving managers the most anxiety as they refocus training is the problem of refocusing the reward system at work. Traditionally, people at work have been rewarded for outstanding individual contribution. Our models of success have so often been influenced by the normal curve, in which only a few scores can be at the tails, that is, only a few can be rewarded for excellence. Or, our models of rewards have been influenced by the traditional A-B-C-D-F grading system found in most schools. Our motivations for excellence have been colored by the sure and certain knowledge, based on our cultural traditions, that only a few can possibly make it to the top. We have grown up in an educational culture that values getting that 4.0—3.99 just won't qualify you to be valedictorian.

An unfortunate corollary to our accustomed learning environment that motivates superstars is the attendant culture of inferiority. If only a few are at the top, then everyone else must be "lower," and certainly there are many, by implication, at the bottom. The system of salary range charts, "quality points" for academic excellence coming into a company, recognition and promotion for outstanding individual performance above that of all others simply have worked in past years to perpetuate the notion that only a few select high performers get the rewards, and that all others at work are there just to earn decent pay, do what they're told, and stay out of the way of those on the fast track.

Some observers have characterized the traditional culture as "low innovation." Recall the Baldrige National Quality Award key themes which have been strengthened, first appearing in the 1993 guidelines. One of these themes is "connection with invention, innovation, and creativity" (1993 Guidelines, p.11) . The new Baldrige Guidelines are one attempt to motivate companies to restructure their reward systems so that the culture of inferiority can be replaced with a culture of pride and self-esteem among all workers. Also, the human resources development and management category of the Baldrige Guidelines places a greater stress on flexibility in work organization and work assignments. Baldrige Guidelines specify that continuous improvement and "cycles of learning" be integral to the activities of all work groups, thus requiring a company to develop a culture of problem solving, analysis, and enterprise (p.10). 1994 Baldrige Guidelines repeat these ideas (pp. 11 and 12, 1994 Award Criteria)

A recent article in *Quality Progress* magazine on "quality change" contrasts what low innovation companies invest in with the investment choices of high innovation companies. Author Rosabeth Moss Kanter says low innovation companies typically spend their human resources budget on recruitment and replacement because of high turnover. High innovation, flexible companies, on the other hand, tend to spend their money on making employees better over time—on things like career development, and on training and education designed to help people be better at their current jobs.[8] High innovation companies foster a culture of pride, and typically feature a reward system that includes abundant praise, many different kinds of recognition, and very public demonstration of pride in continuous improvement. According to Kanter, high innovation workplaces benefit from the publicity value of abundant praise. Because everybody sees what everyone else is capable of, pride in the company and in each other increase. Low innovation companies tend to give rewards in secret because so few are rewarded, and public display of such rewards tends only to reinforce the culture of inferiority and exclusivity.

In our design of motivations and rewards appropriate to high innovation workplaces, we need to be strong enough to shed the dead weight of our intellectual, political, and financial investments in past systems and to think differently about the human resources of economic development and to invest differently in them.

Plan of Action: One place to look for guidance, of course, is the Baldrige Guidelines themselves. This document can give you ideas, but any organizational assessment and problem diagnosis should be a "bottom up" endeavor, originating within the organizations under scrutiny. The point system of the Baldrige Award should be recognized for what it is, a publicity system, not necessarily a recipe for organization development. Use the concepts in the Baldrige Guidelines to create your own formula for assessment of motivations and rewards in your organization.

Another place to find clues to action is in the corporate mission statement and the personal mission statements of those who will be involved in the change. Begin your action plan by finding out what the values and goals are of the people affected by new reward systems. Look for words like caring, integrity, empowerment, support, learning, commitment, contribution, best of the best, quality, etc. Verify with employees that they intend to work to accomplish these goals. Ask the people involved in the change what they *want* their rewards to be.

Find out why people have the jobs they have; find out what about the work itself and the environment of work motivates them to keep working. Find out if they know how to do their jobs better; find out what motivates them to make small incremental improvements, and what keeps them from (demotivates) doing so. Look at incentives, penalties, personal preferences, career goals, and personality-based needs for motivation and rewards. Above all, ask and listen to the individuals who will be affected by whatever change is coming.

Examples: During the summer of 1993, BMW, the German luxury auto maker, began construction of a new kind of assembly plant in South Carolina. In this plant, BMW will turn out many different models of cars at once, a radical departure from the assembly line auto factory of just a few decades ago which produced many cars of only one model. For these workers, a whole new way of doing auto assembly will have to be learned. The work of the group or team will be very important; interpersonal communication skills will be essential; troubleshooting and problem solving will be required as basic skills of the job. BMW intends to replace as many robots as possible with humans. *The Washington Post* reporters who covered the story said this new approach to work "could bring life-altering changes to the American worker, who will have to become more efficient and multiskilled" in order to do the work. BMW's goal is to expediently and cost-effectively bring cars to the sometimes fickle consumer whose demands for luxury cars often change quickly. In order to do this, BMW intends to create a flexible workplace and flexible workers in it.[9]

There is no place in this kind of workplace for the motivation to get the numbers up in order to create shareholder value in the short run. Rather, in such a plant where several different models of cars are being produced on the same assembly line, employees will have to know how to do "every job in the plant" according to the press account. BMW says it located its plant here because American workers are already well trained, are available for lower wages than comparable German workers, and the state of South Carolina provided the company with attractive incentives to locate here. We can expect the motivations and the rewards systems at the new BMW plant to be quite different from those at a traditional auto assembly plant.

Another example of action regarding redesigned reward and motivation systems is the Polaraoid Corporation in Massachusetts, who in 1990, instituted a company-wide "skill-based pay" system for all employees.[10] Polaroid is one of a very few major companies who have instituted a broad-based and comprehensive skill-based pay system. In essence, this new pay system pays employees for the skills they acquire—the more skills, the more pay. This is a radical departure from the traditional pay-for-doing-a-job system, in which each job has a salary or pay range assigned to it. In skill-based pay, there is a new emphasis on both the employee's control of his or her own career and the employer's commitment to a person's individual opportunity for skills growth on the job. Skill-based pay as a reward and motivation system seems to fit with current directions in the employment marketplace where a worker's value depends on how many skills you have and can use, not on what job you hold. Pay for jobs doesn't cut it in today's slimmer organizations where more work is required of fewer people.

The other phenomenon affecting motivation and rewards and demanding a change in the traditional system of pay and merit is the rise and proliferation of work teams. *INC.* magazine recently featured the XEL Communications company of Colorado, a manufacturer of custom circuit boards for telecommunications products. XEL has been a pioneer in structuring its workforce around team-based management, and has seen many successes as a result of working this way.

Among the things that have to change about the way business is done are performance reviews and compensation. Managers interviewed by *INC.* said an important skill that employees need is that of "assertiveness, ambition, or simply an expansive attitude toward work life." XEL's workers must learn a variety of skills and be willing to use them to perform many tasks. XEL's managers say that in team environments, the standard systems for managing people go out the window.

XEL rewards employees by merit increases based on a combination of team performance and peer reviews, a profit-sharing check every quarter, and a skill-based hourly pay system. The motivation system includes banners, control charts, responsibility diagrams, and other public indicators of empowerment, employee involvement, and continuous improvement.[11]

WORKSHEET 1 - 27

A PLAN FOR REFOCUSING MOTIVATION AND REWARDS (PART A)

Directions: Turn the four points below into an individual or composite checklist to be given to each employee, or use this as a discussion guide in one-to-one interviews with employees. Add, delete, and modify any information on the form. This refocusing information-gathering exercise is based on these assumptions:

- You believe in empowerment of all employees
- You believe that high self-esteem is related to good job performance.
- You believe that employee development pays off in continuous improvement.
- You believe that adults can learn new ways of working.

1. **Ask employees what they need to know.** Give them a checklist similar to the one suggested here, or make up your own. Make a chart out of the results.

job skills	*intellectual skills*	*information*
_____	_____	_____
_____	_____	_____
_____	_____	_____
_____	_____	_____
_____	_____	_____

2. **Ask employees what support they need.**

_____ more supplies	_____ different time blocks
_____ different equipment	_____ better workspace/workstation
_____ clerical help	_____ library or information resources
_____ technical help	_____ recognition

3. **Ask employees what motivates them to do a good job.**

_____

_____

_____

_____

4. **Ask employees to complete these statements:**

a. I consider my strengths as a worker to be: _____

_____

_____

b. I consider my personal strengths to be: _____

_____

_____

c. I consider my most important specific job-related skills to be: _____

_____

_____

WORKSHEET 1 - 27 (SAMPLE)

A PLAN FOR REFOCUSING MOTIVATION AND REWARDS
(PART A)

your name: *Frank Earnest*   your job: *Drafter*

1. **What do you need to know?** Check and specify please.

job skills	intellectual skills	information
✓ *CAD skills*	✓ *forecasting*	✓ *on early retirement*
✓ *how to work in a team*	✓ *SPC*	✓ *relocation options*
———	✓ *reading P&L statements*	✓ *health benefits changes*
———	✓ *writing*	———

2. **What support do you need?** Check and specify please.

   ✓ *more supplies—CAD software updates*
   ✓ *technical help—how to write reports*
   ✓ *library or information resources—CAD reference books and catalogs*
   ✓ *recognition—my work within the Big Picture*

3. **What motivates you to do a good job?**

   1- doing my part in a company whose products I value

   2- knowing my work is 100 percent top quality

   3- seeing good results at the end of every day

4. **Please complete these statements:**

   a. I consider my strengths as a worker to be: *dependable, on time, mind my own business, don't goof off, give a solid day's work for a solid day's pay*

   b. I consider my personal strengths to be: *independence, self-reliance, the strong silent type, care about my neighbors, family, and co-workers, have a positive outlook on life*

   c. I consider my most important specific job-related skills to be: *a steady hand, an intuitive sense of what's straight, I work very clean*

HRD person's assessment of employee's needs regarding motivation and rewards:
Frank requires clarity and the security of complete information. Seems to be motivated by seeing daily results of his work and being able to see how it contributes to company's mission. The challenge is to keep valuing his specialized, independent, narrow contributions within the new team environment.

A PLAN FOR REFOCUSING MOTIVATION AND REWARDS
(PART B)

Directions: This worksheet details the types of motivations and rewards you can redesign, based on input from Worksheet 1 - 27 (or a stack of Worksheets 1 - 27). Use this checksheet as a springboard to action as you then take steps to change your current motivations and rewards to more appropriate ones for learning and employee development. Check all items that give you a specific do-able target for change.

MAJOR AREAS IN WHICH TO REFOCUS MOTIVATION

_____ policy	_____ vision/mission
_____ contract	_____ recognition
_____ budget	_____ work flow
_____ training	_____ job design
_____ tools	_____ support
_____ facilities	_____ time on task
_____ procedures/methods	

Notes:_____

_____

_____

MAJOR AREAS IN WHICH TO REFOCUS REWARDS

_____ quality of performance	_____ usefulness to the company
_____ meeting/exceeding objectives	_____ customer relations
_____ depth of skill	_____ experience/know-how
_____ breadth of skill	_____ problem solving ability
_____ accumulation of additional skills	_____ teamwork
_____ communication	_____ decision making ability/good choices
_____ sharing expertise	_____ good use of resources
_____ knowledge	_____ ability to learn
_____ wisdom	_____ facilitation skills
_____ innovation/creativity	_____ integrity
_____ flexibility	_____ ability to teach

Notes: _____

_____

_____

WORKSHEET 1 - 28 (SAMPLE)

A PLAN FOR REFOCUSING MOTIVATION AND REWARDS
(PART B)

Use input from Worksheet 1 - 27 as you select specific areas in which to refocus motivation and rewards to support learning and employee development.

MAJOR AREAS IN WHICH TO REFOCUS MOTIVATION

_✓_ policy	____ vision/mission
____ contract	____ recognition
____ budget	____ work flow
_✓_ training	_✓_ job design
____ tools	____ support
____ facilities	_✓_ time on task
_✓_ procedures/methods	

Notes: *Frank is typical of his job category. Their jobs will be redesigned, requiring more communication skills as they work in teams and on short projects. We need to make it clear that it's okay to take more time to do a job right—that they no longer have to work under the club of a "piece-work" mentality. Maybe we should reward those who take their time, rather than those who bulldoze through a job. We also have to revise the policy very strongly and disseminate it widely so that everyone knows that we're serious about doing work differently.*

MAJOR AREAS IN WHICH TO REFOCUS REWARDS

____ quality of performance	_✓_ usefulness to the company
____ meeting/exceeding objectives	____ customer relations
____ depth of skill	____ experience/know-how
____ breadth of skill	____ problem solving ability
_✓_ accumulation of additional skills	____ teamwork
____ communication	_✓_ decision making ability/good choices
_✓_ sharing expertise	____ good use of resources
____ knowledge	____ ability to learn
____ wisdom	_✓_ facilitation skills
____ innovation/creativity	____ integrity
_✓_ flexibility	____ ability to teach

Notes: *The first level of reward should be for the ability to share, facilitate, and make good choices about new ways of working together. After this, we need to reward the systematic accumulation of new skills and a person's flexibility in using them.*

100

THE PERSONNEL SYSTEM

Opportunity within a Diverse Workforce

Problem: A workplace that is committed to developing its human resource must be characterized by "walking the talk" when it comes to equal opportunity across the spectrum of workplace jobs, society, politics, and culture. The '90s workplace is a seething cauldron of change, described very often by diversity in each of these contexts for work. Currently, the American workforce is made up of about 68 percent women, minorities, and persons from other countries. By the year 2000, that percentage is expected to jump to at least 80 percent.[12] The challenge for each person at work is to be a catalyst for action that makes this diversity a valuable human resource that transfers to the bottom line.

People functioning as trainers often get asked to help with various tasks in building community, eliminating bias, and creating opportunity. Trainers often must run the "awareness" courses and facilitate discussion after employees view "diversity" videotapes.

Plan of Action: Trainers today have an expanded challenge to move workforces from a mindset of tolerance and assimilation to one of mutual and willing adaptation. Old models of thinking that inherently defined a "primary" or "mainstream" culture also, obviously, built in a bias against any culture that wasn't primary or mainstream. Affirmative Action programs have been criticized for their tendency to be based on this model of "bringing people up to speed; of making them fit in." Instead, persons of "difference" (that is, difference from the middle-aged married white male stereotype) today insist that they be seen as just who they are, persons of integrity and ability, within their own cultural wrappings. "I am what I am" is the paradigm of valuing diversity for the '90s.

Action from a trainer's perspective. Trainers are in an excellent position to think creatively about how to help all employees say with pride and confidence, "I am what I am," and to be valued and not penalized for that. These are some of the reasons why trainers usually get a piece of this action:

- Trainers have typically had training in facilitation and coaching skills,
- Trainers have typically had experience working as advisors, counselors, and feedback specialists in one-to-one situations,
- Trainers are the human resources generalists that most often can respond creatively with a personalized problem diagnosis,
- Trainers have typically amassed a "big bag of tricks" into which they can reach for a broad range of specific solutions to human resources problems.

Trainers are good candidates for leading an organization from "tolerable assimilation" to "willing adaptation." If you have no trainers on call around you, try to imagine yourself in the role of trainer with the enabling characteristics suggested by the four points above. Be challenged by the possibility for personal productivity and organizational strengthening by seeing individuals for who they are and for who they can become *as themselves*—their best selves.

Encourage each employee to see the other as a lifelong learner. Help each worker to interact in a substantive way with each other worker, focused on a business objective, with the process goal of continuously learning. Make it clear that communication skills must be developed and must be practiced—written, oral, electronic, body language, communication in appropriate contexts, and communications about significant business matters. Help all employees meet at a core level where values can be explained, shared, and built upon for the sake of organizational development. Spend a lot of time learning to give and receive feedback. See Worksheet 1 - 29.

Action from an organization development specialist's perspective. Another way of focusing on the needs of individuals at work is through a "diversity audit," in which you analyze the organization using a structured questionnaire. This analysis process is similar to a training needs assessment in which the researcher attempts to define the "what is" and the "what should be" in a variety of organizational structures, highlighting the needs of individuals by analyzing the discrepancies between the current situation and the desired situation.

These are some considerations in conducting a diversity audit:

- Are there specific and regular opportunities for employees of diverse backgrounds and values to talk about their culture-based problems? As in all continuous improvement situations, in this case, problems are your friends. Be sure there are opportunities to find them— opportunities for finding problems often create the will to fix them.

- Is there widespread and visible use of the "good words" about valuing diversity? Have you changed the words you use on personnel forms, benefits brochures, job advertisements, slogans, shareholders' reports, sign-up forms, job aids, training materials? Using words that declare the company's intent will help employees believe that the intent will be carried out.

- Do work orders, procedures, methods documents, policies, and job descriptions reflect ways of doing business that value diversity and institutionalize processes that facilitate contributions of all persons?

- Is there obvious and pro-active support from company executives and organizational leaders for celebrations of diversity through ethnic awareness days, variety in cafeteria food, newsletter features, cross-cultural discussion groups and recreational groups, holiday parties? Are the outward and visible signs of leadership support in good taste and in sufficient depth of understanding?

Examples: Here is an outline of areas in which to ask questions in order to assess "what is?" and define "what should be?" regarding diversity issues.[13] Work with a task force or team to create your own interview questionnaire for each employee.

- relationship between employee and supervisor
- mentors/sponsors/advocates
- placement and work assignments
- work flow
- training opportunities
- stereotyping/bias
- communication systems and patterns
- feedback
- cliques and social acceptance
- expectations
- recognition
- rewards/pay
- compliance with Federal law (See Worksheet 1 -30)
  (In case of duplication through state, county, or local law, the stricter law applies.)

Look for specific problems that you can solve and set a course for solving each one systematically. Often, a specific problem identified this way will seem small. Remember always that continuous improvement and continuous learning happen because of small problems having been met head-on and solved before they become big problems. Establish time lines and widely share problem solving responsibilities. Make assignments to specific persons. Expect results.

Example of a small communication problem uncovered and solved during a diversity audit. A large engineering development lab had an extensive proprietary course design operation and training program open to all engineers and professional staff. Technology breakthroughs and state-of-the-art information were shared in these courses. Intelligence gained through participating in such training frequently made an employee worth more on the job, more promotable, and more visible to top management. This kind of training was definitely an opportunity of employment.

A diversity audit regarding training center practices revealed the fact that more than 90 percent of men were signing up for training in the highest leverage courses—the advanced statistics courses which were highly proprietary and designed by the best instructional design staff. The 90 percent-plus figure was not representative of the company's gender-based population distribution which was more like 60 percent men, 40 percent women. Training administrators expected course enrollment, especially for this particular group of high level courses, to have a similar 60-40 gender mix. Other, more standard and lower-level courses, in fact, had a 60-40 breakdown of men and women.

The problem was discovered in the communication system for advertising courses. Lower level courses and standard courses that had been around for several years were advertised through flyers placed in all employees' mail boxes. The newer, higher-level courses never had time to meet the print and mailing deadlines, so were typically advertised through the company's e-mail and electronic bulletin board system.

Upon closer investigation of and correlation with user surveys conducted by the in-house corporate communications department, the trainers discovered that males had a preference for getting all information through electronic media (over paper) in a proportion of nearly 2 to 1, males to females. Males were simply logging onto and responding to e-mail in far greater proportion than females. In the case of this advanced statistics course, the women simply were not getting the course announcement and registration information.

This was a situation where the company inadvertently had built in a bias in favor of men, not because of any overt or conscious favoritism of men, but because they didn't understand the personal preference regarding information usage in existence at that time. The result was an unequal opportunity of employment for the women.

In the '60s, preoccupied with black and white issues, this kind of problem was called "institutional racism," and institutional corrections were sought. The consequences of the communication problem in the case of the engineering lab, left unattended, could have meant big trouble for the company in a short time. It, too, required an institutional, or systemic, solution.

Fortunately, the company took the time and made the *commitment to individuals* to do a semi-annual diversity audit, hunted down and defined the small problems, and fixed them. Those who do diversity audits must always be ready for surprises and always ready to explore yet another avenue to find the small problems that can be solved within the larger context of equal employment opportunity—especially opportunity through training.

Example of a small bias problem uncovered and solved during a diversity audit. Most Americans at work have been acculturated to not be confrontational at work, and to not get involved at a personal level. Our workplace cultural norm is typically to not show emotion, not enter another's personal "arm's length" space, and to be polite, hospitable, and "keep it at a professional level."

A diversity audit breaks all of these cultural rules—it requires disclosure at a personal level; it meets emotions at their most common denominators of fear, hope, sadness, and anger. It talks eyeball to eyeball, hand to hand, and works shoulder to shoulder. All of our cultural images of distance and personal protection are invaded by a diversity audit. It drives change. It is part of the model "I am what I am."

Bias is one of these areas of life like pregnancy—you're never just a little bit pregnant, or a little bit biased. Having acknowledged this, you now can accept the distinction that there can be big bias problems and small bias problems to solve. This is an example of a small bias problem.

A publisher's office had many branches and corridors defining the various departments. Open public reception areas marked the beginning of the different organizations. Although the visible workforce represented a mix of Hispanic, Asian, African Americans, and whites, the persons at work in the open public reception areas were all young African American women.

This seemed very strange to all but top management who insisted that they were doing this to create opportunity for the young women—that all who saw these attractive young women in positions of visibility would then think well of the company for taking such steps to value and promote its diversity.

What most people felt was just the opposite. They felt disgust and anger at management who "paraded"—not promoted—management who just didn't get it—who misguidedly used skin color as a placement criterion. Furthermore, the women in the hot seat felt patronized and abused as female employees. If managers had been brave enough to break the personal distance and emotional norms of their corporate culture and talk directly with *individuals* on their staff, they would have discovered that many of the persons placed in those jobs were neither competent nor interested in doing them, and they much preferred a placement and advancement system based on merit and skills.

The audit did identify this as a problem of stereotype and bias, and one which, fortunately, could be corrected shortly after it became apparent. The example points out that even good, well-meaning leaders who've operated within a certain mindset or cultural norm often "don't get it" and need to be confronted with uncomfortable facts about their progress in diversity management behavior. The clue during periods of rapid change, is to audit frequently enough so that the pace of organizational learning can keep ahead of the pace of change.

In this case, the leaders were still stuck in a '70s mindset which measured success by numbers of target group members in visible positions. The new mantra is "I am what I am"—and I don't want to be "targeted," penalized, or singled out because of who I am.

GUIDELINES FOR GIVING AND RECEIVING FEEDBACK[14]

GUIDELINES FOR GIVING FEEDBACK

Feedback is the attempt to reduce distortions between the message a person intends to convey and the message another person actually receives. It is given and received in a spirit of personal learning and improvement.

These are guidelines for *giving* feedback:

1. Get agreement from both partners that they are willing to both give and receive feedback.
2. Make your comments descriptive, not evaluative.
3. Describe behaviors and actions, not total impressions.
4. Make specific suggestions, not general ones.
5. Include both positive and negative observations.
6. Begin your comments with yourself, that is, "I believe that you . . ." rather than with "You did . . ." Don't accuse; simply report what you have noticed.
7. Maintain smiling eye contact with your partner.
8. Maintain an open, somewhat informal posture; pay attention to your body language and send a nonverbal message of acceptance.
9. Beware of your own biases, attitudes, and hidden agendas, and don't get trapped in your own frailties.
10. Be considerate of the receiver's feelings, readiness, trust level, tolerance limits, and self-esteem. Don't press on if the emotional climate needs fixing.

GUIDELINES FOR RECEIVING FEEDBACK

Feedback is the attempt to reduce distortions between the message a person intends to convey and the message another person actually receives. It is given and received in a spirit of personal learning and improvement.

These are guidelines for *receiving* feedback:

1. Pay attention; listen actively; remain open-minded.
2. Ask for clarification and elaboration of specific points if you want them.
3. Request descriptive information on specific points. (If your actions need changing, it will be much easier to make change if you have an accurate description of very specific points.)
4. Be willing to hear both positive and negative reports.
5. Acknowledge feedback. (It's hard for some people to give feedback.)
6. Ask for your partner's ideas on specific improvement tactics if you believe that you could benefit from them.
7. If you've had enough, tell your partner by saying, "Thanks, that's enough feedback on this item," and continue to the next item. Keep it item-specific.
8. Avoid being defensive. (This is feedback, not salary review.)
9. Be aware of your body language and attitudes so that your partner doesn't become defensive about giving feedback.
10. Sort out and select which elements of the feedback you will act upon. Do this soon after the training session and in private.

WORKSHEET 1 - 30

LIST OF EQUAL EMPLOYMENT OPPORTUNITY (EEO) LEGISLATION REQUIRING COMPLIANCE

Title VII of The Civil Rights Act of 1964

The Civil Rights Act of 1991

The Age Discrimination in Employment Act (ADEA)

The Equal Pay Act of 1963

The Rehabilitation Act of 1973

The Americans with Disabilities Act of 1990 (ADA)

The Pregnancy Discrimination Act of 1978

Executive Order 11246 (Affirmative Action in Government Contracting)[15]

WORKSHEET 1 - 31

CIVIL RIGHTS/EEO CHECKLIST FOR TRAINERS[16]

Directions: Periodically and systematically use this checklist to review your practices and training materials so that you continuously guarantee your employees equal opportunity. Use this yourself, delegate its use to a responsible staff member, and encourage your suppliers to use it regularly also.

Face-to-Face Communication

_____ 1. Take the time to attend to others. Watch for clues in body language, facial expressions, eye contact, personal distance.

_____ 2. Show respect and caring for intellectual or commitment risks that another person is taking. Step back and listen; don't "bulldoze."

_____ 3. Give people a chance to explain. When you seek information, ask open-ended questions. A person of "difference" might need some time to clarify a position.

_____ 4. Verify the messages you receive. Be sure that the other person understands that you understand. Paraphrase, reflect your feelings, check assumptions, use examples.

_____ 5. Protect your own self-worth as well as that of others. Explain your own cultural point of view as well as ask the other person to explain his or hers. If you don't understand, say so, and ask the other person to help you understand.

_____ 6. Be aware of feelings. If something bothers you, tell the other person how you feel; and be open to the possibility that you might hurt someone else's feelings. Feelings and beliefs are powerful motivators at work and should not be denied.

_____ 7. Make sensitive decisions. Develop options and assess their consequences. Consider differences in norms and try to minimize conflicts in values. Involve others in decision-making.

_____ 8. Correct information deficits.

_____ 9. Remove barriers to contribution.

Written Communication

_____ 10. Examine print materials for evidence that no discriminatory language exists regarding race, ethnicity, religion, gender, age, or disability. Look at these kinds of materials:
    _____ • slides and overhead transparencies
    _____ • films, videotapes, and audiotapes
    _____ • computer software, programs, CBT lessons
    _____ • textbooks
    _____ • student manuals, instructor manuals
    _____ • articles, pamphlets, and other handout material
    _____ • promotional materials from vendors and exhibitors
    _____ • conference registration forms, confirmation forms, and all pre-conference publicity
    _____ • artwork (posters, cartoons, graphic slides, etc.—be especially careful about gender and racial stereotypes)

WORKSHEET 1 - 31, continued

Accessibility

_____ 11. Establish procedures for persons to report violations of equal employment opportunity.

_____ 12. Establish procedures to discipline persons who violate protections of equal employment opportunity.

_____ 13. Advertise courses and conferences equally to all persons whose jobs can benefit from it.

_____ 14. Make sure classrooms, libraries, laboratories, conference areas, and all other learning areas are accessible to handicapped persons.

_____ 15. Make sure rest rooms, eating rooms, and lounges are accessible to handicapped persons.

Evaluation and Testing

_____ 16. Solicit written evaluations and make sure you receive one from each attendee. Also, process them equally to give each attendee an equal voice in feedback to improve training.

_____ 17. Make sure testing done to indicate mastery or achievement is directly related to the job.

_____ 18. Review tests to ensure they are free of bias in design as well as in language.

_____ 19. Validate tests and make sure they are reliable.

_____ 20. Make sure tests are administered fairly by competent test administrators.

_____ 21. Make sure test takers are given opportunities to remediate poor testing performance.

_____ 22. Explore alternatives to testing thoroughly before embarking on a testing program in a course, seminar session, or any training event.

Note: Training is considered by many people to be an "opportunity of employment." Every training event that you sponsor must be governed by principles of access and equity according to Federal law.

WORKSHEET 1 - 32

CHECKLIST OF THINGS YOU CANNOT ASK AT TIMES OF HIRING, PLACEMENT, JOB ADVANCEMENT, AND TERMINATION

Federal law and the courts have determined that information in any of these areas can be used to prevent equal employment opportunity.

_____ Race
_____ Sex
_____ Date of birth
_____ National origin
_____ Marital status
_____ Ages of children
_____ Religion
_____ Former name
_____ Parents' names
_____ Birthplace
_____ Primary language/ secondary language*
_____ Arrest record*
_____ Childcare arrangements
_____ Parents' or spouse's occupation*
_____ Religious affiliation
_____ Military experience
_____ Educational background*
_____ Physical limitations*

*unless this information is a requirement of the job

FACILITIES, INFORMATION, AND CLERICAL SUPPORT

Facilities

Problem: As employee development becomes more important to the company, more focused on the individual learner, and more varied in delivery media, employees need to take an objective look at the existing facilities for training to see if they're still relevant. Workers also need to imagine what kinds of learning spaces they personally feel comfortable in, as the new world of continuous learning *at work* and *from work* takes shape.

It's no secret that the combination of computer, telephone, and video technologies is rapidly changing the way in which people receive information. For several decades, a public discussion has been going on over what is entertainment and what is useful information. Educators from kindergarten to graduate school worry in classrooms and in scholarly journals that the proliferation and integration of electronic media have already conspired to seduce viewers and users into believing that they are learning when, in reality, they have been simply watching or playing. Grazing with a video remote control device or skimming the surface of a field of computer icons with a mouse, according to many skeptics, can hardly be called engaging in learning. Critics complain that questionable consumer appetites for more and flashier bells and whistles, and corporate profiteering in a hugely successful consumer electronics market, have spawned an essentially passive entertainment activity that all too often tries to masquerade as education. Those who worry about isolation of the individual as he or she sits in front of a TV screen or at a computer keyboard worry that our society is dooming itself to extinction by importing electronic "bread and circuses" into every home, office cubicle, company car, and workstation.

Plan of Action: To be sure, facilities issues in the learning organization must be debated in the context of communication systems. Consideration must be given to how people at work send information—that is, how an individual initiates the sharing of what he or she knows, needs to know, or deems important. The way language is used suggests clues to the user's capacity to learn. And in an information-intensive work environment, the medium or vehicle for transporting language plays an important part in the facilities' support that a workplace provides to the learner. Employees at all levels would do themselves a favor if they'd take a look inward to their own preferred learning styles and how they most efficiently use information. Individual differences can be expected to be very much in evidence in this endeavor, and should form the foundation for specification of the kinds of information processing technology that it makes sense to provide to an individual in order for that individual to be supported in his or her work. Defining the appropriate "facilities" for an individual's best use of information means thinking very creatively about how and where pieces of electronic gear can be linked together in order to "facilitate" the human relationships that must be part of an employee's contributions to work and continuous learning from work.

Marshall McLuhan warned us a long time ago that "the medium is—(or could become—without careful safeguards)—the massage." With today's ever-increasing speed and capacity for information use, it is more and more important that individuals take the time to reflect upon their own particular relationship to information so that the indisputable power and wily seductiveness of the medium of electronics does not drown out its possibilities as a learning facilitator. It is very easy for the busy worker, suffering from information overload and few maps with which to organize pathways through it, to revert to a highly self-centered and surface relationship with electronic machines, simply conducting business by inputting and outputting data and isolated bits of information, sitting all day in a lonely facility which encourages the medium to bombard *the person* with the message that work is unconnected in a human way with the flesh and blood of the marketplace.

Individuals relating to individuals is the essence of human enterprise, and learning must occur within this relational context. Use of tools and structured environments to support learning is important, and must be updated for the nature of work in today's world. Workplace learners need to analyze the classroom, the laboratory, the conference room, and even the lunch room to see how these facilities support various kinds of learning and whether or not they are being used in appropriate ways. Workplace learners also need to assess their uses of books, tapes, conferences, benchmarking trips, software, CBT lessons, team meetings, and all other tools and facilities surrounding work to see just how each can be supportive of that individual's preferred ways to learn. Facilities support must be determined within this broad context of options, yet within a narrow individual learner set of requirements for continuous on-the-job learning.

Examples: In 1991, Subaru-Isuzu Automotive, Inc., an auto and truck manufacturing complex of plants in Indiana, was faced with having to train a large maintenance staff quickly in dealing with new processes and new equipment. New technologies, new plant organization, new information, and new buildings all contributed to the training challenges both for the trainers and the maintenance workers themselves.[17]

Trainers first approached their training design task by collecting the hundreds of equipment manuals and attempting to see what could be turned into lessons for classroom training. They soon realized that the speed of change in the production schedule and the speed of change in work processes and last-minute design changes in the equipment itself associated with the start-up of the new facilities were too fast to design and deliver training in the usual way. There simply wasn't enough time. The classroom was definitely not a facility option for delivering this maintenance training.

Instead, the trainers turned to the work itself as the "facility" of choice for the training. They chose a structured on-the-job training program that met their requirements for flexibility, completeness, cross-functional skill development, and continuous improvement.

This example illustrates the absolute necessity, within a workplace of rapid change and information abundance, for trainers and trainees to be willing to break the old bonds of familiar times and places for "getting" training. It entices us to think about the inherent learning potential of work itself, and prods us to search for systems, methods, and persons who can guide and "facilitate" the discovery of that learning.

FACILITIES, INFORMATION, AND CLERICAL SUPPORT

CHAPTER 3

Information

Problem: Electronic linkages characterize today's information rich world and alter the relationships between groups and their members. Accessibility to information shifts the manager's traditional role of "information filter" or "informational gatekeeper" to the individual accessor of information, generating a power shift of enormous proportions. But access doesn't mean that users of electronic ports or entryways are producers or shapers of information; use doesn't mean that useful information is being found; and availability doesn't necessarily carry with it a responsibility or a capability to make wise decisions about the information.

The big problem with information is the problem of organization of information, more specifically, of "retrofitting" a practical and effective means to get to the heart of what you need for learning and for working. In addition, data security and control systems are also having to be designed in many cases after the data bases were designed and created. Both retrofit problems leave the user at the mercy of good designers, bad designers, and no designers. Even the most flexible and mentally fit user can hardly be expected to be an efficient user of such information, and, at worst, is probably spending a large percentage of "information-engagement" time in simply cruising through pages of data and random messages.

How to get more out of the information experience is the challenge of the '90s. Talk-radio wonder, Rush Limbaugh's producer is quoted in *US News & World Report* as describing his baby-boomer audience by saying, "I'm convinced these people want to learn, but they don't want to wade through the *New York Times* to do it." He further says that his boomer audience "perceives news and current events as pop culture." One Rush fan is quoted as saying that "Before Rush, I didn't know anything about politics. Rush makes politics fun."[18] Limbaugh's use of information to entertain is smart marketing in tune with his audience's experience in dealing with information.

The challenge of information is the challenge of managing the contradictions in it—enormous availability, yet limited understanding of the active processes required to turn it into learning, and to not be content with its being simply passive entertainment.

Plan of action: One of the clues to personal management of information is the notion that people are designed to learn. Peter Senge, "learning organization" guru, said in a speech at the American Society for Training and Development (ASTD's) National Conference in New Orleans (1992) that he believed the urge to learn was greater even than the urge to have sex, noting that it started earlier in life and lasted longer than the need to procreate. Perhaps the problem with learning from information, or using information as a tool for learning, is that we suffer from too much of a good thing—our coping mechanisms have been dulled by too many words, too many images, too much availability, too many competing information options. We need a plan of action to put ourselves back in the driver's seat. We need to embrace a psychology of self-direction regarding information and the uses of it.

As the Rush Limbaugh producer said, they seem to *want to learn*, but just don't want to deal with the overload. A different kind of thinking about information is required. Here are some suggestions:

1. Think active instead of passive.
2. Think of yourself as a monitor, not one who is dependent on or enveloped by information.
3. Think of synthesis instead of fragmentation.
4. Get the whole into the parts. Define the big picture first.
5. Think in terms of both conceptually-driven information and data-driven information, but not of one to the exclusion of the other.
6. Think of inquiry rather than dogma. Investigate, don't just accept.
7. Make information connections; think network, not formula.
8. Think collaboration rather than competition.
9. Think in terms of management of knowledge rather than in terms of management of information systems.
10. Think relationship, not isolation.

When you hold information at your fingertips, here are some suggestions for getting and using it—up close and personal:

A. Get only what you need. As you gather information, stop periodically to assess whether it is the right information. Necessary and sufficient is the guideline.
B. Don't accept all digital images as truth. Electronics is a field of instrumentation, not a representation of The Almighty. Question sources, check for bias, try to determine the limits to the veracity of information. Be in charge of it.
C. If you need the information but don't understand it, ask for help. Make information work for you. Act upon all information which you possess.

D. Connect new information to old information. Build upon your own unique database of information that has been useful uniquely to you.

E. Trust your intuitive sense, not only your sense of reason. Go down other pathways if you seem drawn to them intuitively.

F. Practice visioning and scenario-building. Play lots of "what if?" games with information. Harness the potential randomness of information and the searching process.

G. Turn crisis into opportunity. Think always of the Taoist yin and yang, light and dark, each with the seed of the other embedded in it. Define your problem, analyze what made it a problem, find solutions to it and choose among them.

H. Keep always learning to ask the right questions. Adopt an inquisitive learning style rather than a style that simply strives to get right answers.

J. Practice self-evaluation during all encounters with information. Take the time to step back and make a judgment about the goodness or usefulness of both the content of your information and of the process by which you choose to travel through it. Do this often as you search. Build evaluation into your information experiences. Be in charge of your information.

Example: One of the great dangers in living within information proliferation is that opportunity will be denied as crises seem too great. When our sensibilities are dulled by the opiate qualities of electronic wizardry and ever more engaging interactivity and responsiveness, we run the risk of confusing the important and the non-important, of perceiving "news as pop culture."

Corporations who own information channels and databases, government regulators, and all persons in authority over access can readily be motivated by factors other than learning when faced with decisions about who gets to log on to the net. We need to remember our altruistic natures and democratic values so that we take steps to ensure that information's on ramps are open to all, and that access is not denied nor a detour shaped by one constituent for another. In times of information crisis, because of rapid growth, inadequate planning, or shallow thinking, there is a built in danger to deny opportunity in an attempt to control a crisis. Indeed, the good corporate citizens of the future just might be the companies who provide information access to public-sector schools, libraries, and service agencies. Corporations have a chance, through information technology and the will to use it for the ultimate public good, to help build society's ability to learn from it. Perhaps this is an evolution in the human individual's cognitive growth; to be sure it is a challenge of the information society, for the learning organization, and to the individual learner.

Some statistics about the Internet illustrate the scope of the information challenge:

Internet is a confederation of computer networks, called by some a kind of "counterculture" to the computer industry. It has more than 20 million users in at least 50 countries around the world. All you need to become part of it is a personal computer, modem, telephone lines, and several dollars per month to buy services. The names of some of the most popular on-line services are MCI Mail, America Online, Genie, and Prodigy. America Online, for example, as of August 1993 charged $9.95 per month for basic electronic mail service plus five hours of network time.[19]

16,000 networks in 60 countries route Internet Protocol packets among nearly 2 million host computers. *Information Week* calls the growth in Internet's core "phenomenal," estimating that the monthly growth in business usage of more than 7 percent per month will result in a user ownership of the network at 50 percent commercial by the end of 1993. The total user base is estimated to be growing at about 10 percent per month. Research, government, and education are the other sectors of the economy currently using "the Net."[20]

No one knows how many of the 20,000,000 users are children, but sociologists, educators, and computer experts agree that the Net is a way to motivate underachievers as well as build bridges across racial, gender, handicap, cultural, and economic gaps that have in the past tended to disadvantage children. Their numbers are estimated at as much as hundreds of thousands. One sixteen-year old boy from Texas is quoted on the front page of *The New York Times* (8/31/93), "On the Net, people are willing to talk to me. It's a huge self-esteem booster. People at school treat me like I'm nothing." And, a New York City researcher speaks of the "virtual neighborhood" taking place because children can interact through the network by playing games, sending and receiving messages through electronic bulletin boards, and by participating in computerized "chat groups." These children of the Net seem to be creating a new kind of "hangout space." Can this be a new learning facility?

Opportunities for self-directed learning are enormous; so are opportunities for consumer abuse and curtailment of individual civil rights. Those of us in the general field of education, and of workplace learning in particular, must be proactive in helping information users understand that access to information doesn't equate to learning—learning requires a mission and a plan.

FACILITIES, INFORMATION, AND CLERICAL SUPPORT

Clerical Support

Problem: The concept of clerical support is surely due for re-definition as information management becomes more personal and self-directed. Old organization charts that automatically attached a secretary to every manager might have to be re-drawn; old office configurations of desks, chairs, computers, telephones, and office doors might also have to be re-drawn as all employees gain access to information sources and use the same kinds of tools to do it. Information usage has the potential effect of blurring the boundaries between "management" and "support." Secretaries who were used to "protecting" their bosses just can't do that anymore when the doors between people are digital and almost everyone has keys.

Of course, the kinds of responsibilities that clerical support staff have typically had are still important. These include things like maintaining documentation, organizing resources, disseminating information, accounting for employees' time, making things run more smoothly. In an information-intensive, electronically networked work environment, clerical staff need to look again at the traditional parameters of these job functions and update the duties of the job. Market advantage in today's world will often depend upon the strength and learning skills of the internal organization—a shift in thinking from "competitive advantage" through manipulating advertising and margins to "organizational advantage" through honing the abilities of employees to learn—and the clerical staff is clearly at the heart of responsibility for creating this new kind of advantage. The challenge to secretaries and support staff is very great indeed, and their continued support is essential.

Plan of action: The mindset to adopt is that of asking the right questions, not of giving back the right answers. Organizational self-renewal can be given a big boost by trusted support staff who ask the right questions, and ask them consistently and persistently. Opportunity for renewal exists at the point at which answers to the right questions define the job tasks of the support staff. These are some critical questions:

1. Is it easy to learn?
2. Is it easy to use?
3. Does this process build in flexibility and options?

4. Is this process big enough/comprehensive enough/powerful enough to carry us into our future and help us to grow according to our vision?

Overlay the answers to these questions onto the responsibilities of support staff associated with forms, methods, resource expenditure, information dissemination, accountability, and operational efficiency and you will define an exciting and viable position that drives organizational excellence. There is a very bright future ahead for clerical and support staff with vision, will, and the personal mandate to first seek to understand and then to be understood.

Example: Gyrus Systems in Virginia has created a software package for supporting the administration of a training operation. Among the many clerical and administrative functions in the package are student records of courses taken, skills certified, degrees earned; courses offered, vendors available, rooms assigned, equipment required; registration history; enrollment fees paid and acknowledged; course calendar and daily schedules. Companies who've used Gyrus's "Training Administrator" software include Kraft General Foods, Texaco Chemical, Johnson & Johnson, Qantas Airways, and Bankers Trust.[21]

Support staff who ask the right questions about any of these functions are very likely to get answers that spark their imaginations about their part in creating organizational advantage. Here's just one example:

If I buy this piece of software, can I change the wording on the default confirmation letter? We like to use the word "learner" not "trainee."

The right question regarding the function of enrollment confirmation is question number 3, "Does this process build in flexibility and options?" If the answer is no, this support person has probably contributed to "organizational advantage" by deciding not to purchase this software. If the answer is yes and the decision is made to purchase the software, chances are that the support person using the enrollment confirmation function will be on the lookout for other areas where customization and flexibility can be employed to make the process and the enrollment product better. In both instances, the no answer and the yes answer, the questioner contributes to creating organizational advantage by asking the right question and having the will, vision, and empowered self-direction to act upon the answer.

MANAGEMENT LEADERSHIP

New Models

Problem: Stephen R. Covey in his best selling book, *The 7 Habits of Highly Effective People,* uses several metaphors to clarify his idea of leadership and differentiate it from management. He says that management is "efficiency in climbing the ladder of success," but that leadership "determines whether the ladder is leaning against the right wall;" that on a project to find one's way through a jungle the manager brings in the improved technologies and procedure manuals for jungle survival, and the leader climbs the tallest tree and yells, "Wrong jungle!"[22]

In dealing with the human resources changes at the personal and individual level in today's workplaces, what we need is "wrong jungle"-type leadership—involved, initiating, risk-taking, paradigm-shifting, and visible.

Plan of action: There are some working models of leadership within sweeping organizational change. One comes from the Total Quality Management (TQM) movement, and includes some ideas worth borrowing. These are:

1. Bring the local goals (for HRD) into the strategic business plan,
2. Systematically review and evaluate progress,
3. Give recognition,
4. Revise the merit standards,
5. Make communication happen,
6. Facilitate continuous improvement,
7. Be visible working with employees,
8. Listen to customers.

These are just some of the requirements for leaders who can be "wrong-jungle"-type leaders for the new personalized human resources development challenges ahead. This particular list of eight responsibilities of leadership is quite a different list from the leadership responsibilities outlined for our fathers and grandfathers (there were few women then and they played by their own rules or those of the men!) as they led American companies in the '50s and '60s. Developing human resources today does require a paradigm shift from the standards of big company/lifetime employment/job security days of the recent past generation. Human resources have changed, and so have the rules for leadership for them.

Another model for leadership can be found in the problem-solving literature. This model is built upon a psychological structure that can help prevent a leader from being simply a cheerleader. The essence of all of the variations of problem solving models is a two-part endeavor: problem finding, and solution finding. On top of this is the concept of the "cognitive monitor," or continuous assessment of progress in both areas by the person who is engaged in the problem. This cognitive monitor concept comes from the field of cognitive psychology, and often is described within the larger notion of "metacognition." These three mental constructs—problem finding, solution finding, and self-monitoring—all require a proactive, involved leader, but one who exhibits those leadership characteristics at his or her own personal level.

The capacity for personal integrity as a problem solver—always a problem solver always behaving the same way regarding problem solving—is expected of leaders who must develop the human resource base of the American economy. These are some of the characteristics required of problem-solving leaders:

1. Stay on top of the situation as you are working through it.
2. Find the problem by defining what currently is and what should be at some specific future date.
3. Observe, infer, withhold judgment.
4. Collect and analyze data about the current situation. Describe the current situation in different ways.
5. Design the desired future state.
6. Generate hypotheses about how to get through the discrepancies to the future state.
7. Specify action options for arriving at problem solutions.
8. Find the solution.
9. Determine the measures of success.
10. Implement the actions for solving the problem.
11. Evaluate the actions and verify success.

The most common and damaging error in problem solving is not taking enough time to define the current situation. Accuracy in problem finding is a common mistake people make. Related to this is the tendency of persons in problem situations to not think creatively about the options for solution. Our previous work culture has valued the quick fix, the decisive and immediate action, the strong, firm leader calling the shots.

This former model of speed and power is no longer appropriate for many reasons, not the least of which is that leaders today are required to engage in a different kind of decision-making regarding information than the decision-making models of the recent past which focused on thorough review of all available information. That old rationalistic model of decision-making has been adapted to a more intuitive one for today's decision-makers. In former days, before the proliferation and bombardment of information, chances were that leaders could know all of the parameters of a problem. If leaders then were bright, motivated, and knew where to find the information they needed, chances were that rational decisions based on all the facts could be made.

In today's world, though, a more creative, constructing, sort of mental process is required for decision-making. Leaders today simply have to be more intuitive, synthesizing, and creative in the way they define problems and make decisions. There is so much information available and accessible that one leader's brain and schedule could never get it all. Instead, problems must be defined—not by the rationalistic model of getting it all—but by a creative filtering and adapting approach. Today's leaders must be able to construct realities based on admittedly partial information.

This, of course, makes some leaders uncomfortable. It somehow feels good if you think you're operating under complete and well-organized information. It's the nature of the human resources paradigm shift to a personal self-directedness that seems to be at play here in our requirements for leadership too. Command and control leadership just doesn't work anymore, and this is very clearly illustrated by the new requirements for leaders regarding problem solving. Above all, leaders today must model in their own actions at work the self-directedness regarding *their* jobs that they expect of employees in *employees'* jobs.

The third model which contains some ideas for leadership in the new human resources development arena is the systems thinking model. Systems thinking has been around for a long time, and has had many permutations and adaptations throughout the decades of its popularity. At the core of the model is a circularity rather than a linearity, a model that is usually represented by a circle or at least lines referring back to some beginning point. Feedback and subsequent use of that feedback is usually built into systems thinking. Often, the system of reference is a "living system" such as the human body, which people understand as being always changing within at the same time it is changing in its movement through an external environment. The Instructional Systems Design model (ISD), used for decades in training, is one example of a systems model. The "within" as well as the "between" representations are standard fare in systems thinking. Inputs, throughputs, and outputs are familiar notions.

The other key characteristic of systems thinking is that it emphasizes a dynamic representation—always changing—rather than a static representation. Contingencies, discrepancies, and options are all typical terms found in systems thinking. Systems thinking requires leaders who can deal in change, and who see the value of developing personal, organizational, and corporate flexibility. It requires leaders who can relinquish the control that often comes through dealing in details. It requires leaders who can think in terms of fluid organizations moving toward goals. It requires leaders who can be open to surprises and who can see *business* value in creating opportunities for their employees to be innovative. Systems thinking requires people to get beyond the event-based, task-based, or activity-based experience and concentrate instead on developing and refining processes that can continuously work to make a company stronger.

Examples: The first example is a composite from the TQM area. It illustrates how leaders were bold enough to revise the standards for performance and to appropriately reward those who changed their behavior to meet or exceed the new standards.

Shortly after the first Baldrige Quality Awards had been presented, a group of thirty U.S. Congressmen commissioned the U.S. General Accounting Office (GAO) to do a study of corporate change in those winning corporations as a result of changes they had made because of the stimulation of the award and the preparation for competition for it. The Congressmen wanted to know whether or not "quality" should be the strategy of choice for regaining national competitiveness.

The GAO study looked at a host of factors and results. Among the findings was the impact that a different kind of leadership had on the communication system and the reward system. These are some of the indications of the kind of leadership that was required in order for a company to change its patterns of business as usual to quality management, Baldrige Award style:

- Credit for courses taken was not awarded until the employee demonstrated use of new skills on the job,
- Praise and wide visibility were given for employee suggestions for quality improvement,
- Money and temporary technical support were given to employees whose projects were chosen for follow-up, and
- Time was allowed during work hours for employees to leave their job sites to think about new opportunities and new ways of doing things.[23]

In each case, leadership was required to start the process rolling for facilitating a new paradigm in human resources development. Guidelines for thinking this way can be found throughout the TQM movement in the words of the recognized quality gurus, the motivation of national awards and certifications, and in the thousands of quality mission statements and plans now prevalent in many U.S. companies and agencies. Congress apparently was pleased with the demonstration of strategic potential in the quality movement promoted and diffused through the Baldrige Award.

A second example illustrates some of the new leadership behaviors stemming from the problem solving model. Specifically, leadership at Allstate Business Insurance made a dramatic organizational change within the information systems operation based on a way of thinking about the problem that featured observation, withholding of closure, collecting data, finding the right problem, and then finding the right solution. In this case, leadership finally had had enough of business as usual and was willing to adopt a different—problem-solving—mindset about the situation.

Allstate's 200-person information systems operation had become out of touch with its customers throughout the corporation to the extent that the various business units, agents, and other internal customers were defecting to outside consultants and suppliers of information systems services. Allstate's leader in charge decided to go visit the customers and find out what the problem was. He found out something he didn't expect to find out, namely, that his I.S. group in fact had current skills and could serve its internal customer base well from a knowledge and skills perspective. Work he was losing to the outsiders was not because of technical incompetence. The problem-solving leader was still in a problem definition stage, and still not ready for closure.

He also spent considerable time thinking about what he wanted his organization to look like in the future in order to regain its competitiveness. He got the external suppliers and consultants to give him presentations about their companies and their approaches to business, and then "creatively swiped"—as Tom Peters would say—ideas about the qualities of I.S. delivery organizations that appealed to *his competitors'* stated business values. He took the time to design his ideal future and figure out ways to work through the discrepancies in order to make that ideal a reality.

The rest was fairly easy, once the problem and the solution had been found. The new Allstate organization he created featured "engagement managers" and "dynamic pools of talent" instead of the traditional hierarchical groupings of workers traditionally found in data-intensive companies like insurance companies.[24]

The third example comes from the mind of a leader who was immersed in systems thinking, the president of a large electronics company in Japan. This man is credited with saying that he believed that the next generation of product improvements at his company would be found in technology itself, and that, furthermore, Japanese leadership was committed to finding the "seeds" of ideas anywhere in the world they looked for them. He, particularly, was a creative problem solver with a grounding in the kind of systems thinking that shaped his "living systems" approach to organizational analysis.

He spoke of trying to get rid of the pyramid of the traditional organization—an organizational structure in which the bottom layers cannot see the top layer because too many people are always in the line of vision. He, instead, thought of his company as a spinning top with the stem comprised of manager-facilitators and the flat round balance plate near the bottom of the spinning top as the employees—all of whom could see each other and all of whom depended upon each other as they spun through space and time together. He described his own role as executive as "to connect" the spinning parts and make the spin stable.[25]

This clearly was a leader who lived his responsibility for a different kind of thinking about his company. He was also clearly part of the unprecedented leaps forward that Japanese companies were demonstrating in the 1980s. He was a "wrong jungle!" kind of leader.

WORKSHEET 1 - 33

BALDRIGE AWARD CRITERIA FOR LEADERSHIP

This worksheet illustrates differences between the 1993 Baldrige criteria for leadership and the 1991 Baldrige criteria for leadership. This comparison is suggestive of a direction for leadership as the '90s progress into a more personalized expectation for leadership behavior, consistent, perhaps with a more personalized expectation for empowered, self-directed behavior of employees. Note also the greater numerical emphasis on the worth of the leader's behavior in sub-category 1.1 in the 1993 criteria over the 1991 criteria. The following are quotes from the Award Criteria published by the U.S. Department of Commerce.

1993 Baldrige Leadership Category 1.0 (95 points out of 1000 points)
The *Leadership* Category examines senior executives' *personal* leadership and involvement in creating and sustaining a customer focus and clear and visible quality values. Also examined is how the quality values are integrated into the company's management system and reflected in the manner in which the company addresses its public responsibilities and corporate citizenship.

1991 Baldrige Leadership Category 1.0 (100 points out of 1000 points)
The *Leadership* category examines how senior executives create and sustain clear and visible quality values along with a management system to guide all activities of the company toward quality excellence. Also examined are the senior executives' and the company's quality leadership in the external community and how the company integrates its public responsibilities with its quality values and practices.

1993 Baldrige Leadership Sub-category, 1.1 Senior Executive Leadership (45 points out of 95 points)
Describe the senior executives' leadership, personal involvement, and visibility in developing and maintaining an environment for quality excellence.

1991 Baldrige Leadership Sub-category, 1.1 Senior Executive Leadership (40 points out of 100 points)
Describe the senior executives' leadership, personal involvement, and visibility in developing and maintaining an environment for quality excellence.

The *1993 criteria* also include a note of explanation of "activities" which might include leading and/or receiving training, communicating with all employees, benchmarking, customer visits, interactions with suppliers, and mentoring other executives, managers, and supervisors. The *1991 criteria* contain no explanation of "activities."

Note: 1993 was the year of the greatest change in criteria from previous years. The 1994 Award Criteria are very similar to, and in these leadership categories, the same as 1993 criteria.

WORKSHEET 1 - 34

PROBLEM-SOLVING ANALYSIS GRID

Directions: This chart is meant to be read in three columns: the first column represents problem finding, the second column represents solution finding, and the third column represents the actions required to work through the discrepancies between what is and what should be. Use this grid to make notes to yourself as you engage in problem solving. Make cells in the grid larger as needed.

The stated problem: _____

Date: _____

1.0 *Problem Finding:* Succinct description of the current situation:	2.0 *Solution Finding:* Succinct description of desired future state.	3.0 *Action* Hypotheses about how to get to the future situation.
1.1 Observations on the current situation:	2.1 Design of the solution:	3.1 Options for action:
1.2 Elaboration/ mental expansion or different descriptions of the current situation:	2.2 Measures of success:	3.2 Steps to follow in solving the problem:

Therefore, the discovered problem is: _____
_____

Therefore, the discovered solution is: _____
_____

PROBLEM-SOLVING ANALYSIS GRID

The stated problem: _group over-staffed, not current in skills, losing internal customers_
Date: _____ 7/12 _____

1.0 Problem Finding:	2.0 Solution Finding:	3.0 Action
Succinct description of the current situation: · 189 employees · wide range of I.S. competencies · deep experience · loyal employees	Succinct description of desired future state. · same people enthusiastically doing work they know how to do	Hypotheses about how to get to the future situation. · motivation and rewards might have to change · a new customer base could be developed · former customers are our best customers
1.1 Observations on the current situation: · too many boxes—cubicles, org. chart, etc. · too many pass-offs · too much red tape · low morale · wasted time	2.1 Design of the solution: · retain all staff · eliminate bureaucracy · re-draw the org. chart · organize vertically, each organization under one customer	3.1 Options for action: · allow overtime pay · tear down walls · reorganize into customer-based service teams
1.2 Elaboration/ mental expansion or different descriptions of the current situation: · look at numbers (189) and time differently · deep experience could be beneficial · visualize org. chart with only vertical lines	2.2 Measures of success: · numbers of customers returning · pre- and post-reorganization employee attitude survey	3.2 Steps to follow in solving the problem: · design and administer pre-reorg. survey · identify customers · prioritize accounts · throw out org. chart · make up project teams for each customer account · implement a customer based marketing plan

Therefore, the discovered problem is: _**group organization doesn't serve customers**_

Therefore, the discovered solution is: _**reorganize staff into customer service teams**_

EVOLUTION OF SYSTEMS MODELS FOR LEADERSHIP

Directions: Use this as a transparency master or other visual aid to remind any employee who is required to or wants to be a leader that leadership requires some mental exercise, specifically thinking in terms of wholes first, then of parts. Especially in the human resources area, leaders must think in terms of social science integration, just as natural scientists are exploring integration.

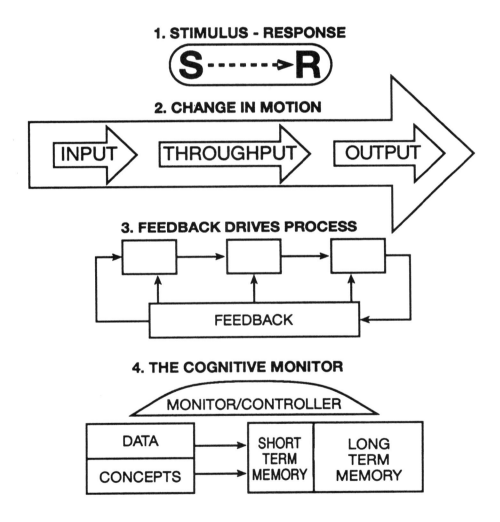

MIND BENDERS FOR LEADERS

Directions: Use this as a transparency master or poster to remind any who would be a leader that new ways of thinking are required.

Think big; act small.

Think universally; act personally.

Bring the whole into the parts.

Integration, not fragmentation.

Systems are elements in mutual interaction.

Find or create your own point of leverage.

LEARNING ORGANIZATION

Description

Problem: If there is to be a revolution in the internal structure of business, there obviously has to be in place after the revolution a structure or way of organizing that contains the germ of the organization's future growth. Such a structure has been generally referred to as "the learning organization" or "the knowledge creating organization" or, even Deming's "joyful" workplace.

What this self-renewing workplace looks like is the subject of this problem statement. The problem is seeing organizational structure from a developmental perspective which starts with the individual worker's desire to learn—and this is a whole new point of view from our traditional way of organizing workplaces by the *influences on* an organization.

We are looking at the challenge of imagining that work begins in the intellect of workers, not in the out-basket of a boss. We are further looking at the challenge of creating this workplace out of the sometimes frayed fabric or weary battlefields of current structures that have outworn their usefulness.

Plan of action: So we ask the question, 'what features distinguish the learning organization?,' and we look for answers first within ourselves because it's at the level of self that many changes must occur in order for the learning organization to thrive.

First, training has to be redefined as learning. The structures, methodologies, and tangible trappings of traditional training (books, videos, CBT, slides, etc.) have to be recast in the minds of everyone at work as learning aids. Trainers must help employees see that work itself, its disciplines and challenges, must be viewed as the foundation for learning, and they must guide workers into learning more from what they do and how and why they do it. Traditional trainers must think about training in a more individualized way, and abandon the old standard of filling up classrooms as the standard of success. Trainers must help learners break their old habits of thinking that classrooms are boring and resenting that "formal learning" on the job is taking them away from their work.

Trainers, by their commitment, their vision, and their craft, must convince employees that learning on the job is the job. Furthermore, *continuous learning* on the job is the goal. Improved performance is an individual matter first and foremost, and trainers are the best prepared change agents to spearhead the attack on the status quo of organizational culture. Training is the critical existing organizational structure from which companies can create the new structures required in a learning organization.

So, we ask again, "what are the features of a learning organization?" "How do we know one when we see it?" For sure, it has an "—*ing*" character about it: It's happen*ing*, mov*ing*, generat*ing*, creat*ing*, seek*ing*, talk*ing*, listen*ing*, study*ing*, think*ing*, reflect*ing*, find*ing*, improv*ing*. It's a place where time has a flexible quality to it and persons are viewed as infinitely renewable resources, each uniquely endowed with capacities to interact with time and work in ways beneficial to themselves and the company.

The learning organization is a place where there is evidence that individuals are valued for their ideas, the labor of their hands, and their social contributions in their interactions with others at work. It is a place where things have changed so that individuals have a chance to be seen and heard, to contribute, challenge, and make things happen. It is a company not built on fear, but rather, on the joy of creative potential.

It is an organization in which those in charge of facilitating learning are everywhere. Trainers have an unprecedented opportunity to truly serve their companies by being catalysts for change through the instructional design, presentation, and evaluation skills they so carefully have developed during the last several decades. Trainers have an unprecedented opportunity to be facilitators, internal communications consultants, and instructors for employees at all levels who would become better teachers and learners. The learning organization should have the characteristic of "classroom training in transition." The traditional structures through which training has been delivered in the past should obviously be changing, and the learning potential and individual growth potential should be obvious in the interaction of persons and the work that they do. All persons at work should be becoming teachers and learners.

Trainers need to be at the forefront of facilitation to bring about these changes. Trainers need not be shy about spreading their passion for learning throughout the company.

Example: In 1990, General Electric opened a new factory in Bayamon, Puerto Rico to make power surge protectors. This plant was envisioned and implemented as a "different" approach to human resources. It illustrates how the structures of traditional human resources development and training were used as a springboard to a new, more personalized, and more learning-focused workplace. G.E. calls it "rewarding learning and performance in a self-managing environment." *Fortune* magazine called the factory a "perpetual learning machine."[26]

Traditional training delivery structures were maintained in the form of vocational courses related to jobs in the factory. The thing that changed was that every employee on the floor every six weeks was required to rotate out of his or her job to perform different job tasks, and to sign up for and complete specific job-related courses. In addition, the compensation plan changed to accommodate and reward the acquisition and demonstration of new skills and knowledge. G.E. called this its "Pay for Knowledge" and "Pay for Skills" program. Persons in this workforce advance because of increased skills, not because of increased time on the job or seniority. The workforce of 200 hourly workers all have the same title, "Associate Producer." Only 15 salaried employees support this workforce. A "Pay for Business Performance" incentive plan was also instituted to enable employees who exceeded meeting their business goals to share equally with the company in profits. General Electric reports that results of the first year of operation showed a productivity figure that was twenty percent higher than its nearest mainland equivalent company.

The noteworthy change here is that traditional training delivery structures were seen to have in them the possibilities for facilitating personal job-related growth. Along with this, the other human resources management structures of reward, compensation, and job assignment were rearranged in such a way as to support individual learning. G.E. Bayamon has won some major battles in becoming a knowledge-creating organization, and they've done it by valuing each person's work and each person at work, by re-shaping traditional training structures, and by re-thinking some pretty traditional personnel administration standards. The lessons here can be instructive to all of us.

LEARNING ORGANIZATION

Requirements

Problem: Behind the adjectives that describe a learning organization are the question words about how to mobilize intellectual resources at work. It's no secret that many people today characterize these resources as having been dormant, dulled, or otherwise reassigned to places other than workplaces. Tom Peters, for one, talks about "the great blight of dullness" in American workplaces. For years, many employees and employers alike have tried to outfox the other, giving less than a day's work for a day's pay, whittling away at benefits and support systems, contributing to surely a less than "joyful" environment. As recent as the late 1980s, employers were known to systematically "dumb down" the work, using computers, robots, and expert systems to do both the labor work and the thinking work of human beings. National assessments of high school graduates as recent as the early 1990s indicated downward spirals in nearly all measures of academic success, and millions of American adults were found to be functionally illiterate. Clearly, there were signs of trouble in the intellectual base of the American workforce as the century marched on to its close.

A related concern to the description of a learning organization is the concern over the requirements of a learning organization. Those who would be leaders and facilitators of the kinds of organizational changes that must occur must see clearly the requirements for their companies, and be brave enough to change operational structures within their companies to allow individuals to meet those requirements. The question is, "what are the organizational requirements that must surround persons and organizations seeking to learn at work?" The words development, knowledge, and learning are all loaded with "increasing one's capacity" for more development, knowledge, and learning. Fascinating terms they are, so circular in connotation and so different from the psychological underpinning of the one-way "in at nine and out at five." The organizational structures supporting on the job learning require this circular, creative base, and not the linear uni-directional structures upon which so much of the hierarchy and job design of business in past years have been built.

Plan of action: These are some of the requirements of a learning organization:

- That the barriers associated with levels of employees be torn down. An organization of learners must have access to each other.

- That there is excitement and energy about why and how work is being done. Upon being asked, "What is your job?," any employee should be able to respond with enthusiasm and a sense of purpose.

- That people are not penalized for finding mistakes. In fact, an intensive search for finding errors early before they blossom into complicated problems should be the obvious and preferred way of doing work. All employees need to be encouraged to encounter their work with a critical and judgmental eye. Conflict and problems are not bad; they are good. Recognition and reward plans might have to be changed to support this.

- That people know what the "big picture" is; that they think in terms of bringing the whole into the parts; that they see their contributions to work as a piece of the totality of work.

- That individuals think in terms of contributing their best to the group's best. Teams, task forces, work groups, organizations, departments, committees, boards—all these groupings of people can develop excellences of their own that are greater than the excellences of individual members. Working excellently together in groups must be recognized and rewarded more than individual excellence working alone. To make this happen, people have to understand each other's work.

- That individuals commit to knowing themselves better as workers; that individuals commit to continuous improvement of their own unique competencies and capacities for learning.

Trainers who want to be engaged in the exciting process of organizational change leading toward a self-renewing knowledge-based workplace can begin by doing these things:

1. *Dialogue.* Talk, talk, talk. Listen, listen, listen. Get out of your office and onto the floor. Move your desk into the middle of the action if you have to. Send e-mail. Install an 800 number. Ask for suggestions. Open the visible dialogue with many other people; do it yourself and keep at people until they do it with each other.

2. *Explore.* Investigate, search, look, generate options. Take the time to snoop, look under things, rearrange things, try things out according to unusual procedures. Do things differently just to see if you can. If you are uncomfortable "playing" at work, start out by setting yourself a limit on playtime, for example, one hour each day, or 20 percent of your most pro-

ductive hours. Increase this systematically until it becomes your way of working. Use the change-making, facilitation tools with which you are so familiar to lead yourself and your company into new ways of working. This, after all, must be a revolution from within.

3. *Reflect.* Monitor, check, assess, evaluate. Don't do anything just because somebody tells you to do it. It's your job, your time, your commitment, your self-esteem, your mind that's really in charge. Apply that mind in all its uniqueness and with all its experience to your work. Make assessments and judgments after you try something different. Give yourself feedback. Use that feedback to progress in another dimension or to a deeper level of quality.

4. *Personalize.* Think him, her, me; he, she, I. Customize and personalize your ideas and approaches to work. Think of how what you do can affect "him" or "her." Think of how the small incremental changes you make in your work can be used specifically by one specific other person. Imagine how incremental changes that one specific other person could make might affect you and make your work better or different. Think small, and think personal. Invest the energy and intelligence to personalize your work's output as well as its inputs. Commit yourself to building the organization one by one by one.

Example: MIT's *Sloan Management Review* contained an article written by Peter Senge around the time of publication of his best seller book, *The Fifth Discipline: The Art and Practice of the Learning Organization,* in which he analyzes his work at Shell Oil Company from many different perspectives. One of these is the view of corporate planning.

Senge says that the planners finally began to make progress when they had gotten to the point of re-conceptualizing their basic task as fostering learning rather than as devising plans. Shell, reportedly, has been able to develop group planning and has adopted the mindset of "planning as learning." This is one example of a facilitator group within a corporation taking the time to explore different ways of looking at their jobs and boldly taking action that would forever have a more personalized character. Shell's planners were quoted as saying, "We no longer saw our task as producing a documented view of the future business environment five or ten years ahead. Our real target was the microcosm (Senge's 'mental models') of our decision makers."[27]

Endnotes for Chapter 3
Notes 1 through 27

1. *Workplace Basics: The Skills Employers Want* by Anthony P. Carnevale, Leila J. Gainer, and Ann S. Meltzer, U.S. Department of Labor, Employment & Training Administration, and the American Society for Training & Development, October 1988.

2. *Op.cit.*, p. 8.

3. "Reengineering Aetna" by Glenn Rifkin, *Forbes ASAP*, Oct.11, 1993, p. 78.

4. See, for example, T.F. Gilbert's *Human Competence: Engineering Worthy Performance*, New York, McGraw-Hill, 1978.

5. Information about NSPI publications, conferences, and services can be obtained by contacting the national office: National Society for Performance and Instruction, 1300 L Street, NW, Suite 1250, Washington, DC 20005, (202) 408-7969.

6. NSPE survey of 1,000 employers reported in "Trends" column of *Technology Review* by Mubarak Dahir, edited at Massachusetts Institute of Technology (MIT), August/ September, 1993, pp. 14-16.

7. For more information, contact Robert Dockendorff, Director of Education, New England Technical Institute, New Britain, CT (203) 225-8641.

8. "Quality Leadership and Change" (Fortune Forum II) by Rosabeth Moss Kanter, in *Quality Progress*, February 1987, p. 47.

9. "BMW's Experiment Could Begin Revolution" by Frank Swoboda and Warren Brown of *The Washington Post*, reprinted in *The Berkshire Eagle*, July 27, 1993, p. D1.

10. "Skill-based Pay Gains Momentum" by Mary Rowland, *New York Times* News Service, reprinted in *The Berkshire Eagle*, June 7, 1993, p. D1.

11. "What the Experts Forgot to Mention" by John Case, *INC.* magazine, September 1993, pp. 66-77.

12. *Info-Line: Basics of Intercultural Communication*, Alexandria, VA, ASTD, 1990.

13. For a complete discussion of diversity audits and a detailed case study of the Avon cosmetics company audit, see *Beyond Race and Gender* by R. Roosevelt Thomas, Jr., New York, AMACOM, 1991.

14. Adapted from *Trainer's Complete Guide to Management and Supervisory Development* by Carolyn Nilson, Englewood Cliffs, NJ, Prentice Hall, 1992, pp. 255-256. Reprinted with permission.

15. For succinct discussion of each Federal law, see, for example, *EEO Compliance for Supervisors and Managers*, Bureau of Business Practice (BBP), Simon & Schuster, Waterford, CT, 1993. In addition to these major pieces of Federal legislation, expect to see some major healthcare legislation which includes regulations on employers and guarantees of equal access for diverse groups of employees. Contact your Senator's office for copies of Federal legislation.

16. From *Trainer's Complete Guide to Management and Supervisory Development* by Carolyn Nilson, Englewood Cliffs, NJ, Prentice Hall, 1992, pp. 80-81. Reprinted with permission.

17. Subaru-Isuzu's story is reported by Barry J. Martin in the October 1991 issue of *Technical & Skills Training*, pp. 24-28.

18. Articles on Rush Limbaugh by Amy Bernstein and by Steven V. Roberts in *US News & World Report*, August 16, 1993, pp. 35 and 36.

19. "The Keyboard Becomes a Hangout For a Computer-Savvy Generation" by John Markoff in *The New York Times,* August 31, 1993, pp. A1 and D5.

20. *Information Week,* August 30, 1993, pp. 17 and 54.

21. Gyrus Systems, Inc., 1525 Huguenot Rd., Midothian, VA 23113, (804) 794-4033. Promotional brochure picked up at ASTD Conference in Atlanta, May 1993.

22. Stephen R. Covey, *The 7 Habits of Highly Effective People,* New York, Fireside, Simon & Schuster, 1989, p. 101.

23. Report GAO/NSIAD-91-190, U.S. General Accounting Office, P.O. Box 6015, Gaithersburg, MD 20877. The report is free, and can be ordered by mail or telephone (202) 275-6241.

24. A complete report of the Allstate case is found in the article, "The New Work Force" in *Retooling, New Skills and Structures for Changing Workplace Technology,* A Ziff Institute Executive White Paper, Cambridge, MA, August, 1993, pp. 16-17.

25. Personal notes from a keynote speech presented at AT&T Bell Laboratories' Quality Day Program, Holmdel, NJ, October 17, 1985.

26. "General Electric's Perpetual Learning Machine," in *PEPI Update,* Positive Employee Practices Institute, Minneapolis, MN, Lakewood Publications, June/July, 1993, Vol. 4 No. 3, pp. 1-2.

27. "The Leader's New Work: Building Learning Organizations" by Peter M. Senge, in *Sloan Management Review,* Fall 1990. Reprinted as a conference handout by the American Management Association, Human Resources Conference and Exposition, Boston, April 1993.

DESIGN, DEVELOPMENT, AND IMPLEMENTATION OF PEER TRAINING

This section leads you into and through a training design and development process whose entire focus is on developing individuals at work to increase their individual capacities as learners. The worksheets and text in this section use the best of what we've learned from past training techniques and field-dependent research and experience. We explore, reflect on, and personalize decades of work as instructional designers, presenters, and evaluators to synthesize what we know of the ever more challenging arena of human resources development.

CYCLES

It is useful when designing instruction to think in broad terms of cycles, or gently moving circular interpretations and applications of design and development techniques. For example, the 1994 Baldrige Award Criteria application guidelines booklet describes what it calls "interrelated learning cycles." The booklet talks about improvement at all levels and in all parts of a company through these interrelationships, and of the need for "alignment" regarding overarching goals. The Criteria call for "interconnecting and mutually reinforcing indicators" that the cycles are moving through the parts. According to the Criteria, "speed, innovation, and empowerment " are fostered within such cycles and such alignment.[1] In organizational terms, the Baldrige criteria have borrowed heavily from Deming's "plan, do, check, and act" cycle for continuous improvement.

The traditional design tool of trainers is very much built out of the same ideological raw material as interrelated learning cycles. The trainer's Instructional System Design (ISD) model features the interrelated processes of assessing, designing, developing, implementing, and evaluating. Like the Deming cycle or the Baldrige quality cycles, design, development, and implementation action functioning in an ISD framework cannot happen unless assessment (planning) precedes them and evaluation (checking) follows them. That is, no action without investigation and reflection. Ever. Good instructional systems are cyclical, whether the target learner audience is a classroom, as in past training operations, or an individual person, as in future learning organizations.

Educational psychology is full of concepts that view learning with a cyclical perspective. One of the fundamental notions in the study of educational psychology, especially as it involves learning, is the idea of individual differences—and, more specifically in vocational psychology, the idea of differing competencies. It is widely believed that individuals, simply because we are human, each possess something of all, or, said a different way, creativity, ingenuity, intuitiveness, and so forth, are all present in each person to some degree, along some continuum. Heredity, environment, opportunity, will, practice, and a host of other factors, all affect the manifestation of these traits in individuals. The very concept of instructional design, after all, comes from the belief that specially trained technicians can address these individual differences through the exercise of their craft.

Thus, design models have been devised to facilitate and encourage learning. For a number of administratively convenient reasons, much of the instructional design effort over the last three or four decades has been focused on group or classroom instruction. But business times have changed, as the century moved on. We know more and we need to know more about our competitors around the world; our tools for assessment and information gathering and processing have changed. Stable American industries that were labor-intensive have metamorphosed into unstable industries that are knowledge-intensive; our need to build and operate machines has changed into a need to manage machines. Our huge available pool of young workers ready for work has shrunk to a much smaller pool of workers not necessarily ready for work; generalized employment needs have given way to specialized employment needs. Quantity of work has changed into quality of work, but our instructional design models are, for the most part, still being applied as if quantity were still the prevailing requirement.

This is not to say that the models are inadequate, but, rather, that they must be used in a different, more personal, way that can more effectively serve business as it currently is today. Our models need to be updated to support improved performance one by one. This section, specifically, will attempt to do this.

Instructional designers as they reinterpret the wisdom of their experiences from classroom to individual can borrow from other familiar cycles. The product development cycle, engineering cycle, project management cycle, and marketing cycle are some of the most obvious ones. Each contains the provision that growth and progress can happen only after feedback has been given, received, and applied. These cycles, like the instructional design cycle, have built into them the capacity for facilitating learning. A brief comment or two about each cycle may be useful for illustrating how the cycle works to improve performance.

The typical product development cycle specifies a dimension of time for each phase of the cycle, for example, getting the product "concept" can take about four months; the product "design" can take six months; product "development" as much as one year; and "introduction" can happen over several months beyond that. Product designers, like other facilitators of processes, view their jobs as dynamic, moving from one phase to another, always changing and moving forward within a phase over time, as the total cycle plays itself out. In big companies, many product development cycles exist side by side, not necessarily in parallel, but always moving through time and changing within phases as they go. Each product development phase within a cycle builds upon the other, taking from the previous phase and delivering something on to the next phase.

Basic engineering cycles begin with "functional specifications," often for software as well as hardware. Setting systems objectives, designing data bases and flow diagrams of all sorts generally follows. Then comes implementation of all sorts, including a particularly favorite engineering process, "optimization." "Acceptance testing," "documentation," and "maintenance" complete the cycle. Engineering, too, sets the parameters of its field within what could be seen as a learning process—a hypothesis-generating, experimentational, building-upon-itself sort of endeavor.

The cycle of project management also is a useful model as we consider the broader design and development—and learning facilitation—issues in workplace learning. The traditional project management cycle is a descriptive organizational device that generally features the elements of "content, cost, schedule, and control." Keeping a project on target generally means that at periodic intervals (such as every two weeks) each of these elements gets reviewed regarding its current viability. Whether project management is computerized or done by hand, the forward-moving quality of the project is evaluated. The systematic use of monitoring, assessment, and feedback for improvement is built into the project itself. This is a useful design for facilitating business-driven, continuous, incremental, positive change.

And finally, marketing's standard behavioral change cycle provides a personalized analogy. In the marketing cycle, individualized, personalized, behavioral change (that is, purchase and use of a product) is the goal. Marketing typically proceeds from "recognition of a need" through "trial" and eventual "adoption" of the product. Marketing cycles are aimed at all three levels of cognition: the intellectual level, the attitudinal level, and the behavioral level. Each element of design in a marketing cycle is purposeful, targeted to a specific objective, and takes into account the probability of individual differences in its audience. Marketing plans rely heavily on the systems approach of input-output-feedback at every stage of a marketing cycle. The marketing cycle can give us some suggestions about how to design performance cycles for individuals.

The notion of cycles, especially those described above, contains within it the notion of self-renewal, a critical concept associated with the development of human resources. It is this aspect of self-renewal, and the associated concepts of self-awareness and self-confidence, that is often targeted as woefully lacking in the American workplace that is still stuck in the linearity of the mass production mental model of our recent past. Innovation and creativity seem to be stifled without self-renewal. This is why a training design and development effort must be focused on the individual at the one by one level.

NETWORKS

Closely related to the idea of business cycles for various kinds of work (product development, engineering, project management, marketing) is the notion of networks, or information dissemination and diffusion webs of interconnectivity.

The mental frame of a network is very different from the mental frame of an assembly line. It takes its shape from the structure of neural networks found in the brains of living creatures. It is fleshed out by traditional problem solving techniques like brainstorming and newer elaborations of it such as mind-mapping. In all of its uses as metaphors for a learning environment, the network illustrates its capacities for divergent thinking, development of hypotheses, and choosing to connect to seemingly implausible jumping off points. The interrelatedness of the network complements the interrelatedness of the cycle. Both contain within them a certain kind of wisdom required for understanding and being capable of acting upon the complex problems of modern business—or of modern life, for that matter.

HIERARCHIES

In addition to the circular connectedness of various business cycles and the expansive interrelatedness of networks, a third fundamental way of thinking about the learning potential within work is the notion of hierarchy. All three ways of looking at work contain the seeds of individual growth in them, and each is different from the other. Each can foster learning to learn. Together these models can provide the instructional designer with a myriad of ideas to make learning on the job and *from* the job effective and profitable.

Hierarchies have the particular quality of building blocks: they are construction tools, each of which depends upon the other. Hierarchies are typically represented in linear and vertical fashion, as a child playing with blocks might build a tower. The final construction is an entity comprised of related parts, neither circular nor networked, but connected to each other in some sort of prioritized fashion. Hierarchies meet the quality test of being parts of "interrelated learning cycles." Being mentally agile enough to deal with them can be part of learning to learn.

Those of us who are students of instructional design have grown up with various taxonomies and ways of organizing information that form the theoretical base of the discipline. Those of us who would become instructional designers through occupational necessity can learn quickly the principles behind the theory and determine some options for action based on them. Understanding the hierarchies that typically have been used to represent information can be an attractive place to start to develop the personal skills to design instruction in which anyone can readily engage. Some of these include hierarchies of problem solving elements, hierarchies of basic human needs, hierarchies of readiness for change, hierarchies of objectives in various domains of knowledge such as cognitive, affective, and psychomotor. These will be explained more fully in the problem statements found later in this chapter.

CHOICE

Choice is one of the most fundamental characteristics of American life, including life at work. Job tasks, ways of doing things, and the environment of the workplace itself in which choice is *not* present have spawned discontent, mistrust, lethargy, and deceit. All too often, our rush to automate, computerize, downsize, and drive up return on investment has resulted in the creation of fewer choices about work and in work. Often the great hustle to compete "on the numbers" has left our workforce bored, unhappy, and definitely uncreative. If we want to recapture the American worker's spirit of inventiveness, one sure way to start is to redesign work and work processes around the simple notion of choice.

Workers need choice in fitting the tools of their work to themselves, in the places that they find they need to do their best work, in the people with whom they interact as they work, and ultimately, in the kind of work that they do. People at work need to be encouraged to first know themselves, and then to boldly pursue a total working environment which brings out their best efforts and results. Creativity demands a certain bold independence; lack of choice is a certain downer when it comes to fostering innovation. Developing training that fosters creativity, innovation, and invention must be built around choices among all of the support functions mentioned above, and around choices within the content and processes of the thing being learned.

RESPONSIBILITY

It could be argued that a corollary of choice is freedom, and with freedom comes responsibility. Americans resonate with these ideas. We apply them to our family life, our religious life, our relationships with our neighbors, our behavior in social situations, our dealings as consumers, and our lives as citizens under the rule of law. We have somehow managed to not be able to apply them as well in our lives as workers, to the great loss of both our employers and ourselves.

Part of the challenge of the new human resources development in the workplace is to redesign work with more choice built into it, and with its complementary requirement of responsibility as its joyful burden. Deming and his followers have had a great deal to say about this, and consistently take the position of advocating vigorous, broad-based programs of education and self-improvement based on the individual's responsibility for change in areas of his or her greatest influence. Deming consistently has advocated on the job training that fosters pride in work, workmanship, and joy at work.[2] He also urges removal of quotas and other arbitrary work drivers that discourage personal responsibility for one's work. The challenge of creating and developing training that has a foundation of personal responsibility is the challenge of creating peer training from which all who teach and all who learn can grow personally and continuously learn from work. It's an opportunity whose time has come. The good news is that there are platforms for design and development from which to build new structures for learning, and there are many experienced builders already at work. What they need is the courage and some guidance to think about workplace learning differently. The mission of this book is to engender that courage and provide that guidance.

ENGAGEMENT

The last fundamental structure, or mental model, upon which to base a new kind of workplace learning is the phenomenon of engagement—that psychological notion of purposeful involvement in ideas and mental processes. Persons engaged with their work do more than perform it well: they initiate all kinds of inquiry about the nature of even the smallest job tasks as well as the biggest problems of their work; they move easily between leadership and followership around the tasks of work; they identify and remove barriers to their own effective performance; and they, above all, monitor and manage their own involvement with the guts of their work. Of course, they have supervisors or team mates or customers or others in an accountability loop with themselves, but when it comes to the nature of the work that they do, engaged workers manage themselves, and independently and uniquely interact with the disciplines and freedoms of work. If our workplaces have destroyed the ability or incentive for persons to engage in work, it is the instructional designer's impassioned call to revolution from within that might have a chance of restoring it.

Design and development tools for creating training one by one are presented in the pages that follow these introductory sections of this chapter. Many of the tools and techniques of this training will seem familiar to the reader because these are the tools and techniques of the trade. They are cast here in a different mindset within newer organizational models and business realities. They are customized to facilitate individual, personalized learning on the job.

Some of the design tools and the issues surrounding their use are:

- the Instructional System Design (ISD) model for peer training;
- adult learning preferences;
- personal effectiveness;
- learning mastery;
- designs for individual learning, including:
  cognitive learning, active and passive styles of learning, flexibility, problem solving, creativity and innovation, sensory learning, and experiential and reflective thinking, and symbols and representations.

Some of the development structures and techniques are:

- lessons, including lesson plans and objectives;
- presentation options and teaching methods, including:
  mentoring, coaching, one to one, small group, cross-training, correspondence courses, apprenticeship, conferences, teams, laboratory, self-directed learning;
- the psychology of the teacher/learner interaction, including:
  formality, informality, facilitation, and feedback;
- timing and scheduling.

CHAPTER **4**

DESIGN ISSUES IN PEER TRAINING

Peer training is a time-honored—and often misused—technique of training found in nearly all U.S. businesses, non-profit agencies, schools, colleges, places of worship, community centers, and homes. From time to time in our various societal institutions, peer training has been given formal attention, as in the 1960s when it was a favorite "program" in high schools to pair up gifted students with those not so gifted, or several decades before that when a missionary educator, Frank Laubach, envisioned his very successful "Each One Teach One" literacy and Nobel Peace Prize nominee program and heavily implemented it around the world. Teenagers and adults got formal training in how to teach another person in those programs. In businesses, too, there have been attempts to formalize one-to-one training through mentoring programs, and "train the trainer" courses. Technical organizations, especially, seemed to be always worrying about how to use SMEs (subject matter experts) to best advantage. As technical jobs proliferated, so did SMEs, and trainers were on the constant look out for better and more effective ways to tap in to their expertise. The seminar brochures from consulting companies frequently had courses and workshops on how to use SMEs in training design and delivery. The design of expert systems, using structured software programs, in the 1970s and '80s was yet another illustration of our abiding interest in teaching and learning one by one. The uses of coaches and teams in training situations in the 1990s point to our persistence in trying to help each other learn on the job.

There's a certain kind of comfort in being able to talk about our "old friend," peer training, although she's surely due for a face lift, an exercise routine, and a hefty dose of vitamins. Peer training is, in fact, a useful concept for workplace learning. What it needs is a make-over so that it is more attuned with today's workplace challenges and reflects new thinking about how organizations should be structured and how adults learn best.

This section on design issues in peer training gives this new look to the design considerations in peer training. These design issues flow from several key premises:

- that individuals are valued for who they are, who they were, and who they can become;
- that improved group (team, unit, department, company) performance is the goal;
- and that work itself is a rich source of continuous learning.

In addition to these three assumptions, the methodologies for peer training design that follow in the coming pages rest also on the premise that instructional technology can be applied to the process of peer training to make it more effective and attuned to today's workplace.

As in earlier chapters, each new idea is presented in problem format to encourage focus as well as elaboration. Worksheets follow problem statements where appropriate.

DESIGN ISSUES IN PEER TRAINING

Instructional System Design (ISD) Cycle for Peer Training

Problem: The ISD way of doing business in training has been around for nearly fifty years, and it has served the field of human resources development very well. The 55,000 member American Society for Training and Development (ASTD), world's largest organization of professional trainers, who implement ISD throughout the world, as an indication of this longevity and viability, celebrates its 50th anniversary at a national conference in 1994 in San Francisco. ISD practitioners are many and strong.

The problem with ISD is that it is generally still focused on bigness—the corporation, the organization—when it should now focus on smallness—that is, on the individual person and the very specific learning needs of that one person. ISD, like OD (organization development), was a model that spawned huge consulting empires and internal organizations who relentlessly investigated the big movements and structures that affected organizational growth. Big systems were described whose major components were seen as drivers for growth, and ISD was right in there in the most forward-looking companies with its model for large-scale corporate needs analysis at one end and evaluation at the other end. ISD during the expansion years between 1960 and 1980 served the field of training well because it helped to organize the essential functions of training management during years when plenty of training management was needed. The company in which I worked, for example, during those years had literally four feet of orange binders known as the "Training Development Standards" which spelled out in great detail the path to follow in implementing ISD for the sake of corporate growth and well-being in the human resources arena.

The orientation in those years was decidedly growth and expansion. As recently as 1988, a list of steps in managing organizational change included items like, define the target group, develop a research design, determine how to collect and analyze data, develop a strategy for tabulating and analyzing the data, prepare the organization for receiving the diagnosis. All these interventions are targeted at the big organization poised for growth in markets, in numbers of employees, in profit. Organization Development and Instructional System Design have a tradition of bigness about them that worked for expanding organizations.

The issue now in using ISD and other systems approaches to human resources development is the issue of narrowing the focus. The concept of a self-improving system is still very appropriate today, and the components of the classic ISD are as useful as ever. What has changed is the environment for doing business and the nature of work itself. One of the paradoxes of this change is that while work is getting more specialized the environment for doing business is demanding that fewer people be able to do more. The push for efficiency, effectiveness, and rightsizing is throwing trainers into the horns of a dilemma—how to assure that individuals can do more difficult work as well as more work, and continue to be prepared for growth. The new notion of growth is not the earlier wide focus of organizational growth, but the narrow focus of personal growth.

Plan of action: One of the first things a trainer can do to help to narrow the focus of traditional ISD is to think of it as a circle rather than as a linear flow-chart. An example of the new "ISD Cycle" is shown in Worksheet 2 - 1 following this section. The circle representation can be helpful in placing the "system" within a concept of integration and personal wholeness. It can be a useful metaphor for the individual learner.

The new ISD Cycle is seen as actually two concentric circles, the center circle of which is the "activator" driving the processes of design, development, and evaluation. The center circle contains the functions of monitoring, feedback, and modification that interact with each process of the design functions represented in the outer circle. This outer circle contains the traditional ISD functions of analyze, design/develop, implement, and evaluate.

The following suggestions are spelled out in relationship to each of these traditional ISD functions, but here with a narrow, individual focus rather than the customary broad corporate focus of the recent past. Contrast between the two approaches is included to help clarify the change.

Analyze. The analysis phase of traditional ISD would typically look at company positions related to market share, systems requirements for upgrading and potentials for increased services, projected impacts of environmental legislation on profits, and would deal with long range planning documents and large potential target audiences for classroom training throughout the corporation. Research designs and planning for data collection were necessary components of the needs analysis phase under this scenario. In this way of looking at organizational needs, the company was seen as a confluence of social forces and technical forces that had to be sorted out in order for design functions to follow that would serve the socio-technical system that emerged according to the analysis.

The new analysis phase of the ISD Cycle might include questions like, "What is it about the work that you do that excites you most?" or, "What kinds of work do you think need to be done in order to achieve this objective?" and "Who should do this work?" or simply, "What do you need in order to do your job better?" The new needs analysis questions should be focused on the positive outcomes of individual labor and the learning facilitation problems that must be overcome in order for a person's best work to be realized.

Design/Develop. Training design and development under the traditional ISD framework were almost always focused on developing courses to be delivered in corporate classrooms. Hundreds of big companies and the entrepreneurial consultants who served them created "presentation" and "training delivery" seminars that helped instructors know how to teach classrooms full of people sent off to corporate training centers around the country. Companies often had staffs of both "instructional designers" and "course developers." Course manuals were often scripted so that almost any "instructor" off the street could "teach" a well-designed course. Companies today still often think of a good presenter as a good instructor. Seminar and course evaluation forms today still focus on the skills of the "presenter," not the validity or viability of the learning content. Train-the-trainer courses today, in companies of all sizes and in promotional brochures from vendors and consulting companies, almost all focus on classroom training techniques.

One has to wonder how Americans at work can ever hope to *learn to learn* when the efforts of designers and developers have been so ubiquitously focused on the techniques of presentation. The large group/training management approach to design and development must give way to a personalized "design for learning" approach. The myriad of technologies through which to deliver training need to be used to their best advantage in facilitating individual learning. Designs for learning must absolutely eschew the practice of dumping information onto a classroom in the name of training. Designs for learning must be based on an analysis of what someone needs to know in order to do good work. "One by one" should be the motto for organizational improvement and the new challenge for instructional designers.

Implement. The implementation phase of traditional ISD was almost always centered in the corporate classroom. Media, manuals, attendance procedures, corporate charge-back accounting, certifications, and even promotions were all often dependent upon the implementation of training in a classroom.

New ways to implement training must take up the "one by one" gauntlet. Peer training is ready to be exploded with possibilities for creative implementation. Information technology and a diverse workforce are just two of the major factors which should come into play as the new ISD Cycle moves around from analysis and design through implementation.

Evaluate. Traditional ISD featured end-of-course evaluation forms that were glanced at by the instructor and perhaps the training manager. If the same instructor were asked to present the same course again for a similar audience, and if the training manager's publication schedule, staff, and budget could handle revisions, perhaps the end-of-course evaluation comments could be used to improve the course. Chances were, however, that this kind of "continuous improvement" never happened, and that the evaluation forms were used as simply a "smiles test" for the instructor's popularity and an indicator of the comfort level trainees felt with the training room. In ISD as usual, the process of evaluation was seldom used for the purpose of educational decision-making, and it tended to become an administrative trapping of the bureaucracy of "big training" that had no effect on either learning or continuous improvement.

Evaluation in the new ISD Cycle is seen as individualized regarding the person in the learning cycle and directed at the content of the learning encounter. If we agree that learning to learn is the skill of choice for the '90s, and that the knowledge resident in and possible through the workforce is America's competitive edge, then evaluation must become the quality-enhancing process it was intended to be within the instructional system. A revised view of ISD can serve us well as we plan for an unprecedented development in depth of our very rich and varied workforce.

Example: ASTD's *Training & Development Journal*[3] contained an article about a shift in focus in the Coca Cola Company's management training. The article begins with a finding from the Center for Creative Leadership in Greensboro, North Carolina which stated that when successful executives were asked about key *developmental events* in their careers, no one mentioned a management training/development program. The author, a director of executive and organization development at Coca Cola in Atlanta, then goes on to talk about management training programs at Coca Cola and explains how they diagnosed and treated the problem of the relevance of training to management competence.

The article's bottom line is that instead of designing and delivering training about some topic "of interest," management trainers should design and deliver training that has the capacity to support corporate strategy. By this, the article means that training has to give managers the skills to assess their own "current knowledge and skill base against what they will need for success," allowing them to "manage their own development." Also built into the design of the learning base of the new training is the peer to peer dialogue with other managers over what they need to do differently. The learning encounter is designed to create competence rather than simply awareness. The author draws a distinction between the old model which created training programs around job descriptions, and the new model which must create training around "current and future business challenges." The author sees training as "a means to an end rather than an end in itself."

Coca Cola's application of an ISD model came to the conclusion that looking inward to the individual manager's "gap" between what he or she currently knew and could do and what he or she needed to be able to know and do was the kind of "AHA!" conclusion that is implicit in a more personalized interpretation of traditional instructional systems design. Coca Cola believes that this "right focus" to management training will enable training to support the company's competitive strategy.

INSTRUCTIONAL SYSTEM DESIGN (ISD) CYCLE
FOR PEER TRAINING

Directions: Apply this model to training design at the personal level rather than at the organizational level. Tie it to business strategies and the individual's learning requirements.

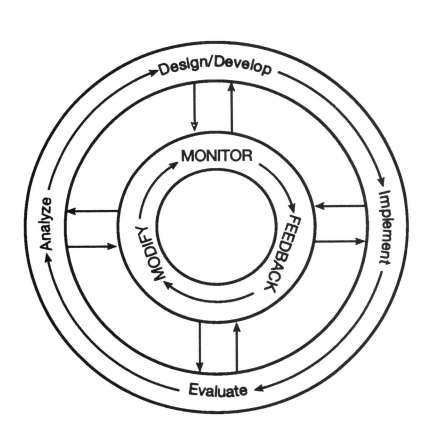

DESIGN ISSUES IN PEER TRAINING

Adult Learning

Problem: Approximately twenty years ago, Americans began to pay a great deal of attention to adult learning, particularly to the recognizable differences between the way children learn and the way adults learn. Various pieces of Federal education legislation, starting in the mid 1960s, had provisions for special program development for adults, and the decade of the 1970s brought with it a renewed interest and emphasis on adult and continuing education in visible aspects of our public life. Public school programs for adults blossomed during those years, and public and private R&D monies were channeled into the field of adult education. English as a Second Language programs for adults gained in popularity, as did a variety of recreational, professional, and academic programs. The Continuing Education Unit (CEU) was born.

Workplaces, too, began designing and developing instruction around some of the interesting findings about how adults learn and prefer to learn. One of the obvious things we discovered was that adults differ from children in the fundamental measure of "experience in life." Adults simply have been around longer and have experienced more out of life than have children. Those of us who paid attention to the trends during those years perhaps recall that much was made of the pedagogy of teaching children through a "developmental psychology" approach—very future-focused, designed around the predictable stages of a child's growth. Popular writers, too, during those years, began talking about adult stages of growth.

However, adults at work, unlike children at school, probably have more of life behind them than ahead of them, and the future-focus of developmental psychology isn't as appropriate for adult development as it is for child development. In much of workplace learning which originated and proliferated during those years, there was the tendency to focus on "the future," and often on an undefined future that manifested itself in training courses that were the latest buzz words—nice-to-knows, rather than need-to-knows. The problem is that much of our training has a tendency to invalidate the adult learner's past and thus loses the richest data and experience base for future high quality learning, that unique accumulation of knowledge and skill resident within each person at work.

Plan of action: Peer training design and development depend upon tapping into the experience base of teachers and learners. Our view of adult learning must be based on valuing the work experience and the life experience of individuals on the job. Designs of lessons and practice exercises must be anchored in a worker's past and present skills, and build upon demonstrated competencies as learning moves forward. Training delivered by peer instructors works because each person's experience is important for its content and process knowledge, and is full of potential for further learning. In addition, peer training works because of people's need for collegiality; "we're in this together" is often a motivator for focus and problem solving.

When designing peer training, keep in mind these principles of adult learning:

- Adults bring to any learning situation an enormous memory bank of information which can be useful in further learning. This includes memory for:
  — knowledge gained through trial and error experimentation,
  — patterned responses,
  — data, numbers,
  — words, information, concepts,
  — smells, tastes, sounds, sights, tactile memories,
  — spatial relationship memories,
  — approaches to problems that work for them and those that don't work,
  — preferred learning styles.

- Good designs for adult learning will tap into any or all of these memories in order to enhance an individual's learning ability. Peer training is especially good at doing this.

- Adults like to be active rather than passive during learning. They resent being dumped on or looked down on by other adults.

- Adults come to work to work, not necessarily to learn. They respond better to on-the-job learning than they do to structured formal learning in classrooms. Time spent in classroom training is still considered by most companies to be "time off the job" and therefore, time wasted or at least not optimally spent. The secret in increasing the skill levels of workers is to facilitate learning from work, at work, on the job. Peer trainers are a large available source of learning facilitators—on the job.

- Adults like to be in charge of how they learn. Peer trainers, because of the one-to-one nature of instruction, are ideally situated to help workers engage in learning according to the way they do it best.

- Adults like to see a personal payoff from the time they spend teaching and learning. If teaching and learning are not their regular jobs, they'll expect some kind of obvious reward (more pay, compensatory time off, gold stars, lunch with the boss, etc.), or ideally, teaching and learning would become so integral a part of everyone's job that all of the recognition and reward systems would be revised to reflect this.

- Adults expect learning on the job to be directly related to the job. Peer training is the best way to fulfill this expectation.

Examples: Companies that have "gotten into" teams during the last few years under the impetus of the empowered employee movement have, no doubt, also either unexpectedly or on purpose gotten into peer training too. In fact, one of the most popular strategies for maintenance of effective teams and building quality into the processes of work is the strategy of peer training. Working effectively in teams often means that team members teach and learn from each other daily as they work out problems together. Unfortunately, because quality improvement has been the motivation for team organization—and not necessarily *learning*—many teachers and learners in teams are not paying enough attention to the most effective learning techniques because they're preoccupied with *quality* techniques.

Working in teams has brought with it such strategies as "just-in-time" training, whereby learners learn what they need to know as close to the time they'll need the new knowledge or skill as possible. "Cross-training" is another popular training technique that is often practiced in teams in which each member must know the job of each other member in order for the team to remain flexible in dealing with business issues and accomplishing business objectives. Peers training each other can handle these kinds of training very well, and with the correct instructional design help, can tap into all of the most attractive characteristics and preferences of adult learners.

An example from my own experience as a new "group" member illustrates how one organization intentionally promoted peer training, and in the process recognized that the group's learning potential was infinitely greater because of the active participation in learning by its members from the enormous memory bases of its collective experience.

Within the first hour of my employment at AT&T Bell Laboratories as a Member of Technical Staff, an instructional designer in the Systems Training Center, I was escorted to my office, shown my computer, and handed a stack of manuals, user guides, and corporate directories. I was given a chart with mail and telephone numbers of my work group and the immediate fifty or sixty persons located under the same roof. I was told only one thing about how to do work and that was this: "The only thing we don't like around here is if people don't ask questions." It was made clear to me that the organization valued its people and the wealth of all sorts of information each brought to it. This was an organization of highly educated, creative, experienced learners, and to the company's credit, each was expected to learn from the other. In such an organization, it is tempting for individuals to consider themselves specialists and to retreat into cubicles, laboratories, or corners of the library. "If you don't know the answer, go find out" was the mode of operation. It is one of the reasons why Bell Labs has been able to continuously build and improve upon its knowledge base.

One final example of a training experience designed two different ways will help to illustrate the old way of doing things and the preferred new way of doing things. This is an example of typical objectives in a management training course:

Old way: "Managers will demonstrate different leadership styles in a role play exercise using prepared scripts." Note that this kind of objective involves not much more intellectual engagement than reading a definition out of a dictionary. It probably is at the lowest level of cognitive interest to trainees, even though it is an "interactive" exercise. Its design violates two essentials of adult learning: it does not elicit involvement with the trainees' own rich experience base, and it does not allow trainees to be in charge of their own learning. This training experience will be seen as "Mickey Mouse" training, probably boring, and definitely not worth the time or money.

New way: "Each manager will create a definition of his or her own leadership style after having worked for 45 minutes in a problem-solving team of three members around question #2 following the case study from the auditor's log. Trainees may use the Myers-Briggs materials or other reference materials provided to each team for ideas if they need them." Note that this objective is based on several of the principles of adult learning: it is based on a real situation from company files, it requires trainees to learn from and with each other, it provides stimulation to encourage active inquiry, and there's a personal payoff to the trainee, his or her own identified leadership style.

Well meaning instructional designers in the past have all too often fallen into the trap of the first example, and mistook learning about something for learning something. This kind of lowest level "identify and define" learning was often couched in "active training" surroundings. It was often promoted heavily as the "newest ideas" in training, and offered around companies as something that people surely were going to need in the future. This kind of training often had the overtones of a misinterpreted developmental psychology about it. New instructional designers make use of the company's real work and facilitate the development of new skills and knowledge out of the present challenges and past strengths of trainees.

Even the unwieldy Federal and state employment and training agencies have been known to be responsive to newer calls to value past experience of "deep" workforces. In my own region of Western Massachusetts, the base of small and mid-size manufacturers has been steadily disappearing in recent years. Active public job training and re-training programs have been proliferating to help the unemployed and laid off workforce. However, recently an unusual infusion of public "jobs money" was provided to Martin Marietta Defense Systems as an incentive to keep the skilled workforce intact and in the geographic area in which it developed its knowledge and skill base.[4]

In this unusual funding of an experienced, aging, workforce with deep rather than broad skills, three state agencies combined their resources to fund two high-priority training programs to broaden the skills of existing workers. In this case, public-sector money is being seen, apparently, as an investment in an experienced worker pool of talent in order to help a private company remain productive and competitive. By these actions, state and Federal officials demonstrate their commitment to enhancing the value of the learning potential that comes from a deep experience base.

DESIGN ISSUES IN PEER TRAINING

Personal Effectiveness

Problem: The popular and business press are full of commentary about the decline of values, the disintegration of our institutions of church, school, family life, and community, and the lapse of the American worker into being simply a follower and not an initiator. All these criticisms add up to the conclusion that our "personal effectiveness" as people is lacking. When we look for general reasons behind this and try to make a succinct problem statement regarding this, we are tempted to blame the future and complain about how complicated life has become, and with no end in sight—so much violence, so much grief, so much sadness, so much fear, so much information, so much world out there. If we stop thinking here, we run the very real risk of becoming powerless in the face of such an overwhelming future.

Perhaps a place to look for wisdom about personal effectiveness is to our past. Historically, America has been a place of "the frontier." Both geographically and psychologically the concept of always having more territory to conquer and claim has been a vital part of the American concept of who we are. The explorer, the scout, the rugged individual setting out to "get there" have all been images within our visions of ourselves. They have *informed* our habits of thinking. We relate to "the lone ranger."

The problem is there isn't any more geographic frontier and the complexity of problems demands an interdependent, not an independent, solution. The essence of personal effectiveness is purposefully moving from independence and isolation to interdependence and connectedness. We need to think about problem solving differently.

Plan of action: There are ways to do this in order to come to grips with the difficult job of changing habits. Believing that "you can help me and I can help you" is the first step. Realizing that habits are learned behavior and that they can be unlearned is the second step. Being willing to do the hard work that learning and unlearning require is the third step. Anyone who's tried to lose weight and keep it off, or anyone who's tried to stop smoking forever knows just how insidious is the development of a habit and how much work it takes to unlearn the behavioral and the cognitive bases of it. Stephen R. Covey, author of bestseller, *The Seven Habits of Highly Effective People,* (Fireside, Simon & Schuster, NY, 1989) says, among other things, that effective people are products of their values and decisions, not their moods and conditions. We need the wisdom to be able to discern the difference; and often, the anguish or confusion we feel regarding current conditions blinds us to being able to articulate and live by our values and to be decisive. Our old habits of thinking like a lone ranger don't help much, and it's always easier to be acted upon than to act.

Peter Senge, author of bestseller, _"The Fifth Discipline: The Art and Practice of The Learning Organization"_ (Doubleday/Currency, NY, 1990) offers some insight too. He challenges readers to see interrelationships and commit to wholes; to listen to other people's points of view and visions for themselves; to step back and reflect on assumptions before bulldozing into action; and to engage in joint inquiry into a variety of views of reality. He suggests that there is a "creative tension" pulling between one's vision and current reality, and he urges persons who would develop "personal mastery" to constantly try to clarify their definitions of both ends of the pull. He also suggests that "only mediocre people are always at their best."

If you are willing to agree that there is some truth to popular writings which sound the alarms about the need for a change in the way Americans relate to each other in our institutional life, and are willing to respond to some of the challenges, then perhaps considering redesigning training as peer training might be a way for you to begin to change your workplace habits regarding personal effectiveness. Peer training has in its structure—its design and its methods—the potential for helping people get out of the "lone ranger" habit of problem solving and on the path to a more effective and personally satisfying habit of interdependent communication, thinking, and problem solving. The learning organization at work must be created one by one, together.

Covey uses terms like "think win-win," and "seek first to understand . . . then to be understood;" Senge says "try truth" for starters. Each of these is a seemingly obvious admonition, but most of us who've been around America's workplaces for a few decades unfortunately haven't seen much of any of these three. The old "conquer or die" mentality surely had winners and losers. "Do as I say because I know and you don't," has an all too familiar ring to it. "Things are so bad that you don't really have to know all the details" also seems quite logical to a workplace of lone ranger thinkers. A workplace of learners teaching and learning through purposeful, vision-based peer training can help to change some of these old habits by introducing its new behavioral practices and philosophies which clearly depend on interdependence rather than on independence.

Example: Shortly after the divestiture of AT&T's "Baby Bells" from the parent company and its attendant downsizing of organizations, several of the new AT&T lines of business got involved with outdoor/sports psychology training for their managers and executives. Change of great magnitude had been forced on AT&T, and the new company simply had to explore all avenues of workforce renewal and survival. Attitude changes and behavioral changes were required of those still employed after the rightsizing. Outdoor training was one approach to get the former hierarchical-type managers thinking more in terms of teams. Hundreds of AT&T managers and executives were trained at remote outdoor centers around the country. Thousands of employees in large and small companies have also gone through this kind of training.

It's probably fair to say that during the months leading up to divestiture, most AT&T managers were surely not thinking win-win, they were probably trying to make anyone who would listen understand them, and it certainly was hard to figure out what the truth was. These folks indeed probably could benefit from stepping back to reflect on their habits of managing and decision making, and from purposefully engaging in different ways of thinking which might be more appropriate for the new company that they now were.

One of the first paradigm-shifting requirements of outdoor team training is acceptance of personal responsibility for one's decisions and actions—from admitting that the pole climb is just too scary to recommendations regarding who should be first over the wall, where the rope is placed, to one's choice for breakfast. One of the first and most difficult actions for many managers faced with paradigm-shifting thinking was simply being able to face the truth of saying at the start of each physical challenge of the outdoor adventure, "Yes, I want to do this," or "No, I do not want to do this."

Whatever else it was, this requirement of seeking truth, accepting the reality of the current situation, and seeing the whole—of the challenge, and of the team's resources—was surely an exercise in developing personal effectiveness.[5]

DESIGN ISSUES IN PEER TRAINING

Learning Mastery

Problem: Closely related to the development of personal effectiveness is the individual development of learning mastery. Some definitions are in order: a simple definition of learning is the capacity to get what you want—from experience, from a database, from a story, from a metaphor, from one's emotions, and so forth. It carries with it the notion of initiative and an active process of engagement with the subject at hand. Said more eloquently, perhaps, learning is an individual's response to informational stimulation of all kinds which, through processing that response, enables or empowers that individual to act purposefully. Learning begets change and growth. Learning begets more learning. Mastery is the degree of sufficiency and fulfillment that characterizes excellence or quality. Learning mastery in the workplace, then, is a high degree of individual capacity for effective action upon one's work.

Learning mastery in the workplace is a personal goal to be sought after by individual learners. Its conscious development, along with increased productivity, can be a powerful strategy for building a knowledge-based organization. It can also be the value-added factor in high-quality, strategically effective peer training. Said another way, the individual mastery of the best ways to learn can drive the individual worker forward to getting more out of work and to higher and higher levels of achievement because of work.

The problem is how to define and measure, that is, by what factors shall success be determined. Two representations give some clues:

$$\text{productivity} = \text{output/input,}$$
$$\text{and}$$
$$\text{learning mastery} = \text{time expended in engagement/}$$
$$\text{time required for engagement.}$$

In both of these equations, the desirable process is for the denominator to be reduced. For example, if productivity is equal to "2," output / input might be equal to 8/4. If the denominator "4" were reduced by half, that is, to "2," the productivity figure would climb to 8/2, or 4. Likewise, the learning mastery figure would increase if the time required for the engagement of learning (the denominator) were reduced. Individuals—and by extension, organizations—would have a powerful strategy at their disposal if they could systematically and continuously reduce the resources expended at the front end of both productivity creation and learning mastery development. Peer training has the potential to do just this—maximize and ultimately reduce the resources required at the front end.

Plan of action: Central to the concept of learning mastery is the value of the variable of time. At the one end of the idea is the desire to spend "quality time" on the essential task at hand, and at the other end is the drive to enter that task engagement with as much prior intelligence and wisdom as possible so as not to "waste" time.

The role of those who design instruction (training professionals, supervisors, managers, and even colleagues) must be to create the structures within which individuals can work in order to develop that prior intelligence so that individuals come to their work tasks with the best that they can possibly bring with them. Here are just some of the ways in which instructional designers can work on this "input" variable:

1. *Recognize aptitude.* Ask the individual what he or she is really good at. Encourage each person at work to say out loud or write down the five things they know that they can do well. Get them to think in terms of mental exercises or intellectual skills which they know they perform well. The list might include such things as: estimating, organizing, prioritizing, planning, writing, presenting, teaching, troubleshooting, analyzing, drawing, listening, and so forth. Help individuals recognize their strengths, and help each person understand that each is truly unique with a specialized set of intellectual skills. Focus on the notion that the only valid definition of "goodness" is one that measures the individual's intellectual "output" only against the output of which he or she is capable. Recognize too that the desire to learn and grow are built in to the human creature, and that most individuals can and want to learn more. They want to be very good at what they are good at, but they resent being "made" to be good at or "told" to be good at something they have no aptitude for being good at. As an instructional designer, practice the preaching that has always told you that educational designs must account for individual differences. This means at work too. When individuals know what they're good at and know that training opportunities can allow them to be better at those things, chances are that the rate at which they continue to learn will improve and their contributions to engaging in a task will be of higher quality.

2. *Customize instruction.* Because people vary so widely in learning styles, experience base, and information-processing skills, and because the tasks that they do generally are different from those that other people do, learning opportunities should be designed for individuals. Instruction itself, in all of its objective-setting and content delineation, works best and most efficiently when it is customized. Tailor the construction of instruction; one size never fits all. There is all kinds of waste when objectives for learning are inappropriate, too hard, too easy, incompatible with a learner's experience base, or when content is neither necessary nor sufficient, or when the proposed procedures of learning are wrong for that person. As a designer, think in terms of the elegance of design for each specific learning encounter—and that

means consideration of the full learning environment, the individual, the content, the process, and the intended outcome. Learning mastery can be enhanced through economy and elegance of design.

3. *Set up ways for individuals to learn from each other.* An article by Japanese professor, Ikujiro Nonaka, at Hitotsubashi University in Tokyo, which appeared in *Harvard Business Review,*[6] discusses the characteristics of "tacit" knowledge and "explicit" knowledge, how they differ from each other, and how each should be used—and is used in many Japanese companies—to further a company's ability to be a continuously renewing knowledge-creating company.

Professor Nonaka offers definitions of these two kinds of knowledge, the tacit kind generally associated with a person's intuition, ease of performance, and seemingly innate "know-how," and the explicit kind generally associated with formal and systematic structures like procedures, rules, scientific experimentation, and predictable results. He further suggests, from his research, that learners typically move between tacit and explicit knowledge in four essential ways as learners create knowledge.

These four interactions with knowledge most often involve the interaction of two persons, and demand skills such as communication, matching of needs to resources offered, articulation horizontally between new learnings and significant other persons who need to know them, skills of translation, re-ordering, combining, synthesizing, and, of course, the skill of integrating one's new knowledge into one's own base of experience.

Nonaka describes the four interactions thus: tacit to tacit, explicit to explicit, tacit to explicit, and explicit to tacit. Here are some examples:

1. Tacit to tacit- directly sharing tacit knowledge, person to person, as in one's grandchild watching Grandma show her how tomatoes are sliced with a serrated knife and then slicing her own tomato with the knife;

2. Explicit to explicit- combining various outputs or formats of explicit knowledge, as in combining a graph with written interpretations of it, or putting together an annual report from a variety of documents;

3. Tacit to explicit- jumping ahead from a tacit understanding, or a tacit revelation, to translating it into new explicit knowledge, as in using one's tacit knowledge of the predictable harmonies of Baroque music to compose one's own sonata;

4. Explicit to tacit- dissemination and diffusion throughout an organization or from person to person of explicit knowledge to such an extent that it becomes widely used and accepted as good; and then it is acted upon by various individuals of differing persuasions and aptitudes who create their own new tacit knowledge as a result of integrating the explicit knowledge. An illustration of this might be the training needs assessment document

which identified a tremendous need for gap-filling measures regarding the employed workforce, rather than spelling out the measures to be taken for the laid-off workforce. The explicit descriptions and analyses in the report caused those who read it to shift their thinking to "defense diversification" and pursue entirely different program development paths. The explicit knowledge encouraged them to re-order their intuitive knowledge of what good training should be; their tacit knowledge base about training needs had changed forever because of the integration of the explicit knowledge contained in the report.

Training designers would do well to learn from these lessons about the interactions between kinds of knowledge. In order to maximize the opportunities for advantage from these interactions, training should be designed so that individuals have opportunities—offered in a systematic, institutionalized way—to interact with each other in order to learn from each other in a dynamic interplay between tacit and explicit knowledge. Person to person interaction with a learning purpose can dramatically affect an individual's ability to contribute his or her best to work. Effective, purposeful interactions can alter the time factor by upgrading the quality of the learning that goes into the learning mastery formula. More effective, better tuned, deeper and richer, learning approaches will cause less time to be wasted in extraneous or peripheral endeavors. Institutionalizing peer training is one way to develop learning mastery.

Examples: An article in *Harvard Business Review* by two consultants[7] describes their research study into the characteristics of high performing engineers at AT&T Bell Laboratories, and more specifically, into the work strategies which these top performers tacitly and explicitly adopted.

In addition to core skills like technical competence in their fields and taking initiative, the researchers found that the high performers also used networking for direct access to expertise embodied in their peers, assuming responsibility for effective outcomes of teamwork, being willing to be both a leader and a follower, and consciously taking on the points of view of other people such as customers or managers. These are certainly the skills required for learning mastery. The knowledge potential within an already competent workforce was recognized by the employees themselves, and the company supported and facilitated the dissemination of that knowledge base. Companies, who believe in the business potential of a knowledge-creating workforce, must organize themselves so that individuals can do their work based on their strengths and can share their know-how and savvy of all sorts with each other.

Another example comes from the Nonaka article cited previously. Professor Nonaka says that in Japan, the company is seen as a "living organism," not a machine, and a corollary to this is that the human mind is seen as an instrument to use and not a vessel to be filled up. Western workers have tended to see things as linear—in one end and out the other, build hierarchies, climb ladders, keep score. Japanese workers see things as organismic and connected. The Japanese worker is in it for the long haul; the American worker for the short haul. The Japanese individual naturally, culturally, looks to peers for the probability of increasing one's knowledge; the American still tends to be a lone ranger or conquistador.

Nonaka tells the story of the quest for new product development intelligence at the Matsushita Electric Company in Osaka. The job was to develop a new home bread-making machine. After many standard analysis techniques, the key software developer proposed that she go to a hotel in town where the baker had a reputation for producing excellent bread and learn how he did it. With careful observation of the master baker and standing by his side asking questions for days while he baked bread, the software developer found that the way he twisted the dough was probably the secret to the outstanding unique and consistent quality of the bread. She went back to her lab and designed a dough-twisting device for Matsushita's bread-making machine that simulated almost exactly the technique of the master baker at the hotel. The point of the story is that a company, or an instructional designer, must consider the value of the process of movement between tacit and explicit knowledge and must encourage employees to continuously and creatively expand the company's knowledge base by watching and talking to each other as they work within this dynamic force.

Endnotes for Chapter 4
Notes 1 through 7

1. *1994 Award Criteria, Malcolm Baldrige National Quality Award*, U.S. Department of Commerce, Gaithersburg, MD, p. 9 sections 4 and 5.

2. "Integrated Systems: You Can't Gain If You Don't Train!" by John A. White, in *Modern Materials Handling*, Vol. 48 Issue 5, April 1993, p. 29.

3. "Linking Management Development to Business Strategy" by John K. Berry in *Training & Development Journal*, August 1990, pp. 20-22.

4. "State Agencies Will Fund Martin Training Programs" by Lewis C. Cuyler, in *The Berkshire Eagle*, September 8, 1993, p. D.1; Editorial on September 9, 1993, and "Martin Marietta Stays in Pittsfield" headline stories in *The Berkshire Eagle*, October 1, 1993, pp. 1, 4, 5.

5. Observations from conversations with a program participant.

6. "The Knowledge-Creating Company" by Ikujiro Nonaka in *Harvard Business Review*, November-December 1991, pp. 96-104.

7. "How Bell Labs Creates Star Performers" by Robert Kelley and Janet Caplan in *Harvard Business Review*, July-August 1993, pp. 128-139.

CHAPTER **5**

DESIGN METHODS FOR INDIVIDUAL LEARNING

This second chapter on design deals with some of the specific methods of designing training to enable individuals to learn; it complements and logically follows Chapter 4 on the design issues in peer training. Worksheets in this chapter are particularly useful in providing tools for the designer of instruction for individual learners.

The focus in Chapter 5 is on basic generic needs for learning that have been articulated by numerous business writers, critics of the current American workplace, and human resources gurus as the critical baseline learning needs of knowledge workers. These include the needs for flexibility, creativity, ability to identify and solve problems, to be active in one's learning, to understand and exercise one's memory, to make time for reflection, to be intentional and conscious about processes of learning, and to discover in work itself the potential for expansion of knowledge. This chapter addresses the educational foundation of the kinds of workplace learning that must be codified and made practical as training methods.

Information on these next pages is meant to guide the design of methods for learning—tangible ways to help people learn as individuals. The tools contained herein are the first practical and structured help for designing instruction for individual learning. Training methodology specifically designed for one-by-one learning has been missing from most corporate training design operations resulting in a somewhat haphazard learning experience for most workers who have had to learn from a co-worker. This chapter intends to change this typical randomness about workplace learning by providing a solid practical and useful base of technique and *intention* about the design of learning on the job and from the job.

DESIGN METHODS FOR INDIVIDUAL LEARNING

Active and Passive Learning

Problem: The major obstacle in designing training from which a person can learn something is the corporate drive for administrative efficiency. We want our work processes (manufacture, accounting, selling, . . . whatever. . .) to be efficient, to work smoothly along a predetermined path. The *quality* management movement, however, and now the *learning* organization movement, have given us new banners to march under and some different ways of marching.

The problem with training under the efficiency mindset has been that the administrative convenience of the classroom, and indeed corporate training centers full of classrooms, encouraged the proliferation of classroom training. Most of the classic training literature is full of how to manage classrooms, how to present to groups, tricks and techniques for making groups more interesting, how to deal with curriculums and catalogs full of classrooms of training opportunities, how to make money from the other organizations who sent their people to you for training, how to account for time away from the job which those folks spent in your classrooms, how to hone the registration process, how to organize all of the support media. The efficient training operation ran hundreds of students through classrooms, chalked up lots of tic marks on various frequency charts, and made money for the training operation.

The obvious role of the instructor in this familiar model of the training operation is that of lecturer, or group facilitator in the most forward-looking companies—but *group,* nevertheless. The all too often role of the learner was "sitter." Trainees sat around tables or in rows, theater style, or sometimes at computers, but mostly they sat. Learners looked passive physically, and they often were passive intellectually. Instructors typically presented a body of information within a specified time period like two-hour blocks, structuring their presentation so that the elements of the content could be delivered in logical segments. The focus of the instructor/learner interaction was passive. Chances are that the learning itself in this kind of scenario was also passive.

Under this kind of training, instructional designers tried to design elements of dealing with content so that those who sat in the classroom could engage in some mental exercise at least as they moved through the prescribed course manual or textbook. Instructional designers worked hard to get learners beyond the basic levels of simple definition and description that so often was characteristic of the classroom model of training. At its worst, this kind of efficient training was piles of information dumped into the heads of piles of trainees. The efficiency model often drove instructors to move rapidly through material in order to "dump" it all by the end of the day.

Well-meaning variations on the lecture rose up in the form of videotapes which substituted a media-based set of stimuli for the stimulation of one instructor. In many cases, training via videotape required and created more passivity on the part of the learner. It too is efficient, and therefore appealing if efficiency is the driver. All too often, training delivered through either of these methods was confused with simple information. Not much capacity for change is built within a learner who sits intellectually and physically passive during learning; not much ability is created for action upon one's situation; not much empowerment occurs when the learner is given no guidance or opportunity for experimentation with the information.

These are the settings of passive styles of learning, and it is questionable, even, that useful elements are learned in such settings. This kind of training can be characterized as training that focuses on getting the right answers. Information is presented as unequivocal, as truth, or as the right thing. The learning process is marked by a kind of short-loop matching exercise, in which the learner is expected to give back to the instructor just what the instructor just gave to the student. What we need, instead, to deal with work of increasing difficulty and with workplaces with the potential for economic leadership is training that addresses this complexity and focuses on getting the right questions.

We need to apply what we know about the discipline and craft of instructional design to a workplace with standards other than administrative efficiency in its learning processes. We need to focus all of these decades of wisdom and effort in design and instructional technology at the learning process itself—not necessarily at the administration of classrooms. Acts of learning must be efficient, not because of an immediate profit margin or cost per head, but because efficient learning itself can be the best way to create more learning and better learning.

Plan of action: Measures must be taken, and soon, to move away from this passive style to an active style of learning and of training. Learning must be seen as a strategy for change, that is, a planned-for, budgeted-for, measured, and evaluated tool in a company's arsenal of change makers. A company's rate of learning has to be greater than the business environment's rate of change. Standards for what is good training must be replaced by standards for what is good learning.

A place to begin is in the sorting out of the many kinds of mental or physical processes your own work requires. Here are some possibilities:

- estimating
- recognizing patterns
- memorizing
- fitting pieces together
- choosing
- sorting
- prioritizing

- organizing information
- organizing data
- listening for specific sounds
- adjusting tension
- writing
- analyzing
- polishing.

The list could be endless. Sit yourself down and make a list of all of the things your work demands of you. Think of the active mental processes you must employ as you do your job. Recognize that your very own work contains in its structure and its requirements the foundation for learning: work itself presents workers with an opportunity to develop competency in hundreds of active mental and physical tasks. Your colleague's work also contains this opportunity—for him or her, and for you, and for everyone else in the workplace. The instructional designer's role is to help workers codify their work as learning tasks and opportunities, and then to facilitate the structure of the workplace so that individuals can learn quickly and effectively, working with a learning purpose. "Working with learning in mind" is a pretty good slogan.

A word or two should be said about "active training," a term generally used to mean the presentation techniques which classroom instructors use in order to get the "sitters" up out of their seats and interacting with each other instead of just interacting with the instructor. These techniques include such things as role play, simulation, case study analysis, breaking into small groups within the large group, trainees using audio visual media in front of the large group. These are to be commended for their conscious attempt to physically get the trainee moving, but they must always be seen as tools for the traditional classroom instructor who still functions as the selecter, organizer, and translator of *presented*—that is, one-way from teacher to student—instruction.

At issue here is active learning in all of its variety and possibilities.

Example: At this very moment, my work contains many opportunities for active learning. I am using a new software package that is icon-based in a Windows environment, but I have spent a decade of my writing life in DOS. I know that I am a linear information processor, and I actually prefer to work in DOS. However, I share my office with a partner and we jointly made the decision to upgrade our computer hardware and software, and move to Windows.

In addition, I would like to use the graphics commands of the new software to draw the box around this section of the page, and I don't know how. To save time, I'll just insert horizontal lines which I can easily do with the underscore key and pencil in the vertical lines to complete the box.

My work tonight is almost done and I am about ready to backup my day's work. However, I have never done backups using my new system. My partner happens to be out of town and he's the one who always does the maintenance and file management on all of our office files.

With this brief true life mini-case study, I can define many work tasks that I could do better, and if I did them better—if I learned from my work to improve my work—I would be worth more in terms of job knowledge and competency at doing what I do. In fact, I probably could assign a dollar figure, or a worth figure, to my work if it were being performed by me at a peak level. I know that I can learn more in at least these elements of the job:

- I should ask my partner to spend one hour of focused time showing me why he believes so strongly that a Windows environment is better than a DOS environment,

- Maybe I should do some exercises in non-linear information processing to expand my capabilities—if I took just 15 minutes per day for two weeks I could get a good feel for another way of thinking—maybe digging into the software user guide and spending some time using the help menus and tutorials would do it for me,

- It's just plain stupid to not know how to draw the vertical lines to make a box. I probably could have looked up the instructions in the time it's taking me to think about and write about it right now—my work would obviously be of higher quality if I didn't use the handwritten vertical lines,

- I am about ready to close my file for the night and do the backup onto disk. I should have paid more attention yesterday when my partner showed me how to do it—no, I should have practiced in front of him with him coaching me so I got it right. I wrote down the steps, and I intellectually know what to do, but, after all, backup is a psychomotor task and I could have benefitted from having practiced it prior to doing it tonight.

In this very simple description of half an hour's worth of work, I have found four different learning challenges, and I have devised four different plans for meeting them. If I implement these four plans, my work will have improved and I will have learned something new. In addition, my new learnings will help me do better work in the future and will help me continue to learn.

In past times, I would have been tempted to sign up for a Windows course in a community adult school or through a local corporation. If I had done that, my learning would probably have been inefficient because there would have been a great deal of information that I simply didn't need, my learning would not have been customized for me since there were administrative considerations like 29 other people in the class, my learning probably would not have used the exact kind of computer or software I use, and it certainly would not have been set within my own work context. Chances are that I would have been a passive learner, and perhaps not even a learner at all.

Clearly, the learning of choice for my problems was learning of my own definition and design, self-directed, work-centered, involved with my peer—an active learning from every perspective. Design for active learning is today's instructional design imperative.

WORKSHEET 2 - 2

MASTERY CREDO

Directions: Use this checklist to verify your beliefs about adult learners before you decide what you need to learn, how you want to learn it, and from whom or from what you can learn. This credo will help you shift your thinking about what training should be. Test your beliefs against each separate statement.

_____ I believe that each person at work is a capable individual.

_____ I believe that each worker has unique strengths.

_____ I believe that individual differences can be creatively used to achieve business goals.

_____ I believe that people can learn from each other as peers.

_____ I believe that I know what I need to learn.

_____ I believe that instruction can come from the disciplines of work.

_____ I believe that quality in instructional design pays off in quality of learning.

_____ I would like not to waste time when I learn.

_____ I need to know standards for excellence in the various tasks of my work.

_____ I need to know my company's short range and long range goals.

_____ I would like to be able to demonstrate that I have learned new skills or acquired new knowledge.

_____ I need feedback during my learning in order to improve the way in which I am learning.

_____ I believe that consciously and systematically improving my learning will expand my ability to continue to learn.

_____ I believe that individuals who can perform better in their jobs will cause teams, departments, and organizations of all kinds to perform better as groups.

_____ I believe that continuous learning is a competitive tool.

ADULT LEARNER DESIGN CHECKLIST

Directions: Use this checklist as you create new learning opportunities for learning at work. This checklist can be used by those whose job title is trainer or instructional designer, or it can be used by any individual who functions as an instructor for any other individual. It functions best as a peer trainer's job aid to learning design.

1. Build in learner control of learning. Trust the learner to know what he or she needs to know in order to do better work. If new skills are being learned, trust the learner to know what can be brought to the new challenges from his or her experience.

2. Set performance or quality standards for each learning task. Design small. Think in terms of continuous improvement in the quality of learning.

3. Provide a monitoring or assessment checklist or other documentation device for a learner to measure his or her progress.

4. Do not penalize lack of progress; figure out a better way to get there or accept the fact that this learner shouldn't get there if he or she has no aptitude for the new task. Good instructional design can make a difference, and individual differences must be considered.

5. Take the time for individualized needs assessment. Focus on one individual's requirements for quality work and this person's unique needs for learning from work.

6. Provide peer trainers, coaches, mentors, hot line responders to personally provide help during learning.

7. Provide printed reference materials and informational media aids so that individual learners can search for and find information they need for learning.

8. Communicate the idea that learning from work is everyone's job number one. If you have to, suggest that at least five percent of an individual's time on the job should be spent daily in learning—in conscious, systematic, self-monitored learning.

WORKSHEET 2 - 4

INDIVIDUAL NEED TO KNOW ASSESSMENT

Directions: Use this chart to identify and document exactly what a trainee needs to know. This simple matrix can be one of your first individual needs assessment documents as you begin to design a personalized learning plan for an individual at work. Use it at a "job learning" level or at a "task learning" level. Use it at the beginning of a typical business planning cycle, such as at the end of each calendar quarter (March, June, September, December), or at the beginning of each new week. Use the time factor to help facilitate or motivate; choose any that works for your business. Staple a stack of these together to form more detailed needs assessment.

Worker's name:_____ **Cycle:** _____

Job or task being analyzed: _____

learning task	person who can help	resources required

WORKSHEET 2 - 4 (SAMPLE)

INDIVIDUAL NEED TO KNOW ASSESSMENT

Worker's name: _Jeffrey_   **Cycle:** _5 working days_

Job or task being analyzed _client interface tasks of new stock broker_

learning task	person who can help	resources required
draft questions to yield 3 qualifying bits of information per cold call	*Eric x802*	*30 minutes*
introduce one new service per contact	*phone Scott in St. Louis*	*corporate research reports and product information sheets*
allow client to lead the conversation for at least half of each client meeting	*ask Noelle to monitor my meetings and time client leading (6 meetings this week)*	*Noelle's time to help me (8 hours?)*

WORKSHEET 2 - 5

JOB DESIGN MIND MAP

Directions: Imagine that your job exists as a metaphor of your brain, with various parts of the job holding various keys to learning success. Use this drawing as a background for identifying the major intellectual requirements of your job. Post it at your workstation as a reminder to travel from one area to another as your learning on-the-job increases. This is another way to help you make the paradigm shift to thinking of the workplace as a learning place.

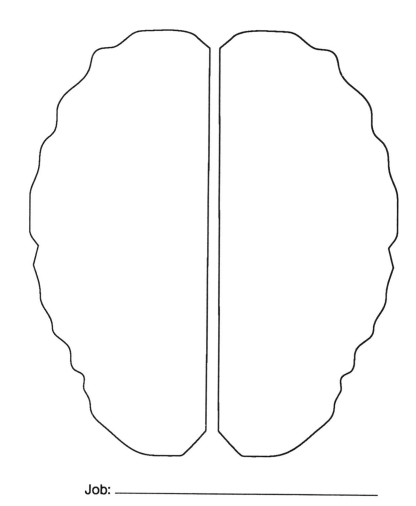

Job: _____

JOB DESIGN MIND MAP

This job design mind map uses information from the job of "trainer"[1] outlined in a report from the American Society for Training and Development (ASTD).

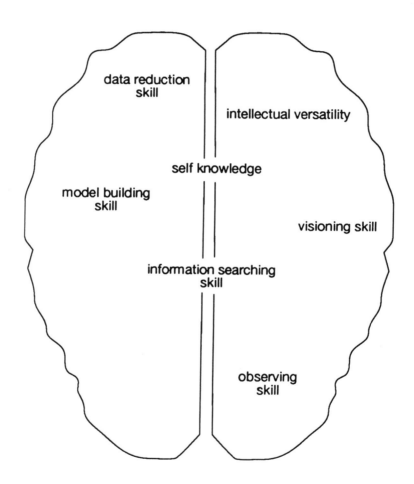

Job: intellectual competencies for the job "TRAINER"

DESIGN METHODS FOR INDIVIDUAL LEARNING

Memory

Problem: Throughout the history of Western thought from Plato to Piaget and beyond, philosophers, educators, psychologists, and neurologists have been fascinated with how we think and how we learn. With modern analysis technology and great advances in information sharing among scientists, and with newer attitudes of communication between natural scientists and social scientists, there have been persistent and always fascinating studies linking psychology and neurology. What Plato surmised from his mental exercises with students, what Locke was so sure he saw (or didn't see) in the mind of a baby, what Skinner observed by running rats in mazes, and what Dewey discovered in his educational experiments, we can now know in a different way as the clarity, surety, and objectiveness that medical science contributes to the "black box" nature and subjectiveness of social science inquiry.

We have seen how human neurons respond to electrical impulse, and we have watched the two brain hemispheres work separately and together with various surgical interventions. We have a history of investigating memory that is rich with the assumptions and questions of past ways of thinking, and is shaped by revelations and truths that have come via scientific findings and medical news. Our understanding of the function of memory in the learning process is informed by both our interpretation of history and by current events.

We have come to believe that memory plays a major role in learning. The problem is that we have seldom taken the time or invested the energy in designing learning experiences that take advantage of the rich body of intelligence we have about memory. Most training deals with memory at only the most elementary levels of our collective theoretical and practical wisdom.

Plan of action: We simply should pay more attention to ways in which to exercise and develop our various kinds of memory in the service of learning. Scholars generally agree that the notion of learning carries with it the element of persistence over time. When one learns, it generally means that one has more or less permanently increased one's capacity to think differently or to act differently. It carries with it the element of being able, then, over time, to continue to build capacity for effectiveness based on that learning.

It's this element of persistence that most directly addresses the instructional design issues around memory use and enhancement. The functions and uses of memory depend upon the quality of the persistence of the images and processes in memory. We should be designing training that helps to create high quality, rapid, unencumbered, direct, and efficient processes of memory manipulation, so that information can stay in—that is, persist in—our memory.

The question becomes, what is high quality memory training? Our answers must always be made with the understanding that the field of memory studies is rich, broad, deep, current, and ever changing. We believe that certain things are true, and so we act accordingly. But as always, current events affect our inquiries and understandings.

For example, there has been a recent resurge of interest in the issue of how credible are child witnesses or witnesses who come forth years after crimes have been committed. *The New York Times*[2] recently contained a major article about the way the memory system works in imagery, that is, in constructing reality out of imaginary events. Academic researchers at the University of Pennsylvania, Princeton University, and Harvard University are finding that the remembering that comes from actual seeing is the same kind of remembering that comes from imagining, and that the same physical areas of the brain are affected in both processes. However, the process of visual perception happens in the reverse order of the process of imagining. The Harvard researcher found that the visual system "maps" imagined objects and scenes precisely, mimicking the real world. The Penn researcher focused on whether mental imagery was just an abstraction or was it actually rooted in the physical biology of the visual system. Athletes and singers have long known that using mental imagery makes them perform better. The lines in this research blur the distinctions between real and imagined, and lead us along new paths of inquiry regarding the functions and uses of memory.

Previous recent research at Johns Hopkins Medical Institutions, also reported in *The New York Times*,[3] discovered that the storage areas of memory, or the "bins" into which we categorize information are quite discrete and appear to be the brain's own natural categories for knowledge. The surprise to the researchers was that "the brain is not necessarily built the way your mind thinks it is." They believe that the neurons actually fire differently according to differing ways of dealing with each category. Different channels for processing information and different circuitry are being studied at Johns Hopkins and elsewhere, as we continue the always fascinating study of human memory and information processing.

Memory is a complex tool for learning, but we have treated it with so little care in the workplace that its capacity to contribute to continuous learning is greatly diminished. With a watchful eye on current psychological and neurobiological research, instructional designers should take a fresh look at memory and at the designs for learning that can maximize its potential for creating a generation of continuous workplace learners.

From our past and present information bases about learning, we believe that information severed from thoughtful action is dead information and not going anywhere (Dewey), that humans are wired to interact with their environment (Skinner), that learning is constructed from our powers of combining, abstracting, collecting, and organizing (Locke), and that sometimes learning is created from a holistic act of insight (Kohler and Gestalt psychology). With all of these informers of our ideas about learning, we accept the common denominator that we are responsible for taking action: it is the individual learner that acts upon environment to take something meaningful from it and that acts again upon environment to give something back to it. It's what happens in between that involves our complex memory.

For those instructional designers who believe that the rate at which people learn is a competitive advantage in today's business world, here are some suggestions for looking at memory in ways to make it work for you as a strategic tool. These are some general instructional design methods for enhancing memory:

1. Use design elements to address short term memory, long term memory, and processing memory. See Worksheet 2 - 6, MEMORY EXERCISER.

2. Differentiate among short term, long term, and processing memory.

3. Design for getting information into memory as well as getting information out of memory.

4. Keep in mind the current research on multiple intelligences (Howard Gardner, Harvard University[4]) and be aware of memory experiences in each of these kinds of "frames of mind." Don't get stuck designing training for only those "types" who have linguistic intelligence or logical/mathematical intelligence. Design learning experiences and memory exercises in all of these kinds of intelligence, because the current research suggests that each learner has some of all kinds of intelligence. A well exercised memory can cut across the various frames of mind and work to get the most into and out of each one, for the ultimate benefit of the learning that results.

Adult learners have enormous advantages over children as learners in that the adult memory system is at its peak—it has an enormous store of patterns, data of all sorts, and experience in ways of using its stores. The adult's memory is one of the greatest untapped resources for learning. As we re-orient the practice of instructional design from an external to an internal focus, the design to enhance the potential of memory should be among the first things we tackle.

Examples: The following examples illustrate that memory is so much more than simply pulling names and definitions out of "the warehouse."

It is probably fair to say that most of our training—as it applies to memory—has been at the very elementary "identify" and "retrieve" levels. We check trainees by asking them to give back to the instructor the name of a new concept, for example, after an explanation of the Pareto Diagram in a TQM course, we might say, 'so, what's the name of this chart?—how do you spell it?—what are its descriptive features (80/20)?'—and so forth. This kind of interaction is typical of corporate classrooms, and, unfortunately of elementary school and high school classrooms too. This is memory training at a very minimal level. It's even questionable in this scenario whether or not the Pareto Diagram ever got out of short term memory, and thus will be forgotten as soon as something more interesting comes along. Too often in this kind of training, we have erroneously misnamed the "activity" between instructor and trainee as active learning, when all it really is is an action upon the external superstructure of training. Active learning means that the internal mental processes of dealing with information, and especially new information, are becoming increasingly complex and integrated with the meaning of work.

This example, on the other hand, illustrates another use of memory—one which encourages the trainee to be aware of action upon his or her memory in a much deeper way. It is this kind of memory exercise that instructional designers should assist learners in performing. This kind of exercise features an active search through memory. It also features a looping mechanism by which optional paths through the problem are considered, sub-problems are identified and solutions to them sought, and the "answer" is finally retrieved from long term memory with the aid of short term memory and processing memory. Awareness on the part of the instructional designer and the learner regarding the nature of memory and the desirability to investigate and exercise its depth can make this kind of exercise an exercise in learning to learn.

The problem solution is presented as numbered steps, for ease of use in discussion later. This is the question:

What were you doing on Tuesday, late in the afternoon in the third week of October twelve years ago? (Don't panic, back off and think about it for a while. Write down your thoughts or tape record them if you like. Think out loud as you work your way through the problem.)

1. Okay, what was I doing twelve years ago?
2. That's 1993 back to 1981. Right, 1981.
3. Let's see, I was a graduate student at Rutgers University in New Brunswick, New Jersey.
4. On Tuesdays, I had a full day because I had to put in 4 hours of time as a research associate at the curriculum lab across town from where my evening classes were held.

5. That means I had to drive across campus (about 3 miles) from my job to the building in which my first Tuesday evening class was held.

6. I usually had just enough time after parking in the student parking lot (I had a blue "full time student" parking decal which allowed me to park closer to the building) to get a quick snack supper before my three evening classes began. Once they started, I did not have the time to get supper between classes.

7. So, late in the afternoon on a Tuesday in October of 1981, I was probably standing in front of the Greek food pushcart on College Avenue in New Brunswick, NJ eating a gyro sandwich.

8. I remember the smells of the lamb roasting on the little spit in that funny little glass and metal shack on wheels, and the great taste of that guy's sesame sauce. In fact, the gyros in late afternoon were one of my best memories of graduate school!

9. Depending on how late in the afternoon it was, I might have been on my way to class. On Tuesdays, I think I had Carl Schaefer's class first.

10. I heard last year that they made all those ethnic food cart people go somewhere else. Too bad. They definitely were a colorful part of graduate education at Rutgers.

From an instructional design point of view, there are numerous opportunities for facilitating this student's active learning from this memory problem. Among the direct interventions might be to help the student separate out the extraneous information that she remembered, like parts of item 4 and item 5, and most of item 6 as she came to the answer to the question, which she articulated in item 7. A facilitative instructional designer might have encouraged her to consider the information in item 9 earlier in her thinking, so that the information in item 9 could have been incorporated into the answer she gave in item 7. She was a little out of sequence here for efficient use of memory. Another instructional design intervention could have been in helping the student craft a new but related problem around her description of the ethnic food carts and Rutgers' graduate education. She seemed to want to say more about this, and her looping through her memory presented the opportunity for more use and a different kind of use of her memory. Or, for efficiency in just answering the question that was asked, the instructional designer could disallow all peripheral information.

The point is that this example illustrates active and deeper processing of memory tasks; the first example does not. The last example encourages the student to learn more by going into other areas of memory; the first example expects the student to stop thinking about the subject at a very shallow level. The last example illustrates how a person can construct a response from memory; the first example illustrates a rather passive response.

WORKSHEET 2 - 6

MEMORY EXERCISER

Directions: Use this as a guide to instructional design to facilitate the deeper and broader exercise of all parts of memory.

Design learning experiences to exercise these basic functions of *Short Term Memory:*

1. Visual scanning
2. Audial scanning
3. Orienting spatially
4. Estimating dimensions of width and length
5. Perceiving variations in speed
6. Concentrating
7. Focusing
8. Chunking information

Design learning experiences to exercise these basic functions of *Long Term Memory:*

1. Recognizing patterns
2. Making associations
3. Verbally comprehending
4. Computing with numbers
5. Reasoning
6. Making modifications
7. Using mnemonics and cues
8. Being original

Design learning experiences to exercise these basic functions of *Processing Memory:*

1. Addressing information
2. Searching
3. Retrieving
4. Signaling and notifying
5. Regulating
6. Rehearsing
7. Organizing
8. Monitoring

LEVELS OF ANALYSIS IN MEMORY TRAINING

Directions: Use the exercise below as an example of the levels of analysis which can be employed during design of learning that enhances memory. Note that each successive task in the list of memory tasks requires a deeper level of processing. Studies have found that the deeper the processing required, the more complete is the recall; that is, if you really want someone to remember something for use later on, you must design training for high levels of analysis that require depth of processing. In your own training design, try always in memory training to get beyond analysis levels 1, 2 and 3 and their psychological equivalents.

The exercise here is to consider each word in the word list separately, one by one. Assume that several of the words are printed in red, green, or blue; the others are in black. The words are listed in no particular order. The memory tasks are listed from low to high.

WORD LIST
accident - tripped - car - driven - money - save - family - smiling

TASK LIST

low

level 1	say what color ink it is printed in
level 2	say how many letters it contains
level 3	say how many letters in this word rhyme with the word "see"
level 4	say whether it is a noun or a verb
level 5	give a word that rhymes with it
level 6	give a word that means the opposite of it
level 7	make a mental image of the word
level 8	make a story that incorporates both the current word and the previous word[5]

high

DESIGN METHODS FOR INDIVIDUAL LEARNING

Flexibility

Problem: Speed of information transfer, rate of societal and organizational change, and the nature of new kinds of work are affecting the individual worker's requirement to be flexible—mentally flexible regarding the work that they do and the person-to-person relationships they develop on the job. Things are happening faster these days, and much of new work has in it the technology that makes old work obsolete. Besides the skills problems, it's scarier and riskier to be flexible these days.

Some background is instructive. A recent issue of *Money* magazine[6] published findings of a U.S. Department of Education survey of college graduates regarding salaries. Among the findings was that there was a great discrepancy between "hard science" graduates and those who studied humanities, education, and psychology in the area of being underemployed: only about 7 percent of the hard science majors were underemployed versus about 33 percent of the other majors. Starting salaries, too, showed a similar pattern: $31,000 to start for the hard science majors; $19,000 for the other majors. *Money* attributes this basically to "an economy dominated by technology," and ends the article with a strong admonition to readers to go out and get the kind of skills that today's economy demands.

The American Management Association says it a different way. An article in AMA's *Small Business Reports*[7] talks about the concept of "skills depreciation" and its link with profitability. This is the notion that skills atrophy over time, and need to be rejuvenated or changed altogether to keep up with new demands of work. The author points out that the effect of atrophied skills has intensified of late because of technology. Rapid advancements in materials, processes, information processing, and communication, have tended to shorten the life span of many products and services, forcing companies to go for greater profit and faster return on more and more short-life-span products and services. Skills to deal with this environment for doing business have to be mentally flexible skills. The AMA article elaborates on how a 40-person manufacturing company devised a "pay for skills" compensation plan partly to encourage workers to upgrade their skills.

And finally, there is the concept of job obsolescence because of the integration of technology: *Harvard Business Review* describes it well.[8] The article contains the phrase "service technology," a strange putting together of words. An explanation follows, noting that clothing manufacturers routinely create permanent-press garments that essentially build in the service of ironing, and at the same time, make that job of ironing obsolete. The microchip, of course, is capable of building diagnostics into operations of all sorts of machines from industrial robots to elevators to copy machines, again rendering the service jobs associated with them obsolete.

In this article, a professor at Dartmouth College's Tuck School is quoted as saying, "leveraged intellect and its prime facilitator, service technology, are reshaping not only the service industries but also U.S. manufacturing, the country's overall economic growth patterns, national and regional job structures, and the position of the United States in world politics and international competition."[9] A further point is made that as more and more companies become part of an "information economy," technology transforms the logic of competition, driving the economic edge right back to the resident knowledge base of workers. Even management sage, Peter Drucker, is quoted as saying that knowledge is the "only meaningful resource today."

The notion of knowledge as a business resource, mind as competitive advantage, and leveraged intellect are surely concepts that demand a good measure of individual mental flexibility as they are applied to business decisions.

Plan of action: The question becomes, just what is mental flexibility in the context of this new work and new competitive environment?

The first thing to consider is the difference between skills and competence. Skills are generally thought to be specific, that is, a person's capability to do a certain thing or to think in a certain useful way. Skills can be collected and combined; they also can atrophy and become obsolete. Competence, on the other hand, is thought to be more generalized regarding one's mental abilities to deal with information as well as one's abilities in interpersonal matters. A competent person is one who can extract big pictures from mounds of data, can let thinking diverge just long enough to get useful points of view out in the open and to facilitate the identifications of options, and who can learn from experience.

In trying to define flexibility, it seems to me that we are looking first for evidence of competency, and then for skills appropriate to a specific job or jobs. We need to re-think some of the major ideas in cognitive psychology. We need to translate into action some of the theories about how people learn complex material, how we become able to make transitions, how we manage conflict, in short, how we *learn* to *learn* how to function in our technology- and information-intensive fast-changing workplaces. There is no doubt that we must be focused yet fluent, organized yet open, firm yet friendly, self-assured and proactive. Mental flexibility is a characteristic that instructional designers should work for as we help individual learners develop the competence and the skills to compete favorably in business as it is in today's changing world. Above all, flexibility demands that we think of our minds as if they were instruments or tools. We need to not be "conformed" to this world, but to be "transformed" by the renewing of our minds.

Instructional designers, of course, come in many different varieties. In peer training, anyone can and should be an instructional designer. Those of us who are "professional" instructional designers, perhaps, can take the lead, but each of us at work must find ways from work itself to renew and regenerate our capacity for flexibility. Here are some suggestions:

- Realize that information is driven by both data and concepts. When you think you're getting overwhelmed by data, turn your thoughts to concepts. Find the conceptual bases of the information processing in which you are so deeply engaged.

- Fit the data into the concepts.

- Realize that humans are infinitely capable of both serial processing and parallel processing. Create exercises for yourself that expand your capacity for doing one, the other, and both. Know the difference. Be open to different ways of processing information. Think of the mental virtuosity of an organist, who reads three staffs of music both vertically and horizontally, pulls stops to change registrations, makes the volume swell or wane, moves hands and feet meaningfully and correctly across keys, and interprets the feelings of a composer to an audience. Don't allow yourself to get stuck in one way of processing information. Look for and learn from models of flexible thinking.

- Use your memory in a conscious way to integrate new knowledge with what you already know. Psychologists call it "tuning," and it involves adjusting your mental models and favorite patterns to allow them to envelop what's new. Think in terms of processes such as add, delete, modify, elaborate, enhance, pare down, and so forth. The idea is to keep what you have and build from it, but to make small structural changes in order for your current memory base to become adequate for your new knowledge. Tuning helps you to become flexible. As you learn from the tasks you are doing at work, think in terms of when you should tune your existing mental models to incorporate new knowledge and create new mental models. It's the active processes going on in the exercise of tuning that help to make you more flexible.

- And finally, as you approach a complex issue or specific work challenge, remember always that you are in charge of it while you are working on it. Flexibility is severely limited when we allow ourselves to "let them do it to us." Individual adults at work have enormous capacity for being in control of their own work processes and their own learning; we have just gotten out of the habit of thinking this way. Instead of waiting for your boss to tell you, your contract to allow you, or your credit card balance to motivate you, take charge of the way you approach work. Think in terms of being a "cognitive monitor" of your own best ways of doing things. "Navigating through the waters" is an apt analogy. Don't be afraid to show or tell someone else how you do it.

Psychology Today even says that "flexibility in midlife is a good indicator of reduced risk of mental decline. Rigid people show declines in mental functioning earlier in life than flexible people."[10] Aside from all of the business reasons why mental flexibility is a good thing, it might just be good for your health too!

Examples: The ASTD/Department of Labor study, *Workplace Basics: The Skills Employers Want,* presents a "Blueprint for Success" regarding design of a program for workplace renewal through training. Among the items in this blueprint is, "Design a Performance-Based/Functional Context Instructional Program."[11] The operative word here is "context." Training should be designed according to the needs of the job or the task at hand, in the total context of work. This is contrasted with textbook-based training in which training is designed around getting to the end of the book regardless of the context of work, according to the rationale that whatever is in the book will be good for you sometime or other, if not now then in the future for sure; or with training that is instructor-led and designed external to the context of work such as in the ivory towers of consulting companies or seminar providers, or even in the offices of corporate trainers.

Remember always that the individual learner at work is the potentially most cost-effective training designer because of all he or she brings to the job and of all he or she can envision accomplishing because of the job. Using job-related materials and the nature of the job itself as the raw material of design has great promise for increasing the quality of workplace performance. Designing for the context of work will almost guarantee that flexibility issues will be addressed. The functional context of work, after all, is multi-dimensional, requiring a host of task-related performance skills as well as competency in information processing and mental model construction.

An example from my own consulting experience illustrates the design issues around flexibility. I live and work in a geographical area which has a long history of manufacturing and assembly work in support of the defense industry. Major government contracting companies as well as many small company parts makers and suppliers dot the New England business landscape. From time to time, I get involved in training design issues in these kinds of businesses.

I recently had occasion to talk with defense workers, men and women who had spent many years in factory jobs doing repetitive tasks under contracts that lasted for years. Their jobs were routine, procedure-driven, narrow in scope, and secure. But times suddenly changed and their entire industry responded to world political changes, shaking up not only the rationale for labor-management relations but also the very nature of the way they worked.

Throughout New England, and in key other geographical areas around the United States heavy in defense contracting, the new buzzword became "Defense Diversification." Workers around my hometown are having to take swift and sure steps to be able to deal, not in long-term contracts but in short-term ones; not in work marked by routine and sameness but by exceptionality; not in procedure-driven work, but in work driven by the market. Mental flexibility is certainly a requirement of work here.

Examples of faults in our thinking about higher-level performance skills, including the skill of being mentally flexible, abound in the literature of competency test design. Such tests are often used in certification and credentialling. My doctoral dissertation, for example, focused on the design of such tests, and found, among other things, that written multiple choice tests certifying competency as an accountant were actually tests of remembering. The tests tested very little of the essence of being an accountant, of doing accounting work. The tests tested verbal skills, mostly at the level of identifying and defining. There would have been no way for the public, for example, to know that an accountant, credentialled by having passed such a test, knew how to do accounting. The consumer of accounting services could only have been certain that the person who passed the test had a verbal facility with the terminology of the field. There was hardly any requirement nor test of the mental flexibility of doing accounting work in those particular tests.[12]

Not that design of testing or design of learning is easy: it isn't. Some classic studies in the 1970s of professional competence in a variety of occupations also illustrate the problems of designing for flexibility. From an attempt to classify the cognitive requirements of medical practice, researchers concluded that the licensing exams in use in the late '70s did not reflect what was known about competence in the field nor about what could be measured by existing tests. These were some of the cognitive skills the researchers found that were probably not being measured:

- analysis of data or application of a unique combination of principles to a novel problem,
- evaluation of a total situation,
- analysis of a variety of elements of knowledge and application to a novel problem situation in its entirety.[13]

These studies were typical of the kinds of studies that attempted to capture and codify the cognitive flexibility requirements of doing specific kinds of work. The competency testing movement in vocational-technical education and professional credentialling is an important piece of the instructional design cycle.

DESIGN METHODS FOR INDIVIDUAL LEARNING

Problem Solving

Problem: A problem, cognitively speaking, is a situation for which a person has no ready or adequate response. Problems generally contain requirements for several kinds of knowledge: development and application of strategy, verbal or semantic facility and agility, and procedural ability. Many discussions of problem solving end up being circular; that is, which comes first, learning certain skills in order to solve problems, or because of possessing certain problem solving skills, one learns better. Whatever the disagreements are in this regard, most critics agree that learning and problem solving are related, and that being good at either positively affects the other.

For the purposes of this book, we will draft this problem statement according to the frame that says there are things one can learn—and teach—in order to become better at problem solving. As an instructional design issue, the problem is how can we re-cast work into "problems" rather than as the content-dependent phenomenon it typically is. We typically go to work in order to accomplish a "to do" list of things we describe as nouns—mail, meetings, memos, outlines, pages, pieces, sales, phone calls, appointments, and so forth. In order to get beyond the simple descriptive mind-set about work, we need to challenge workers to think of work as good "problems" containing the cognitive requirements of at least the fundamental skills related to strategy, semantics, and procedures.

To be sure, much of work has evolved into routine. We think we know how to do the mail, the meetings, the memos, and the rest of it; we seldom consider the possibility of doing meetings differently or for a different purpose (strategy), of constructing our memos around different uses of concepts or with new terminology (semantics), or of handling our mail responsibilities differently (procedures). If we could cast our work tasks within a problem solving framework, we'd have a better shot at getting more out of work and at retraining ourselves and our peers to operate mentally at a deeper and more creative level.

In addition, all indicators point to the disappearance of routine in the work of the future. We simply might not have all that much time to develop new skills for dealing with the non-routine, and must figure out ways to learn these new skills from current work itself. We are likely to be confronted with new work problems—that is, with situations for which there is no ready, adequate response—on a daily, and perhaps, even hourly basis. New work, by all accounts of economists, management gurus, labor leaders, business writers and researchers, and politicians, will be knowledge work; and developing good problem solving skills as individuals and as organizations is at least part of the essential work and work ethic required of knowledge workers.

Plan of action: The use of the computer for mental modeling has contributed greatly to the interest in and study of problem solving. Largely because of the fascinaton of so many academic researchers with the computer ever since its widespread acceptance in the 1970s, there have been many studies of cognition, information processing, and problem solving since those early years. The psychology literature is full of models, investigations, and findings regarding problem solving. There are many avenues to pursue when devising a plan of action for workplace training in the techniques of problem solving. The challenge is to synthesize the wealth of information into some useful strategies and techniques for learning.

We begin with the widest conceptual overview of problem solving, and that is the "Big Memory" and "Big Switch" theory of Allen Newell, a professor at Carnegie-Mellon University in Pittsburgh, PA. Newell and his partner, Herbert Simon, are generally credited with launching the renewed contemporary interest in problem solving with the publication of their book, *Human Problem Solving* (Prentice-Hall, Inc.) in 1972. The early work of these two men focused on the individual as an information processing system when it comes to solving problems, and the essential structure of this system, according to Newell, is a mental organization known as Big Memory and a processing structure known as Big Switch. We too can think of business tasks as having a structure of Big Memory and Big Switch. Problem solving, then, becomes an exercise in pulling from Big Memory just what we need, and activating Big Switch at just the right times. Problem solving has a "power" dimension (effective use of memory), and a "speed" dimension (correct execution of turn on and turn off mechanisms). We could design training, especially peer training one by one, around exercise of Big Memory and Big Switch.

Another way to look at a problem is to define the structural elements common to all problems. These seem to be:

1. a goal or right solution,
2. a set of operations or techniques to achieve the goal or solution, and
3. information unique to the content or context of the problem.

We could design training for problem solving around verification of goals; identification, development, and practice of operational techniques; and elaboration and explanation of the problem's unique information. Anyone at work can develop a self-assessment tool for approaching work tasks within this framework, and can share such a monitoring device with peers.

Another way of looking at work problems is to think of working as information processing, and therefore to categorize the tasks of work as one might categorize information. Within this frame of mind, we might isolate the tasks of work as:

- developing and dealing with concepts,
- processing data,
- establishing or creating structure,

- categorizing and organizing,
- abiding by principles,
- recognizing and working within a process, and
- establishing and following procedures.

Problem solving instruction, then, becomes training in decision-making about and use of information processing strategies. Training in any or all of the information-related skills such as using analogies, being fluent in written expression, matching, reasoning, choosing appropriate definitions, defining opposites, could be useful in increasing one's ability as a problem solver under the information processing mindset.

Simply getting used to asking "why?" or "what if?" instead of "what?" or "what kind?" is another way to re-train your thinking. Changing from "content" into "process" is another mental gymnastic that sometimes works. Putting "-ing" onto the ends of many of the words you use to talk about work is another mind-changing game you can play with yourself or your peers as you become better problem solvers, and better learners.

Examples: Business magazines and journals are beginning to have articles about how to reorganize work in order to become "a learning organization." Many of the strategies described by academics and business persons involve training for problem solving.

One such article is, "We Do; Therefore, We Learn," the keynote article in ASTD's *Training & Development*, October 1993. In this article, a reorganization of information at the consulting company, Ernst & Young is described in a good bit of detail. What prompted this look inward was a finding that the professional staff reported that 90 percent of their learning took place on the job. Trainers at the consulting company reasoned that to win in their business's rapidly changing and highly competitive worldwide business environment, Ernst & Young trainers simply had to provide the system structures and supports for their consultants to quickly get information from and add information to the corporate pool of knowledge. If, in fact, their learning took place on the job, then the job had better be an outstanding source of learning.

The Ernst & Young folks determined that their self-appointed, self-directed learners had certain characteristics as learners, and the trainers took the challenge to devise new ways for those learners to learn. Among the characteristics they defined were: they use business experiences and problems as triggers for learning, they extract lessons out of their experiences, they use feedback to improve their performance on future similar tasks, and they restructure problems by consciously incorporating different approaches or perspectives. In short, they learn from their own experience and from the experience of their peers.

The design for learning had a particular problem solving goal to it, matching the problem solving nature of the work of most consultants. It also was very much focused on the notion that peers should be able to learn from peers, making the most of techniques and information structures that were appropriate to the learner characteristics they had identified.

A key feature of the new "learning to learn" model is a computer database to which all consultants are required to contribute as they serve clients. Consultants enter what worked and what didn't work, and are ethically obligated to share information with their peers. Reportedly, Ernst & Young management is considering incorporating use of the database into standards for the performance review and pay treatment of consultants. Managers note that in a world of experts, it's hard to get workers to stop and reflect, and to admit that they don't know all the answers and it might be good to ask. What they hope to do with this new workplace learning to learn model is to encourage people to practice restructuring problems. And this, they believe, is the key to competitive advantage in their business.[14]

A second example of instructional designs for problem solving comes out of an article by David A. Garvin in *Harvard Business Review*.[15] One of the companies which the article features is Xerox, and the "gritty details" of how it transformed itself into a problem-solving company. The definition of learning organization given in the article includes the idea that it is an organization skilled at *modifying* its behavior to reflect new knowledge and insights, and at *transferring* knowledge from theory into action. These "restructuring" types of processing are often equated with problem solving, and indeed, Xerox's organizational restructure follows a classic problem solving systems model.

Along the route from analysis to action to evaluation (the familiar systems model espoused by instructional designers too), Xerox's learning organization designers insisted that several critical ideas form the foundation of the approach to problems. These are: that data rather than assumptions form the basis for decisions, that statistical analysis tools be routinely and consistently used in problem analysis, and that a specified step-by-step systems procedure be used for diagnosis. Xerox wanted to build in problem solving techniques so that they no longer operated on "gut facts" and sloppy reasoning. Employees there are provided with tools in four areas: generating ideas and collecting information, reaching consensus, analyzing and displaying data, and planning for action. Problem solving was seen as one of Xerox's value-added competitive tools.

Training in the use of these problem solving tools has been done in classrooms and in work team small groups, using the tools to solve real work problems even in training. Xerox reports, in the article, that after a decade of operation under this problem solving model, they indeed have developed a "common vocabulary" and a consistent company-wide approach to problem solving. Employees are expected to work this way, and they do.

WORKSHEET 2 - 8

LEARNING TOOLS FOR PROBLEM SOLVING

Directions: Use this list of tools to help build individual problem solving skills. Encourage their use by individual workers in self-directed learning or for pairs of workers to refine in the give and take of structured peer training. Add other tools as you think of them.

TOOLS FOR DEALING WITH PROBLEM CONTENT

1. Expand vocabulary.
2. Brainstorm.
3. Compare, contrast, use metaphors and analogies.
4. Organize, file, categorize, prioritize, sequence.
5. Define information gaps.
6. Exercise memory.
7. Collect ideas.
8. Design and follow procedures.
9. Seek and use information resources.

TOOLS FOR WORKING THROUGH PROBLEMS

1. Always ask why.
2. Talk out loud during strategy formulation.
3. Experiment.
4. Give cues.
5. Look for cues.
6. Modify: add, delete, expand, contract, reshape.
7. Hypothesize.
8. Identify sub-problems; seek sub-problem solutions.
9. Use part:whole analysis.
10. Listen.
11. Dialogue.
12. Stop and think.

TOOLS FOR ATTITUDE ADJUSTMENT

1. Want to solve problems.
2 Commit to truth, facts, and accuracy.
3. Believe in the expert in everyone; believe also in the expert in no one.
4. Use time as an investment.
5. Initiate.
6. Share. Help others.
7. Dump "Not Invented Here" forever.
8. Take responsibility.

DESIGN METHODS FOR INDIVIDUAL LEARNING

Creativity and Innovation

Problem: Everyone likes to talk about creativity, but few people have any idea of how to back up their talk with action to make it happen. We like to think that if we can learn better we can re-create ourselves, and that somehow, in the right environment of "the learning organization" we will become more creative and innovative.

We are reminded of the parable of "C" and the box.[16] "C" had been very comfortable in the box—in fact, "C" had forgotten that there was an outside to the box until "C" re-discovered the spring in the corner of the box. One day, out of boredom, and after "C" had tripped over the spring long enough, "C" used the spring to jump out of the box. The point of this creativity parable is that workers have to find ways to explore the world outside of their current boxes. The point is echoed by other critics of the business environment who are quick to point out that employee skills have not kept pace with the degree of technological capacity built into many of our business processes nor with the pace of competitive challenge from all corners. "C" got out of the box by practicing using the spring and by a change of will to try the leap.

While there's general agreement that innovation is required in business to balance the disequilibrium caused by so many change factors, scholars disagree that there's a "creative type personality" or that there are specific "creative factors" resident in those who are creative. In addition, most observations about creative acts conclude that creativity usually occurs outside of conscious thought and behavior. The bottom line is that while people want creative workers and workers themselves would like to be more creative, the very act of training and organizing creative learning opportunities could very well be counterproductive to developing creativity. We are generally more creative when we don't need to be creative.

So again we turn to peer training as a design and delivery option that holds promise of being able to foster creative action.

Plan of action: This section is a synthesis of some current thinking on creativity and innovation, with suggested approaches for action in design of instruction to foster creativity.

Creative acts require support. A creative act or result is accompanied by change, and change is always difficult for people to endure. It's hard accepting that change should occur, it's hard living through the act of change while it's happening, and it's hard to implement the planning and long-range execution of change. It's easy to think ill of or to blame the change trigger, and often that change trigger is the innovative or creative person. So, creative acts require support from the work system and from the persons who surround the change maker.

There are training interventions that can be crafted to help people understand and therefore perhaps tolerate change better, and there are other human resources supports that can be put in place so that the work environment is less stressful for workers as they go through change. People can be taught the definitions of various scholars' and psychologists' ideas of some creative factors in an attempt to broaden awareness of creativity; people can be taught to think "divergently" or "to brainstorm" through guided exercises in divergent thinking and brainstorming. People can be taught to see the value of "idea generation" in structured classes on creativity. "Creativity" can be taught much the same way that "Quality" has been taught, that is, awareness-level training in the principles and terminology of the field can be conducted to disseminate information about creativity in the hopes that people will know it when they see it and therefore not be afraid of it.

Likewise, the effects of creativity can be addressed. People can be taught techniques of change management or conflict management. People can be taught techniques of planning and reengineering to accommodate the effects of change. Motivation and reward systems can be tweaked to reward those who have a bright idea, who find errors and give suggestions for fixing them, and who demonstrate unusual facilitative or leadership skills. We can support risk-takers by overt acts of organizational support. We can send the message to employees that loneliness and disruptiveness of being creative is valued.

But we still have not dealt with just how it is that people become creative, and how to train them to do so.

Creative people are vulnerable to the richness of experience. Creativity seems to depend on a willingness to be bombarded by experience and an openness of personality. A sterile workstation, narrowly defined job, confirming orders, and restrictive contract don't seem to foster creativity in people. Organizations who want to encourage creative behavior must broaden work; the current movement to work in teams is a move in this direction. Creativity seems to require a large data base of "messy" information within one's current personal experience. Companies can help create these databases for people by enhancing their jobs and broadening their job information. In the jargon of the creativity literature, this is known as the requirement for "saturation."

Creative people seem to be open to being influenced by what they are doing; some trigger problem, event, or person makes them see things differently. Employers can reorganize work to facilitate openness. Workers can be purposefully paired, they can be assigned to teams, they can function on ad hoc task forces, they can be *encouraged* to talk to each other. They can have assurances that the workplace wants them to be creative. They can be put into situations that have been known to encourage the incubation of ideas.

So far, we have restricted this discussion to the notion of creative productivity, or the result of creative thinking. But what about the personal, mental characteristics that seem to be present in order to get to that creative act? The following list includes the factors that most creativity researchers agree seem to be present in creative people:

- *divergent thinking:* ability to rapidly connect ideas; flexibility in approaching work; ability to modify, turn upside down, elaborate, expand;
- *independent thinking:* ability to be "your own person" while immersed in a mess;
- *tolerance for ambiguity:* a predisposition to suspend judgment; to keep generating ideas when others seem prone to close discussion; to thrive on diversity;
- *capacity to find order:* ability to create order out of experience, to "roll with the punches;" to seek organizing structures rather than having them imposed;
- *ability to analyze, synthesize, and evaluate:* ability to deal with information to tear it apart, put it together, and judge its worth; ability to remove oneself from information and act upon it; facility to objectify information and be in charge of it.

Obviously, these five items are seldom the topic of courses or organized training programs. We haven't paid much attention to teaching people how to be creative, although we say creative people are very much in demand. Perhaps teaching people to work with each other creatively at their jobs is the best way to produce creative people. The following section contains some specific examples of things to do in this regard.

Examples: The two fundamental assumptions upon which these examples have been chosen are that creative people need support and that creativity develops best when experience is rich and varied. Trainers can act upon these assumptions to encourage creativity by pairing people as they work, so that as they do their work and address the problems that surface because of their work they can talk with each other and support each other. "Up close and personal" is one basic structural arrangement that those in charge of human resources development can encourage. It's the simplest, most direct, and most cost-effective way of getting individuals support in an organization.

How you do it depends on your commitment and culture. You can take the percentage of time approach, indicating that 25 percent of each day be spent in paired work, or that two days each week be spent in peer training. Or, if you prefer a "level" distinction, and your company's culture can deal with it, you can take the coaching or mentoring approach, making that as formal or informal as you choose. Or, you can take the subject approach, indicating that paired work be done always when product testing is required, or when procedures are revised, or when the company newsletter is put together—or when any other subject of work is definable. Make the decision content-specific, rather than time-specific.

The point is to get people working together, talking outloud to each other as they work through their work together. While they work, suggest these strategies:

1. Suspend judgment for four consecutive hours; don't defend, argue, pre-judge, or otherwise categorize decisions into right and wrong.

2. List all possible and probable options before choosing a path or a solution; actually write them down.

3. Brainstorm with your partner and even with yourself alone; draw a brainstorm nucleus and start connecting ideas quickly to it; talk with your partner as you do this, or talk outloud to yourself as you do this;

4. Be outrageous; think in metaphors or parables; read reports and journals you don't usually read; talk to people in other departments that seem unrelated to your own;

5. Pretend a box of breath mints is a box of "innovation vitamins" and take one at the time of day when you feel draggy and in need of vitamins;

6. Draw pictures and charts instead of writing words;

7. Try out different roles in teams or group work: be a note-taker, a moderator or leader, a facilitator, negotiator, ambassador, or cheerleader; don't always assume the same role:

8. Take "time out" breaks; use a break from work to step back and think about it; no coffee or tea, and no food; just mentally remove yourself for a short time simply to regroup your mental resources, but stay focused on your objective (don't use time out to do your mail or answer a phone call). Use the concept of monitoring your own work procedures and decision making.

A story is told of eight technical managers at American Cyanamid Corporation who worked with the creativity consultant, A. Osborn, in a brainstorming session. Osborn reports that a 15-minute session produced 92 ideas, or more than six ideas per minute. Osborn's work in the field over more than thirty years has shown that quality of ideas does come from quantity of ideas, and that better ideas grow from the synergy of quantity, pace, and suspended judgment.[17] Brainstorming takes a little practice, but it pays off.

The Walt Disney World Seminar Productions organization publishes a marketing brochure called "Behind the Ear to Ear Smiles: the Disney Approach to Orientation," in which Disney describes its train-the-trainer seminar on how to develop an employee orientation program, Disney style. The brochure itself makes use of metaphor, and already, even in this public relations/marketing piece, the well-known Disney approach to people is obvious. The brochure addresses its reader, a prospective seminar attendee this way: ". . . as an honorary Cast Member, you'll gain an understanding of what it takes to help employees see their roles in an organization, and how to capture their interest and enthusiasm" . . . . and see how the "backstage support teams" play a role in meeting employees' needs.[18] Disney is an entertainer, first and foremost, and all of his training uses the metaphors of the entertainment business—even in this kind of brochure meant to attract the general training professional to a "how Disney does it" informational seminar. Trainers and workers everywhere can borrow this creativity-training technique of using metaphor as a way to transport yourself into the "whole" of a situation. Pairs of workers, talking with each other, can surely explore metaphors of their work, and do it efficiently, synergistically, and with great expansiveness.

Another trick with language is to suggest to employees that they think always of verbs when they're tempted to think of nouns. Instead of thinking "sale" think of "selling;" instead of thinking "customer service" think of "customer serving." The story is told of W.J.J. Gordon, a creativity consultant, who met with a group whose task it was to design a new can opener. Gordon would not let them use the noun; rather he made them think and talk always in terms of "opening," encouraging them to be outrageous in their analysis of models for opening. One such model was the pea pod of the garden pea, a self-opener. This led to the notion of a soft-seam opener and eventually to the design of the vinyl tape opener on a frozen juice can—a product that would probably never have been imagined if the group had begun with the notion of "can opener," the noun.[19] The noun into verb idea is so simple that you wish you'd thought of it a long time ago. Having employees work in pairs or small groups helps to encourage depth at the synthesis and evaluation levels, and, of course, provides the readily accessible feedback and support for risk-taking thinking that is important in the facilitation of creativity. People don't mind thinking silly thoughts with a single person they can trust; they don't like to do this in a meeting, a training class, or a large group.

Another example of something you can do to foster creativity is to encourage everyone to think in terms of substituting prepositions for each other. For example, rather than think about "sending the product *down* the line" think about "sending the product *over* the line, *around* the line, *through* the line," and so forth. The different-ness of the mental image created by the substitution can create a spark for perhaps doing things better. Encourage employees also to think in terms of adding, deleting, modifying, magnifying, shrinking, rearranging. In both of these word games, the important thing to realize is that focus is still on the key object or task; it's the process of working with it that is being changed through creative thinking. Again, this is a creative thinking technique that people can learn and practice one by one; in fact, having a buddy thinking like this too can provide the motivation and encouragement to keep thinking this way whenever a need or urge for change might be in the works.

DESIGN METHODS FOR INDIVIDUAL LEARNING

Sensory Learning

Problem: There is a great tendency when talking about workplace learning to make light of the dissonance between the adult learner's agility and flexibility at mental exercise such as logic, conceptual interpretation, and problem solving and that learner's life experience which is largely uncodified, "chaotic," serendipitous, and heuristic. As trainers and instructional designers, we have paid much more attention to the design requirements of "school learning" type of learning than to the "lessons from life" type of learning. We have paid much more attention to the psychological than to the physical dimensions of experience as we attempt to design for learning.

In addition, the "information-izing" of the workplace—or the "informating" power of the computer, as Harvard University's Shoshana Zuboff says[20]—has tended to make work seem like an abstraction of itself for many people, and has added to the learning dissonances that many workers feel today as their personal involvement with the essence of their work changes because of computerization. Information technology, according to Zuboff, tends to reduce the demands of the task itself, often rendering the person who has mastered the task, and done so elegantly over a span of experienced work, useless or at least helpless.

Her book, *In the Age of the Smart Machine,* contains a section of drawings made by various kinds of employees representing their feelings about their jobs before and after getting computerized. These drawings always show a less humanized conception of work organization and work flow, fewer smiles, less full-bodied drawings of themselves or their supervisors, and even wilted flowers on the "after" set of drawings. As their work became more abstract, they perceived that they themselves became less human than they were before. As the rich and holistic type of contact with peers was replaced by the efficient processing capability of a machine, workers felt a loss that translated into a pall over the joyousness of work.[21]

There is an important dimension of learning that is primarily sensory and motor, or psychomotor, as it has been named by educational psychologists. It is the kind of learning that industrial workers from roughly 1750 to 1950 mastered. It is the kind of learning that many of today's workers have a strong, experience-based memory of, and it's the kind of learning that seems to be more akin to life itself. Capturing the important structures of this kind of experiential learning seems to be an endeavor worth pursuing if we are ever to reduce the dissonance between "book learning" type of learning and learning from work itself.

Our problem is to define and analyze the essential, life-enhancing structures of this kind of learning and to suggest ways in which it can be usefully integrated into the whole of learning. The messy, sensory stimulations of lessons from life must complement the lessons of logic in today's workplaces if we are to optimize our best—our human—resources.

Plan of action: There are some avenues of investigation to travel in the search for contemporary meaning in psychomotor or sensory learning.

First, we should consider the classic definitions in a taxonomy of psychomotor skills;

second, we should attempt to view these skills within a context of the cognitive skills already discussed;

third, we should try to highlight some of the areas of particular challenge to instructional designers; and

fourth, we should suggest some overt steps to take to meet these challenges.

After the publication of Benjamin Bloom's *Taxonomy of Educational Objectives in the Cognitive Domain* in 1956, a great deal of interest was aroused in the notion of hierarchies of objectives for school learning. Vocational-technical educators, particularly, were interested in the psychomotor domain, and, spurred by massive Federal education funding in the 1960s, made many studies of the nature of this kind of learning and its design requirements. One such study was that done by Elisabeth Simpson and published at the University of Illinois, Urbana-Champaign.[22] In this study, she suggests the following classification:

1.0 Perception, including:
    1.1 Sensory stimulation upon one or more of the sense organs: auditory, visual, tactile, taste, smell, and kinesthetic,
    1.2 Cue selection;
    1.3 Translation, that is, the symbolic interpretation of the cues into action;
2.0 Set, including:
    2.1 Mental set, or knowledge readiness to perform a certain task;
    2.2 Physical set, or readying the body to perform a certain task;
    2.3 Emotional set, or being willing to perform a certain task;
3.0 Guided response, including:
    3.1 Imitation of a skill, as demonstrated;
    3.2 Trial and error, under guidance or external motivator;
4.0 Mechanism, or habitual response;
5.0 Complex overt response, including:
    5.1 Resolution of uncertainty;
    5.2 Automatic performance.

Simpson's study was based on the notion that learning these tasks was largely a matter of learning perceptual relationships, that is, becoming adept and facile at choosing the best stimuli, organizing them usefully, and applying them in a coherent and efficient way to the work at hand. Better learning seemed to result with better abilities in perception. Simpson, and others like her, were attempting to deal with the dichotomy of mind versus body, content versus process, and theory versus practice, by codifying the skills it takes to perform work using muscles, tendons, joints, bones, ears, eyes, skin, tongue, and nose. She observed that there seemed to be a "habit hierarchy" of learned skill in things like typing or using a dress pattern, and there was an "efficiency in performance" that came from higher degrees of perception. She concluded that thinking well requires knowing what skills are appropriate and when they should be applied for maximum advantage to work.

Ever since John Dewey's[23] influence in the early years of the 20th century, we have believed, with more or less conviction, in the "active" nature of learning itself and have tried out various instructional techniques that attempted to help learners construct their knowledge. Unfortunately, these worthy attempts in recent decades have been overshadowed by the procedural efficiency mindset in management, and training in the corporation has degenerated to a largely administratively convenient information dissemination activity. The time has come to re-think the conceptual bases of workplace learning and to be bold enough to try to use the vast amount of intelligence we have about learning to implement training programs in a more appropriate and useful way. The diversity of the workforce, the dispersion of the workplace, the globalness of markets, and the nature of work all are pushing us in this direction.

We can help ourselves by thinking about how we interact with tasks other than semantic, or verbal, tasks. Much of life's learnings are other than verbal: we reach and grab, bend and stretch, lift and carry, see and hear, navigate through water, air, forests, and snow. We read maps, charts, posters. We play instruments; we build models. We put together superb tastes for sustenance and social enjoyment. We learn songs; we paint pictures; we communicate with infants. We perform a host of tasks that are not dependent on verbal intelligence. Human beings, and especially adult human beings, have an enormous store of memory for and demonstrated skill for other-than-verbal ways of learning. We simply need to capture and capitalize on this memory and this skill. We need to train for the development of these skills because they are the survival skills of living.

Like any learning tasks in cognitive areas such as problem solving or creativity, tasks in the psychomotor domain of learning present certain challenges to those who would attempt to make these tasks as efficient and effective as they can be. There is a general requirement in psychomotor learning to differentiate features and to choose correctly. For example, what kinds of sounds are required for music instead of noise, or how much light is appropriate light to give the proper cue to behavior, or which movements are necessary and in what order should they be executed to perform the lifting tasks on the loading dock. Feature discrimination is critical to high quality performance, and execution of choice has far-reaching effects in psychomotor learning. Trainers must pay attention to these elements of instruction, so that a learner's prior messy knowledge can be synthesized and organized to benefit work and the worker.

Some of the key areas of difficulty with one's experience base of psychomotor skills is that the learned skill has often been learned in a specific context for only that context. Unlike problem solving, where we tend to believe that there are generic skills that readily transfer to other problem situations, and we design instruction around principles of transfer to those other situations, the skills required in sensory skill development tend to be narrow. For example, a wiring specialist in an electronics factory learns wiring for a specific job. Modification of that technique would typically be slow and require conceptual differentiation as well as physical practice of new ways of doing things. Unlike just "plain thinking," psychomotor tasks take up much more learning time. Also in psychomotor learning, there's a danger that the hierarchical nature of learned behavior will not be attended to in the design of instruction, and that the high-level, value-added, and perhaps even the authentic practices of the behavior will never be addressed in training. We need to spend more time thinking about the design of sensory-based learning because there's so much of it embodied in today's workforce. We are missing a great opportunity for human resources development if we continue to downplay this kind of learning.

Examples: Recently, a trainer from the Upjohn Company's Engineering and Maintenance Division presented a session at a conference[24] in Boston in which she showed the group a chart suggesting the percentages of each of the senses used in learning. In order of most to least, this is what her chart said:

seeing	75%
hearing	13%
touching	6%
smelling	3%
tasting	3%

She followed showing these numbers with the admonition to use training methods that were compatible with the sense or senses involved in the learning task. The implication was that all too often, our training methods have not been appropriate.

Edward R. Tufte, a statistics professor at Yale University, writes often about the ways to present and process information resulting from visual stimuli. In his book, *Envisioning Information,* he raises the important point that visual information is at once "wideband" and "controlled channel"—we can quickly glance at a bar graph, for example, and impute a great deal of rather heuristic information from a straight vertical line representing that information, that is, both wideband and controlled channel simultaneously. We can, obviously, train people to read graphs of all sorts; we are pretty good at designing instruction for the "controlled channel" part of the task. We have not been so good, however, at helping the learner deal effectively with the "wideband" aspects of the task. Chances are that the wideband information brought out of memory was not as well tuned as it might have been, nor perhaps as complete or as authentic as it could have been. To elaborate this idea, he notes that a well-trained colorist can distinguish about one million different colors. Tufte makes the point that there are layers of information presented and received visually, and that the relationship between the layers matters when it comes to both the data and the substance of ideas conveyed.

He points out that as we seek to learn from visual information, we need to be watchful for what he calls "chart junk"—the inappropriate designs, colors, lines, and so forth which sabotage understanding. He always calls for an "active eye" with which to build visual information through appropriate differentiation of features and selection.[25] We should be designing instruction much more carefully so that we capture the essence of visual learning. We are a long way from this in our current corporate classrooms.

One of the most interesting studies of sensory learning was that done by Shoshana Zuboff at the Piney Wood pulp and paper mill. Although hers was an investigation of the effects of computerizing work, she also highlighted some of the salient features of sensory learning in her discussions with workers at the mill. Zuboff talked with process operators at the mill, the people who personally with their own senses monitored the chemical and physical mixing and boiling operations. Noises, smells, and vibrations were all important indicators. In addition, process operators said that they often had other, special, ways of keeping things going correctly. These included things such as propping doors open to give greater cooling or more draft, or tapping on pipes to loosen deposits and encourage flow. She concluded that the kind of intuitive understanding that these special ways of monitoring required came only with experience; their knowledge was implicit and embedded in the action learning that comes from well-tuned senses. She reminds the reader of the power of the term, "know-how;"[26] it is robust, detailed, and highly individual. It is the kind of knowledge that peers can teach each other, akin to the art of storytelling, the product of which only gets better over time with each successive layer.

Another example from my own experience is very much like the Piney Wood example. In the early 1980's, I was manager of simulation training at Combustion Engineering Company. My trainees were among the first operators to make the change from an analog world of reading gauges and adjusting valves in oil refineries to the digital world of reading computer screens in offices. In fact, the name of my training center was the "Digital Technology Center (DTC)." My job was to develop "operator training" courses that would help these individuals make the switch from one world to the next.

My trainees were traditional, experienced plant operators. They intuitively knew when a pump sounded right or didn't sound right, when very fine distinctions in temperature indicated trouble, when a valve didn't feel quite tight enough, when a mix was the right color. They had developed their skills through habit, association, experiencing cause and effect, through a seasoned hands-on involvement of senses and muscles. Many of them had a physical memory in their bodies of what excellent performance meant, and they had a cultural and social memory of how to behave in a workplace that depended upon well-tuned senses.

It was hard for them to sit down in front of a computer screen—yes, hard to sit down to work. It was even harder to scan all indicators at once—pressure, temperature, flow, altogether within ten inches on a blinking green screen. This was very different from the real processes which the operator observed and felt, one process at a time, by walking around the machinery or climbing the ladder. It wasn't immediately apparent which readout on the computer screen went with which process. It became very obvious very quickly that the operator's sensory learning environment of real life was very different from the abstracted environment of his new work.

Instructional designers must find ways to capture the ways in which people deal with life as it is experienced through the senses because it is this kind of learning that is useful in the living of life. There will always be aspects of all work that require well-tuned perceptive skills, and in our current rush to develop higher-level cognitive skills, we can have a tendency to ignore this very important aspect of organizational learning.

Fortunately, there is some movement in that direction. One attempt at teaching thinking skills through a "whole-brain" approach to work tasks is known as the "Neurolinguistic Programming" (NLP) approach which tries to address both the data-driven and the conceptually-driven halves of the brain, the organized analytical side as well as the holistic and subjective side of the brain. Other research follows the work of Howard A. Gardner of Harvard University who has identified six major kinds of intelligence present in all individuals to some degree, including bodily-kinesthetic, spatial, personal, and the more traditionally studied linguistic, logical-mathematical, and musical. The other most well-known approach is the "Accelerated Learning" movement which practices techniques to heighten sensory awareness as procedural or conceptual learning is occurring.

All of these movements have substantial followings among training and educational professionals. Although each approach has some components of training for sensory learning in it, each also somewhat dilutes that focus because of its integrative framework. Those who design learning opportunities for workers would do better to focus entirely on the depth and accuracy of skills in the psychomotor domain of learning. A structured, intentional program of peer training in this regard makes a great deal of sense. Peer training is a natural vehicle for encouraging and facilitating the kinds of dialogue and inquiry that help to deepen and verify the embodied skills associated with sensory learning.

DESIGN METHODS FOR INDIVIDUAL LEARNING

Experiential and Reflective Thinking

Problem: Throughout the history of thought, there have been experiments and opinions about how much and what kind of thinking produces the best results. Academic researchers, school teachers, and corporate instructional designers have been among the most interested investigators into the dichotomies between the various forms of teaching—directed instruction, guided practice, individual inquiry, trial and error, and so forth. Those who are focused on the useful results of "good" thinking, such as corporate human resources department specialists, are constantly trying to balance the forces driving toward the quantified results of the bottom line against the forces pushing for quality in the acts of thinking. Economists have joined the bandwagon lately and have seen the concept of "learning to learn" as a competitive tool. We are challenged both from inside and from outside to make workplace learning appropriate, comprehensive, creative as well as full of content, all that's sufficient but only that which is necessary—efficient as well as effective.

The problem is as designers of instruction, we know that efficiency sometimes seems sacrificed in the search for effectiveness; that building quality in costs time. We search for approaches to learning design that can help integrate our needs for being grounded in the thinking that comes from experience with our needs to jump out of that experience and observe and reflect upon the uses, products, and future for that experience-based learning. We need both action and reflection. We need a mental framework for transporting the familiar to the uncharted, a way of thinking that can help us get beyond where our feet seem planted. We need to find ways to exercise the stores in our memories for thought patterns and movement patterns, and to find ways to transport ourselves on the magic carpet of those memories to yet unknown future challenges. We need to approach learning tasks from these points of view together—memory *and* imagination, problem solving in the here and now *as well as* constructing the future.

Plan of action: What we're talking about here is an approach to learning, not a description about various components of learning or learning styles. We're talking here about conceptual differences, differences in approach to design—similar to the debate over DOS and Windows, for example.

We know some things we can do to facilitate a person's experiential and reflective thinking. We know that we have to:

1. Set the thinking task within a big picture context of expectations or challenge,

2. identify and define parts,

3. assemble related information,

4. make choices about what features are significant or important,

5. expand, rearrange, modify, compare and contrast, play what-if games,

6. question assumptions and formats,

7. plan and take action,

8. look back, see what you learned from the way you approached this task,

9. and above all, tell somebody.

John Dewey, perhaps the grand master of reflective thinking, wrote in 1933 that "we should concentrate on developing attitudes and habits" rather than on "studies" like geography, history, piano playing, or other areas of content.[27] W. Edwards Deming and Walter Shewhart echoed Dewey when they called for a *thinking process* in the development of quality: "Plan, Do, Check, and Act" is, after all, not a body of content or specific studies, but is, rather, an attitude and habit that these other grand old men of modern American thought—and an increasing number of their followers—are still pushing more than half a century after the ideas were introduced. Economists and politicians today are saying the same thing when they call for "learning to learn" as an economic development strategy for Americans.

Dewey puts forth some other concepts about learning that are worth repeating. He suggests that genuine education *proceeds* by engaging the mind, and that education *terminates* in discipline; that there is a difference, perhaps even a natural tension, between the process of inquiry and the organized or disciplined result of that process. It was important to Dewey that the learner be demanding of himself or herself, so that the inquiry process as well as its conclusion be characterized by standards at every step of the way. Carefulness, thoroughness, and continuity were the essential components of Dewey's logic.

Corporate training too long has concentrated at the end of the process, the "discipline" part. We have too long focused on structuring courses around the content "studies." We have largely ignored the "engaging the mind" part of the learning situation. We need some updated and more integrative models for designing the learning task, and we are looking back to our own very American thinkers, Dewey and Deming. We need the courage to use time differently in learning. We need to be smart enough to not be fooled by the distractions of entertainment media posing as "instructors" that serve only to dull our abilities to be active learners and to engage our minds in learning. We have to always remember that good technology serves what is essentially human about us; that good tools always allow people to be in charge of them, not the other way around.

Examples: Professors at the University of Texas, Austin, and at Columbia University, New York, have been frequenting the human resources national conferences of numerous professional associations recently, and have been heavily promoting the idea of "Action Reflection Learning" in their speaking and in their writing.[28] Among the design ideas contained in their work are the ideas that individuals at work must learn to learn daily, that shared learning should be experienced on the job, that management must reward and encourage individual and continuous learning. AT&T, one company that is trying to incorporate these ways of learning on the job, reported at the Ziff Institute 1993 On-the-Job Learning Conference in Boston that some of the results of doing things this way include better listening, honest and open communication, ability to give and receive constructive feedback, and a bringing of self to the job as well as an increased encouragement of others' participation.[29]

When President George Bush was in office, he launched an "education strategy" known as the New American School Development Corporation, calling on the nation's businesses to collaborate in funding research for a new generation of American schools. The first group of grants were awarded in the summer of 1992. Newspaper publicity about the project followed in papers around the country.

One of the grants was awarded to a project known as the Atlas project. This project featured, among other things, a testing model which requires students to perform "real-world, meaningful" kinds of tasks, rather than the traditional pencil and paper tests—an attempt, no doubt, to get at the experiential, process-focused kinds of learning instead of the traditional content-based learning which most tests test. Brown University's Theodore Sizer, one of the principals in Atlas, in a press release said that the goal of Atlas schools will be "to develop the habits of heart, mind and work which will enable all students to live effectively in and contribute positively to a democratic society." "Such habits include logical reasoning, an ability to formulate and pursue useful questions, reflection on one's own efforts, persistence, a respect for quality and discipline, a pride in accomplishment, an understanding that good work takes time, a respect for others, a generosity of time and spirit, and a fierce commitment to genuinely democratic ideals and practices." Project documents further indicate that in Atlas schools, "...students will engage in active inquiry; they will learn by doing, by seeking out experts in the school, at home and in workplaces, by consulting primary resource materials, and by devising and carrying out experiments."

The Atlas project is being tested in public schools in Lancaster, PA, Norfolk, VA, Prince George's County, MD, and Gorham, ME. The findings and results of systematically working under such an "experiential" and "reflective" thinking design are worth watching in the years ahead.[30]

Endnotes for Chapter 5
Notes 1 through 30

1. Trainer competencies adapted from *Models for HRD Practice: The Research Report*, by P. McLagan and D. Suhodolnik, ASTD, 1989.

2. "Seeing and Imagining: Clues to the Working of the Mind's Eye" by Sandra Blakeslee, *The New York Times*, August 31, 1993, pp. C1, C7. In this article, the work of psychologists Dr. Martha Farah, Dr. Stephen Kosslyn, and Dr. Marcia Johnson was reviewed.

3. " 'Hole' in Tumor Patient's Memory Reveals Brain's Odd Filing System" by Philip J. Hilts, *The New York Times*, September 15, 1992, p.C3. Dr. Barry Gordon, Dr. Ronald P. Lesser, and Dr. John Hart contributed to this article.

4. Howard Gardner, *Frames of Mind: The Theory of Multiple Intelligences*, New York, Basic Books, 1985. Gardner's "Frames of Mind" include these kinds of intelligence: linguistic, musical, logical-mathematical, spatial, bodily-kinesthetic, and personal.

5. Exercise adapted from *Human Information Processing: An Introduction to Psychology* by Peter H. Lindsay and Donald A. Norman, New York, Academic Press, 1977, p. 356.

6. "Get On the New Fast Track" by Denise M. Topolhicki, *Money*, December 1993, p. 148.

7. "It's What You do That Counts" by Paul Williamson in *Small Business Reports*, October 1993, pp. 16-20.

8. "What's So New About the New Economy?" by Alan M. Webber in *Harvard Business Review*, January-February 1993, pp. 24-42.

9. *Op. cit.*, quote from Professor James Brian Quinn, p. 26.

10. "How the Mind Ages" by Kristin White in *Psychology Today*, November/December 1993, p. 41.

11. *Workplace Basics: The Skills Employers Want* by A.P. Carnevale, L.J. Gainer, and A.S. Meltzer, Alexandria, VA: ASTD/Department of Labor (JTPA), 1988, p. 19.

12. Doctoral dissertation, *Cognitive Correlates of Problem Solving Measures in Student Occupational Competency Tests* by Carolyn D. Nilson, Rutgers, The State University of New Jersey, October 1983.

13. *Defining and Measuring Competence* by P.S. Pottinger and J. Goldsmith, eds., New Directions for Experiential Learning series no.3, San Francisco, CA: Jossey-Bass,1979, p. 33.

14. "We Do; Therefore, We Learn" by Erica Gordon Sorohan in *Training & Development*, October 1993, pp. 47-55.

15. "Building a Learning Organization" by David A. Garvin in *Harvard Business Review*, July-August 1993, pp. 78-91.

16. *C and the Box: A Paradigm Parable* by Frank A. Prince, San Diego, CA: Pfeiffer & Company, 1993.

17. Diane F. Halpern, *Thought and Knowledge: An Introduction to Critical Thinking*, Hillsdale, NJ, Lawrence Erlbaum Associates, 1984, p. 329.

18. For more information, call Walt Disney World Seminar Productions at (407) 824-4855.

19. Morton Hunt, *The Universe Within: A New Science Explores the Human Mind*, New York: Touchstone, Simon & Schuster, 1982, pp. 309,310.

20. Shoshana Zuboff, *In the Age of the Smart Machine: The Future of Work and Power*, New York: Basic Books, 1984.

21. *Ibid.*, pp. 142-155.

22. Elisabeth J. Simpson, *The Classification of Educational Objectives, Psychomotor Domain,* contract no. OE 5-85-104, Vocational Education Act of 1963, July 1, 1965–May 31, 1966.

23. John Dewey, *How We Think,* Lexington, MA: D.C. Heath and Company, 1933.

24. Presentation by Lynn Peterson, trainer at The Upjohn Company, at the On-The-Job Learning Conference of the Ziff Institute, Boston, MA, September 1993.

25. Edward R. Tufte, *Envisioning Information,* Cheshire, CT: Graphics Press, 1990.

26. Shoshana Zuboff, *op cit.,* pp. 52, 53.

27. John Dewey, *op.cit.,* p. 82.

28. Comments taken from a speech by Dr. Karen Watkins, University of Texas, at the 1993 ASTD National Conference, Atlanta, GA, and from a speech by Judy O'Neill, Education Manager at AT&T, Morristown, NJ given at the 1993 On-the-Job Learning Conference of the Ziff Institute, Boston. The work of Dr. Victoria Marsick, Columbia University was referenced in both presentations.

29. Ziff Institute On-the-Job Learning Conference, September 19-22, 1993, Boston, MA. "Results" slide presented by Judy O'Neill, Education Manager, AT&T.

30. " 'Best of the Best' picked to redesign US schools" by Robert A. Frahm, in *The Hartford Courant,* July 10, 1992, p. 1 and p. A10.

DEVELOPMENT STRUCTURES AND TECHNIQUES FOR PEER TRAINING

The following pages focus more specifically on how to do it—that is, on the development structures and techniques that can make peer training happen. These pages will also deal with some of the learning aids and instructional media commonly used in training, suggesting adaptations appropriate for use in peer training.

There are several very important issues to be dealt with before methodology can be discussed. These are the issue of trust, the issue of commitment, and the issue of the value of time. Human resources development professionals and managers must meet the issues of trust and commitment head-on, and take conscious, overt, specific steps to build trust and commitment through communication strategies, rewards, social interventions, work re-design, or whatever it takes before peer training can be effective. If you choose to use peer training as an experimental variable in the building of trust and commitment, be aware that you're conducting an experiment and be ready for acceptance and analysis of whatever results you get. Peer training can be a development strategy, or it can be a "program" all its own. Just be sure that your goals and definitions are clear before you embark upon the development structure that will allow it to happen.

The other knotty issue that must be dealt with before you develop your peer training structure is the issue of how you value time at your company. Time is a critical variable in the foundation of a business's resources. How management shapes that variable is key to the success of peer training. Helping management see that the way time is valued—literally assigned dollars and cents to it—is essentially tied to the effectiveness of peer training.

A macro-view is instructive. National training policy developers in several countries over the past few years have been wrestling with the "training tax levy" idea whereby employers would be required to spend annually an amount of money equal to a certain percentage of their payroll costs, for example, 1.5 percent, on training across the company as a whole or contribute an equivalent amount to a national training fund. Australia is currently implementing such a policy, and we in America are considering this kind of option as the Clinton administration goes forward with its jobs agenda beginning in 1994. Other options at the Federal policy level in America are: tax credits to individuals and to companies designed to encourage new kinds of training; creation of individual training accounts similar to Individual Retirement Accounts (IRAs); and promotion of excellence in training practices through establishment of a national training award similar to the Malcolm Baldrige National Quality Award.[1]

In these kinds of training structures, time is the variable to watch. A closer look at each policy option reveals that nowhere does it say that more time must be spent in classrooms or seminars; nowhere does it say that time off the job for training has to be traded for time on the job for work. In fact, the ideas behind each of these macro-level motivators for training encourage human resources developers to think creatively about how they structure the time element of training. For example, 1.5 percent of payroll could mean any of these things:

1. A certain amount of training per day for everyone,
2. 1.5 percent of each person's work hour to be spent learning,
3. an amount of training equivalent to 1.5 percent of weekly payroll, for some one week, for others another week, and so forth through the year,
4. funds equal to 1.5 percent of yearly payroll dispersed to managers or team leaders to buy training materials targeted to specific work groups,
5. funds equal to 1.5 percent of payroll for consultant help in instructional design or organizational development, in re-engineering a company's human resources development or training programs, and so forth.

When training managers and instructional designers think of "contact hours," that is, actual hours of interaction between a teacher and a student, they assign a pricetag to each hour. Hours of consultant time have another kind of pricetag. Time in writing a course or time in doing a training needs assessment, or time in evaluating a training program are all other ways of dealing with the cost of time in the development of training. There are many ways to reach a sum equal to 1.5 percent of payroll. These Federal initiatives, at a policy or macro-level, purposely leave the variable of time to the local or micro-level of development. The definition of this variable is crucial to the viability, excellence, and bottom-line value of any training program.

The first major task in the development of peer training is to gain consensus on the value of time from all persons affected by peer training. If the total workforce can accept the notion that learning and working are running side by side and interacting often, they can then perhaps see that training time can be scheduled during work time. If employees can be helped to see the learning potential in the company's work itself—their work and their peers' work—then training time doesn't have to be accounted for as time off the job. If each worker can teach another worker something about the essence of his or her job, his or her special way of doing things, or the particular way in which that job contributes to profit or making work easier for the next person in the process, then training time doesn't have to be scheduled at "other" times, that is, when work perhaps is not so pressing. If training and working are seen as integrally bound together in a synergy for learning, then time as a variable takes on a whole new notion of value. Whatever that value is, it must be agreed upon before a full-scale peer training "program" can be started.

With the issues of trust, commitment, and the value of time defined and dealt with, instructional designers can begin the work of figuring out just how to institutionalize peer training. The rest of this section of the book is meant for anyone who must function as a designer of instruction, whether your job title is instructional designer, manager, supervisor, trainer, consultant, or any other worker who is put into the role of instructional designer. Development structures to support peer training and techniques of instruction are presented so that all those persons with an interest in peer training can use this book as a development guide.

WORKSHEET 2 - 9

TIMING AND SCHEDULING OPTIONS FOR PEER TRAINING

Directions: Use these ideas to spark your own creativity about scheduling peer training. Choose as many as apply to your situation; modify them; add your own ideas to the list.

1. Organize the entire workforce into peer pairs. Change the pairs periodically, such as every 6 months. Maintain normal supervisory/reporting structure.

2. Set aside a period of time for training the trainers, that is, develop a peer training awareness and skills training program for the entire workforce. Run this much as you would run a Total Quality Management awareness and skills training program, for example, one day per week for 4 weeks to launch the peer training. (See Worksheet 2 - 10, page 228 for Train the Trainer topics to include in a peer trainer workshop.)

3. Ask for volunteers to be part of a pilot program in peer training if you don't want to take the big step all at once. Run peer training as an experiment for a specified period of time such as 3 months or 6 months. Design it carefully, monitor progress carefully, collect and interpret data carefully. Be clear about what you want to know as a result of the experimental program.

4. The 25 percent approach: 15 minutes of each hour to be spent in intentional learning:

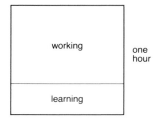

5. The 50 percent approach: Half of each day to be spent learning:

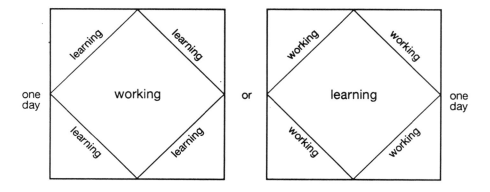

220

TIMING AND SCHEDULING OPTIONS FOR PEER TRAINING

6. The 10 percent of project approach: Project documentation is not complete until project staff tell what they learned at the end of each reporting period, such as every 2 weeks. Think of each 10-day span of work as a unit; think of learning equivalent to about one day's work during that period. Add the "what I learned" section to your regular project accountability forms.

7. Allow at least 15 minutes at regular group/staff/team meetings for peer pairs to report what they learned since the last meeting.

8. Keep individual learning journals. Build time, for example 10 minutes, into each day for all employees in peer pairs to write down their reflections on what they learned that day. Make it brief, not intimidating; suggest one page per day.

   Include this information on each page:

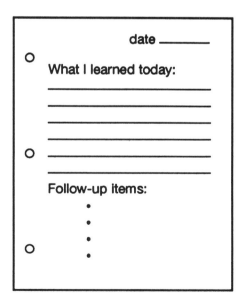

9. Help people establish a journal-writing habit. Regularly review journals in peer pairs with a supervisor and human resources professional so that learning is recorded and follow-up items addressed. Do this once every pay period, for example, once each week or once every two weeks. Follow up swiftly on any training needs identified in the follow-up section of the journal.

TIMING AND SCHEDULING OPTIONS FOR PEER TRAINING

10. In an optional or "selected" peer training program (e.g., one department only, one job description only, or one product line only) you might want to give extra support to the peer training effort by when and where you schedule the peer training. For example, establish a Peer Training Room, or Peer Learning Center, outfitted with study carrels to accommodate two persons side by side, several small conference tables, several arrangements of comfortable chairs and coffee tables, a coffee pot, a juice dispenser, several flipcharts, a VCR, a PC, a copy machine, a supplies shelf, a telephone, and a clerical or administrative support person on duty at specified times (e.g., 10 a.m. to 2 p.m.) each day. Encourage the peer training to happen in this place. Have the room available at all times to any peer pairs. Get the workforce used to seeing learning happening; maybe the rest of them will want to be involved too.

11. If a Peer Learning Center is new to your organization, you might want to have a sign-in /sign-out sheet by the entry to the room so that supervisors can monitor who is using the place and when. Include on the sheet a column for sign-in, a column for sign-out, and a wide column for "learning topic." Employees should get the message that it is a serious place for learning activities and not a social place; they should be praised and emotionally supported when they engage in learning in this place. Supervisors have a responsibility to provide this support.

    Many companies provide financial incentives for being in a peer training program, such as a grade level step increase or a flat ten percent of salary increase while either instructing or being a student in a "selected" peer training program. Many companies incent only those who function as peer trainers.

12. If peer trainers work from a task list, in which tasks are indexed for their difficulty or their value, you might want the scheduling for peer training to reflect that index system. For example, you might counsel peer trainers to be sure to teach the most important tasks first, making sure that all prerequisite tasks have been learned first. If a peer trainer is new to the job of being a teacher, he or she will need some guidance in how to focus on what's important. Most new teachers have a tendency to give equal stress to everything and tend to concentrate on the data-type information that's easiest to learn, often to the exclusion of the conceptual information that's harder to teach. The way in which tasks are scheduled within a training period makes a difference to the quality of the learning that results. See Worksheets 2-10 through 2-14.

DEVELOPMENT STRUCTURES AND TECHNIQUES FOR PEER TRAINING

Training the Peer Trainer

Problem: The fundamental issue in peer training is the issue of "intention." Teaching is always an intentional act. It is not a haphazard happening. Of course, there are shades of gray: we can make the learning environment more or less formal; we can stick to a rigid time schedule or just let time flow as long as "everyone's having fun"; we can facilitate open questioning and divergent thought or be very analytical and focused; we can appeal to the emotional core or the logical thinker; we can show and tell, or we can structure a gestalt-type holistic experience as a training "delivery" method.

The problem is that the participants in peer training, the instructor and the student—peer trainer and trainee—and everyone else, must view the peer training experience as a structured learning endeavor. Those immediately engaged in learning should both be aware of objectives for that training session, and they should be aware of when the training begins and ends. Accountability for training is still important at this point in our evolution regarding workplace learning. (Perhaps the time will come when we all are expert teachers and learners, but that day is still in the distance!)

Peer training sessions must not become just friendly chats, gripe sessions, or self-esteem builders—although these characteristics of one-to-one interaction can be present. Trainer and trainee must know when they are in a learning mode and when their face-to-face encounters are something else. Friendship, gripes, and confidence-building can all be springboards to learning, and peer pairs should be able to recognize and deal with these as such.

The task for those in charge of peer training, then, is to create a train-the-trainer program for all those participating, whether as trainees or as trainers. Worksheet 2 - 10, following, contains some suggested topics to include. Customize these to fit your situation.

Plan of action: These are some things to consider as you develop a train-the-trainer class or small group session for peer trainers and trainees:

1. *Facilitation*—Trainers will need to practice facilitation skills. There are many ways to do this, among the most common being:

    • by practice during a role play situation,
    • by working on a real problem while being observed by a trainer during classroom instruction,

- by videotaping a facilitation practice session and using the playback for instruction, or
- by "expert" peer instructor observation of and feedback to a new peer instructor actually on the job.

One of the learning aids you might want to construct for your peer learners is a checklist of facilitation behaviors to use during your train-the-trainer sessions. These behaviors are based on the concept that adults at work are experienced learners, and, therefore, that the primary role of an instructor of another adult is to facilitate learning, not to lecture or to dump information. Adult learners need help in learning via the same ways in which they learned other things previously, either at work or in other aspects of their lives. They need steering in certain directions of thinking and reasoning in order to refresh their memories about how they learned. They need help in building upon what they already know and can do. That's facilitation.

These are some facilitation skills your peer trainers should develop. A monitoring checklist can be created around these skills for use during train-the-trainer sessions, and for use as they themselves become peer trainers back on the job:

Monitoring Checklist

_____ 1. Says or does something to make the trainee feel at ease.

_____ 2. Gets "housekeeping things" out of the way quickly and without any fuss. Such things are: assembling books, tapes, equipment, models; lesson plans, monitoring checklists of various sorts; time sheets and accountability documentation forms.

_____ 3. Creates an expectation for learning by quickly reviewing the previous peer training session's accomplishments and relating those accomplishments to the trainee's work progress, and by starting the lesson by getting agreement from the trainee about what today's objective is.

_____ 4. Gives the trainee a chance to establish his or her credibility as a worker or as a learner; is supportive and reassuring regarding the trainee's past successes.

_____ 5. Answers trainee's questions.

_____ 6. Leads trainee to self-directed learning by suggesting references, contact persons, alternate "what if" paths, options.

_____ 7. Shows patience: pauses; gives clues; reviews difficult material.

_____ 8. Gives corrective feedback often during a lesson—at least once every ten minutes. Keeps a balance between explaining, practice, and evaluation during each peer training session.

_____ 9. Reestablishes the worker to worker relationship after training is complete, that is, as peers both working for the business goals of the company.

2. *Process as well as Content* - For most peer trainers, teaching the content is the easy part. It's "process" that gives new instructors the most grief, and it's these process skills of instructing that must be carefully taught during train-the-trainer sessions. Instructional processes, of course, are tied to the points of content, and process action always takes its cue from some point in the content being covered during the lesson. (Development of content is explained in the next section of this chapter.)

Together with facilitation skills, the skills associated with *presenting* the content, skillfully mastered, can form the foundation for generating the kind of continuous intellectual agitation that helps people be continuous on-the-job teachers and learners. Well-tuned facilitators and process experts are essential as builders of learning organizations because they are *active* learners.

Here are some ideas regarding techniques in developing process skills:

1. Suggest various ways to present the content: for example, use a working model, draw a diagram, walk around the shop floor and observe, create a checklist for customers and ask for their opinions, interview someone in another department who has some remote or direct interest in your work, create a case study involving all elements of content, do research together around the content to be covered, make a video or slides of things you want to teach and critique the pictures. Help your peer trainer to become a creative and flexible presenter of content; help your peer trainer to use many resources to get the content across to the trainee.

2. Check your peer trainer to be sure he or she knows how to use media to support instruction. Have your peer trainer show you that he/she can use a flipchart without getting in the way of the writing and knows how to operate any models or machines to be used during lessons. Be sure that your peer trainer knows where in the company to locate reference materials and how to use them. Take a few minutes during training-the-trainer to verify that the new trainer can handle all media support with ease.

    Don't underestimate the importance of this point. Employees who have traditionally been "the forgotten ones" in terms of having been to training classes in the past are simply not used to dealing with instructional media—as are managers and sales persons, for example, who typically have had the lion's share of training in past years. Operators, line workers, maintenance employees, technical specialists, clerical workers, and a host of others have simply not had the advantage of much training in the past; when these employees become trainers, they will need help in dealing with instructional media, even in a one-to-one training situation.

3. Be sure that your peer trainer knows that he or she must be sensitive to "the negatives"—the trainee's body language of frowns, folded arms, nervous finger-tapping; the "I don't get it" silence; the "no way!" exclama-

tions; the "we never did it that way before" comment; and other negative actions or pronouncements. Be sure that your peer trainer is emotionally prepared to absorb these kinds of negatives; be sure that he or she understands that negative feedback is just that—feedback, and that all feedback is useful.

The secret is to let the negatives be a trigger for the peer trainer to "rise above it" as soon as it appears, and to use the negatives as a clue to what the deeper *learning* problem actually is. The blocking behavior and killer comments are generally a signal that the trainee is on the threshold of learning something new. Help your new trainers to be able to not take these things personally, and to see them as signals to awakened awareness and as triggers to new learning. Peer trainers must realize that trainees will spontaneously interact with the content on an emotional level, bringing all kinds of emotional baggage with them from past bad experiences with schooling. This emotional-level reaction is normal and to be expected; sometimes, however, it surprises a new trainer if he or she has not been warned in advance. Be sure your trainers see it as a cue to rise above it and look for the learning that most always follows.

4. Help your peer trainer be an evaluator. Be sure that peer trainers know about the Instructional System Design cycle of analyze, design/develop, implement, and evaluate. See Worksheet 2 - 1, page 153, to refresh their memory. Evaluation is hard for most peer trainers and trainees because we don't like to "criticize" each other—our culture has taught us to mind our own business at work, be independent, and don't get involved with somebody else's problems. But making a judgment, that is, evaluation regarding the trainee's actions and understandings is essential to making improvement and to meeting standards of excellence. It is the last process which trainer and trainee must engage in during instruction in order for learning growth to occur. Sometimes it's a good idea to pair people off during a train-the-trainer peer training session and simply have them look each other in the eye at a two-foot distance from each other and say, "No, that's not right." "Did you ever consider doing it like this?" or "How about thinking about it this way?" or "Try again" or "I think I heard you say . . . is this what you meant to say?" Sometimes people have to practice being involved this way at close range before they can comfortably take on the role of peer trainers. Peer trainers must be able to make evaluative judgments about the trainee's relationship to the content of the lesson during the lesson.

Examples: Bob Filipczak, in his "Frick Teaches Frack" article in *Training* magazine,[2] surveyed seven companies and several training consultants across the country in research for his article on "structured" peer training. Early in the article, he makes the point that the people doing the training "are deliberately chosen, trained and supported." Companies featured in the article include T.J. Maxx, Walt Disney World, Morgan Guaranty Trust, Merrill Lynch, Golden Corral Restaurants, British Petroleum, and International Flavors and Fragrances. Each company has a slightly different way of implementing peer training, and all have train-the-trainer instruction for the employees-become-trainers. All view instruction as an intentional act. All recognize and deal with the issue of organizational support.

British Petroleum even trains the trainees: they require the learner to be able to explain to the peer trainer what he or she *intends* to do before operating a machine during instruction. At T.J. Maxx, top performers are chosen to be peer trainers for those employees who are involved in opening new stores. Peer trainers are taken off their regular jobs for a four-week period to be on-site with trainees at the new stores, given five days of train-the-trainer instruction at national headquarters, and get a lot of exposure around the corporation. International Flavors and Fragrances got rid of their TQM consultants in favor of peer trainers to get the quality message across more effectively and at lower cost.

WORKSHEET 2 - 10

TRAIN-THE-TRAINER TOPICS FOR PEER TRAINING

Note: These are the topics most often included in a train-the-trainer course for peer training. The list is equally appropriate for an entire workforce which is embarking on peer training as an avenue to learning and continuous improvement, or to participants in a peer training program that is experimental or to those specially selected to participate. Customize these topics to fit your own situation.

1. Adult learning theory
2. Facilitation skills
3. Questioning skills
4. Giving and receiving feedback
5. Establishing standards and performance criteria
6. Relating learning goals to business goals
7. Elements of a lesson
8. Objectives for learning
9. Choices in presentation methods
10. Job analysis
11. Specific technical skills
12. Managing instructional media aids
13. Evaluating peers

WORKSHEET 2 - 11

PERSONAL CHARACTERISTICS OF GOOD PEER TRAINERS

Note: If your would-be peer trainers don't have these characteristics, help them to develop them. Above all, provide administrative and organizational supports for peer trainers in the form of time, incentives, relaxation of quotas or work rules, visibility, and thanks.

1. Patience
2. Focus—ability to stay on track regarding learning objectives
3. Flexibility—willingness to try different approaches
4. Confidence—secure in what he or she knows and can do
5. Willingness to share
6. Tolerance for personal relationships—(peer training is "up close and personal")
7. Self-esteem—proud of work accomplishments
8. Reliability—has good work habits and attitudes, can be counted on to perform consistently and well

DEVELOPMENT STRUCTURES AND TECHNIQUES FOR PEER TRAINING

Lessons

Problem: The instructional sessions that are at the heart of peer training must be planned and conducted with some foundation of structure. That is, the peer trainer must know where he or she is going with the content so that there's a beginning and ending place related to content—not related just to the clock. In the language of instructional design and development, there must be a lesson.

Lessons are two-way affairs. They are not just the instructor's responsibility, nor are they just the student's responsibility. Especially when teaching adults, and most particularly in peer training, there should be a constant back-and-forth interplay between teacher and learner. Since the peer trainer is generally the leader or facilitator during training, the responsibility for planning the lesson falls to the peer trainer. If lessons are designed well, the peer trainer can get sidetracked by circumstances during a lesson and easily return to the right place in the lesson plan and go forward. Organizing the totality of the content of training into smaller units known as lessons is the surest way to promote learning from peer to peer and improve performance one by one.

If the content of training is not organized into lessons, accountability suffers, business goals are stifled, and training sessions risk becoming unwelcome social encounters. The pages that follow show you why lessons should be developed and how to do it.

Plan of action: The first consideration in developing lessons is to think of the totality of the content to be taught and learned and the time allotted in which to do it. You can start with the broad scope of the content, such as that which might be taught and learned over a one week period in daily sessions of two hours each. Or, you might think of the content that must be taught and learned during the next hour; or, the content that must be taught and learned during 15-minute segments as peer pairs work together in teams each day for the next three months.

Whichever way you think of the content, it is necessary that you identify chunks of content (ideas, concepts, skills, etc.) that seem logical to teach and learn as a unit. Some people use index cards or post-its™ as an aid to organizing and prioritizing content. In instructional development language, this is the requirement for dealing with the "scope and sequence" of content. Any adult who is competent at the tasks of his or her work knows what's important about doing the job—*what* needs to be done (that is, the content), and *how* it should be done (that is, the process).

Part of your train-the-trainer program should deal with helping peer trainers develop content and turn it out into lesson plans. A good way to get into this is to ask your trainees to analyze their own jobs—list the things they typically have to do every day that make their job and the way that they do it special. Then ask them to separate the content from the process, the "knowledge-based" things they need to know from the "skills-based" actions that they have to know how to do. Ask them to code these content items and these process items according to what is most valuable to the company, what is hardest to do, what takes the most time, etc. Figure out your own coding and rating system. The point in all of this analysis is to get your peer trainers to think in terms of what small items of content can be isolated from each other and taught—and learned—in a thorough way. Small is beautiful in the development of lessons. Most people can think this way with a little guidance and reinforcement; most people pride themselves in doing the little things that make their work special—those little things that allow others to know one person's unique and special "stamp" on their work. It's those special ways of doing things that should be shared, and that can be the foundation for widespread learning and increased capacity for learning.

The last assignment for the developer of peer training is to organize the content into actual lesson plans—pieces of paper that provide an outline of each peer training session. A rule of thumb is that a lesson should take about 15 minutes of time and a lesson plan should fit in outline form on one piece of paper. Peer trainers should be prepared to teach in 15-minute segments around a single lesson, paying attention during those 15-minutes to covering content that's outlined and to engaging the learner in the various interactive processes of facilitation, evaluation, and feedback. Worksheet 2 - 12, following, contains the elements of a lesson plan.

A lesson generally follows this format:

1. Trainer and trainee agree on what they hope to accomplish during the next 15 minutes during peer training.
2. Trainer verifies that trainee knows terminology, labels, names of parts, etc. that will be used in the lesson. (Point to things and have the trainee tell you.)
3. Trainer shows and tells in logical order; doesn't skip around.
4. Trainer explains and elaborates by using analogies, examples, stories, drawings, flowcharts, etc. Trainees relate to new content in a variety of ways; trainers have to be flexible in presenting alternatives and options for getting the trainee to the point of understanding.
5. Trainer illustrates by non-example too. Backing into the learning is often an easier way for trainees to "get it."

6. Trainer gives clues, suggests applications, is helpful. There's no point playing "I gotcha." You are not there to embarrass each other. The trainer's objective and the trainee's objective is to get through the content in an efficient and effective way, according to a previously well-thought-out plan for this particular lesson. It doesn't have to take a lot of planning time—just quality of thinking!

7. Trainer dialogues with trainee. Remember, each is peer to the other; each has good ideas and many workplace successes. The overarching goal is learning to learn from each other.

8. Trainer and trainee interact many times during a 15-minute lesson in describing and explaining, demonstrating and practicing, and in evaluation and feedback.

Examples: The following job, that of a food server in a restaurant, is chosen to illustrate the development techniques of analyzing a job, separating the learning challenge into job content and job process, and creating a lesson plan.

Job Analysis

Analyzing a job can start with making a simple list of things that you do. If you are new to the job of trainer, you might want to start small and list the things that you do just today, or that you do every Monday. Limiting the scope is good discipline until you get the knack of job analysis. Here's the example of the job of food server, for the limited aspects of serving food and wine for one meal:

1. Establish rapport with the seated customers.
2. Give them information about:
   • the menu for this meal
   • the wine list
   • the restaurant.
3. Take customers' orders for food and wine.
4. Place the orders in the kitchen.
5. Get and serve the food as it is ready from the kitchen.
6. Get and serve the wine.
7. Remove empty dishes.
8. Prepare their bill and present it to them.
9. Take their money or credit card; settle the account.
10. Say goodbye.

There are other duties the typical server must accomplish behind the scenes, but this part of the job analysis is saved for another time. We assume that the peer training lesson will involve teaching the trainee only about meal service. Encourage your own trainers-in-development to think specifically about what it is that they must teach. Peer training will fall apart if peer trainers begin by thinking too broadly. Learning that sticks is built on one small revelation at a time!

After the initial listing of the things you do in a job—for the specific peer training assignment—organize them into some priority listing. Here are two different ways of organization; there are many more that you can think of yourself and adapt to your own situation.

A. *The difficulty index* (difficult = 3, medium = 2, easy = 1). This rating can help the trainer adjust the teaching strategies accordingly, making sure, for example, that the trainee is not tired when the difficult things need to be learned.

B. *The people-data-things index* (P, D, TH). This rating can help the trainer choose presentation options that fit the kinds of things to be learned; for example, with "people" duties of the job, the trainer might choose role play or case study; with the "data" duties, the trainer might want to demonstrate the correct way to do it and have the trainee copy it, giving feedback during the exercise and talking aloud when trainer and trainee work together.

In preparation for developing the lesson plan, have the peer trainer make a chart something like this one:

duty #	difficulty index	people-data-things index
1	2	P
2	3	D
3	3	D and P
4	1	D
5	2	TH and P
6	2	TH and P
7	1	TH
8	3	D and P
9	3	TH, D and P
10	1	P

The next step as the peer trainer plans how to teach and what to teach, is to circle all of the "difficulty = 3" items, that is, duties number 2, 3, 8, and 9. Each of these duties requires a bit more effort in planning instruction; do this planning first. For item #2, for example, you might want to use a "job aid," the actual menu and wine list. You might want to take the trainee on a side trip to the wine cellar and have him or her talk with the wine steward. You might want to go over each item on the menu to be sure that the trainee can pronounce all the terms and quiz the trainee informally to be sure he or she knows what everything is. Go to the kitchen and let the trainee see each sauce or special piece of veal. Be sure that the trainee knows the difference between the kinds of fish. If you really want to get into it, show slides or videos or CD-ROM information about meat cutting or fish handling. Set up a role play in which you play the part of an inquisitive customer; then play the role of a "dull" customer whom you would like the trainee to "draw out" in order to place a bigger order or a more personalized order. Be sure that the trainee, in fact, has more than enough information about the menu, the wine list, and the restaurant so that he or she can answer customers' questions. As a peer trainer developing a lesson—or lessons—realize that these ten duties learned well will be a great asset to the company's human resource base; well trained employees on these ten duties of the job of food server can bring in big bucks.

It should be obvious that the training outlined in the chart will take more than a few hours to do it right for maximum learning and maximum return on the investment of training. The job analysis and organization of job duties is just the first step in developing learning that makes a difference.

Job Content versus Job Process (Skills)

The next step is to separate out the content topics from the process or skills topics. Content is taught differently than skills are taught. Again, make some kind of chart or matrix listing content in one column and process (skills) in the other column. Tie these to the duties identified in the previous listing of job duties. Such a chart might start out looking something like this:

duty #	content	process (skills)
1	principles of personal communication	approaching the customer
		using body language
	psychology of customer service	making "small talk" that pays off
8	the bill ("check") for food	itemizing clearly
	the bill for wine	using abbreviations
	tax	calculating restaurant costs
	gratuities	calculating tax
	basic math	clarifying gratuities
		presenting the bill to customers

These two items from among the ten duties listed further break down each duty that must be taught and learned. This time, the breakdown lists the areas of content, or things "to cover" during a lesson, as well as lists the action or process things one must do in order to do the job correctly. Content is taught through verbal options such as description, explanation, drawing, graphing, using analogies and metaphors. Skills or process items are taught by demonstration, guided practice, and hands-on kinds of exercises. Too often, unless such an analysis is done, the inexperienced peer trainer will try to teach everything the same way—generally simply describing everything. Head off this error by insisting that lessons be well-thought out and planned in detail.

The Lesson Plan

A lesson plan puts down in specific terms what you expect the trainee to accomplish during the training session. It specifies the changes in behavior that you expect the trainee to be able to demonstrate, and it lists in some kind of order the things that you will teach. A good lesson plan will have some kind of time notation on it, for example, "these six lessons together should take approximately 90 minutes." It will also have a notation about any peripheral materials that are needed, such as reference books, maps, videos, or in the case of our food server example, the menu, the wine list, a blank pad of bills, the credit card machine.

Each lesson plan should cover about 15 minutes of instruction. Staple a group of lesson plans together to form "units" of instruction. Two fundamental rules of thumb in developing lessons are:

1. Write lesson plans from the learner's point of view.
2. Think small.

It is very tempting for inexperienced trainers to write from their own point of view as an instructor, for example, "Teach the student about the restaurant's history." This kind of thinking can be discouraged by always-always-always making sure that all writing of instructional objectives is from the learner's point of view. For example:

"Be able to tell five things about the restaurant's history when asked by a customer."

"Be able to tell three things about the restaurant's history when customers have been seated even if they don't ask."

Call this exercise an exercise in writing "Learner Objectives," rather than an exercise in just writing objectives. Reinforce the idea that you are all trying to create a learning organization—not one that just cares about administrative or leaders' points of view. Worksheet 2 - 12 on the following page contains elements of a lesson plan. The section following this worksheet details the thought processes and techniques for developing instructional objectives.

WORKSHEET 2 - 12

ELEMENTS OF A LESSON PLAN

Overview

The lesson plan is the final element in the development of a lesson that can be taught and learned. It is one more level of specificity regarding work performance that can be made better by a network of teachers and learners. The lesson plan functions as a guide for peer trainers as they prepare to teach, and it serves as an "instructor manual" to follow during contact with the trainee. It suggests the direction for monitoring the trainee's progress as well as the basis for evaluation and feedback. It is the foundation of accountability documentation for learning.

Preparation

The lesson plan should be prepared by the peer trainer, with help from a corporate training specialist or instructional design consultant. Management must allow adequate time for development of lesson plans and other planning activities if peer training is to be successful. Experts in the content field should be available on call as needed.

Rules of Thumb

1. Write lesson plans from the learner's point of view.
2. Think small.

Time Span for a Lesson

Each lesson should be designed for about 15 minutes of teacher-learner interaction. Mastery of that lesson is the goal; being thorough and efficient in design and development of learning is the means. A lesson plan should fit easily on one page. Many lesson plans can be stapled together to form a cohesive unit of instruction.

Format

Lesson title: _____

Materials and teaching aids required for this lesson: _____

_____

_____

Learner objectives for this lesson:

     1. _____

     2. _____

     3. _____

Outline of content, procedures, and skills to be taught during this lesson:

1. _____   4. _____

2. _____   5. _____

3. _____   6. _____

DEVELOPMENT STRUCTURES AND TECHNIQUES
FOR PEER TRAINING

Objectives

Problem: The discussion of objectives for learning must be centered on a discussion of performance and the various tasks that must be mastered in order to do new work—or to perform at a higher level in present work. Most definitions of learning include the requirement that the person who has learned must act differently as a result of having learned—that is, a person who has learned behaves differently and performs differently in the future. For learning to persist, change in action must occur. If no change in action occurs after training, chances are that learning did not occur. Improved performance is the goal of learning.

The problem new trainers have—and that is most peer trainers—is that they have no idea about hierarchies of intellectual skills or motor skills, or have never thought about how improved performance in work attitudes or values happens. The essence of the problem is a need for both trainer and trainee to understand the classification schemes for tasks, so that learning opportunities can be effectively designed to promote the kinds of behavioral changes that result in performance improvement.

There is really no mystery about learning taxonomies, and there is plenty of experience in the instructional design world from which to draw. In the early 1950s, Benjamin Bloom, a professor at the University of Chicago, devised a taxonomy of objectives in the "cognitive domain" of learning. Bloom devoted most of his adult life to a search for better ways to teach school children; his theories and classification system have persisted to the present day and have pervaded curriculum development and educational testing in schools and instructional design in business and industry. Bloom's followers in the 1960s and beyond extended his ideas about cognitive objectives into two other "domains" of learning, the "psychomotor domain" dealing with eye-hand coordination and small and large muscle performance, and the "affective domain" dealing with values, attitudes, and emotional adjustments. Bloom is a towering figure in terms of influence on the design of instruction to promote and ensure learning.

The basic problem that peer trainers have is that of being able to step back from their work in order to analyze the tasks of work and identify which tasks are basic and must be taught and learned before other tasks can be tackled. Training developers must plan lessons so that the elementary tasks, or the ones lower on the hierarchy, are mastered first, before the advanced tasks are attempted. Improved performance happens because the worker has securely and confidently mastered all of the tasks necessary for doing the job. Improved performance—learning—will not persist if instruction is pitched at too high a level for the level at which the trainee currently operates.

Adults are very good at going through the motions of schooling—of mimicking learning. One of the reasons why peer training has such great potential for improving performance is that at such a personal level, the trainer can accurately assess what that trainee's competence level really is, and instruction can be appropriately designed and developed to assure that all of the elementary tasks have been mastered before going on to advanced tasks. In classroom training, it is nearly impossible to truly figure out where each learner is within the spectrum of tasks. Peer training has the potential for making learning more direct, more honest, more efficient, and more immediately useful.

Plan of action: There are two parts to a plan of action to address the problem of task awareness as a development prerequisite. One is the ordering of the job tasks in a similar fashion as tasks have been ordered in each of the three classical domains of learning, and the other is the construction of action objectives based on the job tasks as a convenient and practical instructional device.

Examples: First, a consideration of the ordering of job tasks into cognitive domain, psychomotor domain, and affective domain. Worksheets 2 - 13, 2 - 14, and 2 - 15 contain more detail about hierarchies of tasks in each domain. The easiest way to think about this is to think about high-level tasks, mid-level tasks, and low-level tasks. For example:

Cognitive domain- If a trainee were required to translate a document from English to Spanish, these are some of the cognitive tasks required, from lowest level task to highest level task:

- recall or be able to find equivalent Spanish words in a dictionary,
- define terms in English so that the document makes sense to the translator,
- apply rules of English grammar and composition to evaluate the form and style of the document in English for accuracy and adequacy,
- make corrections or modifications to the document in English
- translate the best edition of the document from English to Spanish.

Psychomotor domain- If a trainee were required to bend a wire around a steel pin in an assembly operation, these are some of the psychomotor tasks required, from lowest level task to highest level task:

- find and feel the correct wire and pin,
- position hands, fingers, shoulders, neck, back, hips and feet properly,

- prepare the workspace correctly in terms of distance, angle, lighting,
- use tools correctly: clippers, fan, tweezers, brush,
- place the wire and pin in position for optimal assembly,
- bend the wire around the pin.

Affective domain- If a trainee were required to think differently about standards for quality in customer service and to hereafter incorporate these new standards into serving customers, these are some of the affective tasks required, from lowest level task to highest level task:

- demonstrate interest in standards,
- tell what current standards are,
- identify characteristics of excellent customer service,
- describe characteristics of current customer service,
- accept the facts associated with the gap between what should be and what is; list the problems or effects of the discrepancies,
- agree through consensus or negotiation that the problems associated with the discrepancies should be solved,
- make a commitment to solving one or more of the problems,
- establish a plan or timetable for carrying out the commitment,
- do the work,
- assess the results,
- set the new standards for customer service.

Persons charged with the development of peer training will quickly realize that each of these discrete, hierarchical tasks in cognitive, psychomotor, and affective domains can be taught and mastered. All too often, a willing and enthusiastic peer trainer will jump into training somewhere in the middle of a hierarchy of tasks, totally unaware that the trainee who has never done such a thing before actually needs to start at the beginning of the task list. It simply never works to go directly to ". . . translate the document from English to Spanish," ". . . bend the wire around the pin," or ". . . set the new standards for customer service." Trainers who are unaware of the differentiation of tasks force their trainees to only partially learn, learn the wrong things, waste time in trial and error learning, make costly mistakes, and turn off to training and to learning. The personal capacity to continuously learn is created from the accumulation of small learning successes—of small, discrete tasks that, taken together, lead to improved performance and learning that lasts.

The second thing a peer training developer must do before approaching a trainee is to design an "action objective" for the learner based on each task to be taught. Some books on instructional design techniques will call this the "behavioral objective" because it focuses on a desired change in the behavior of the learner.

The point in creating objectives is to structure the task so that the learner knows exactly what he or she is supposed to be able to do—and by what standard that accomplished action is judged to be correct. I prefer to call these objectives "Learner Objectives" so that there is never any doubt for whom the objective is written. This is the format for a learner objective; notice that it has three parts:

DO THIS   TO THIS   IN THIS AMOUNT

Here are some examples of **Learner Objectives** from the previous lists of tasks:

(Cognitive) Write out......the names of all acronyms......throughout the
                                                                    whole document.

(Psychomotor) Bend......the wire around the pin......twelve times with no
                                                                    errors in spacing or
                                                                    tension.

(Affective) Recite......the current standards...... according to the "Process
                                for customer service   Quality Manual"

Forcing yourself to think so specifically about what you expect your trainee to learn will allow you to validly evaluate whether or not your trainee has accomplished anything during training sessions. To prevent peer training from becoming uncomfortable encounters, everyone involved must structure the learning situation ultimately around the very specific objectives for the lessons to be learned. Think again of the Instructional System Design cycle as it applies to individual persons—analyze the training need, design and develop a plan of learning, implement it, and evaluate the learner's progress. The wonder of instructional design is its application to this smallest element of learning—the task-based learner objective, and its great potential for improving performance.

LEARNING TASKS FOR GAINING KNOWLEDGE
(COGNITIVE TASKS)

Reference: Bloom, B.S., ed., *Taxonomy of Educational Objectives: Book 1, Cognitive Domain.* New York, Longman, 1954/1980.

Cognitive tasks form the basis for what we know and how we mentally integrate information. It can be argued that all other kinds of tasks (psychomotor and affective) have some cognitive task requirement in them. Mastering lower level cognitive tasks is very important to one's ability to continue learning.

The following list is extracted from Bloom's hierarchical listing of cognitive tasks, from lowest to highest. There are many other tasks that could be listed at each level in this hierarchy; this list is just a beginning. Develop your own similar list based on the nature of the job or job tasks to be taught and learned. Check your trainee on mastery of all lower level tasks before proceeding to higher level tasks.

(low)	1.	Define, describe, list, identify, label
(low)	2.	Explain, illustrate, translate, represent
(mid)	3.	Apply, abstract, generalize, relate
(mid)	4.	Analyze, deduce, differentiate, summarize
(high)	5.	Synthesize, combine, strategize, plan
(high)	6.	Evaluate, assess, judge, conclude

WORKSHEET 2 - 14

LEARNING TASKS FOR ACQUIRING SKILLS
(PSYCHOMOTOR TASKS)

Reference: Simpson, E.J., *The Classification of Objectives, Psychomotor Domain.* Urbana, IL: University of Illinois, 1966. See also the section on "Sensory Learning" in Chapter 5 of this book.

Psychomotor tasks are those which often begin with sensory perception following a purposeful stimulus to one or more of the five senses (sight, hearing, smell, touch, taste). These kinds of tasks typically involve the use of muscles, large or small, and very often involve eye-hand coordination. There are many psychomotor aspects of working with computers, for example; and often we ignore these in the rush to get computers to help us with knowledge-based tasks. Psychomotor tasks are generally taught through observation and demonstration, and plenty of guided practice. They've tended to be the "poor relatives" of cognitive tasks, and have had far less attention paid to them. However, in many learning challenges, it's the mastery of psychomotor tasks in addition to mastery of cognitive tasks that makes the difference between short-term ability to perform and continuous capacity to perform over time.

Psychomotor tasks very often involve the use of tools or models, switches, lights, sounds, smells, and textures. They are often abbreviated by simply calling them "skills," because of the connotation of their requiring the skillful use of tools and machinery. Like cognitive tasks, psychomotor tasks must be mastered at low levels first before advancing to higher levels. The following list is adapted from Simpson's hierarchy of psychomotor skills. Verify that your trainee has mastered lower level tasks before advancing to higher level ones.

(low)	1.	**Perception of stimulus through sensory receptors**
(low)	2.	**Preparation for action**
(mid)	3.	**Response on cue, under guidance**
(high)	4.	**Habitual, patterned response with no guidance**
(high)	5.	**Disciplined, automatic, reliable performance over time**

LEARNING TASKS FOR CHANGING ATTITUDES
(AFFECTIVE TASKS)

Reference: Krathwohl, D., Bloom, B., and Masia, B., *Taxonomy of Educational Objectives: Handbook II: Affective Domain.* New York: Longman, 1964.

Affective tasks are most closely associated with personal, professional, and corporate values. For decades, educational psychologists and instructional designers have searched for better ways to define affective tasks and to measure their implementation. It seems difficult to learn values in the same hierarchical fashion as learning cognitive or psychomotor skills. The most common way to assess affective learning seems to be some kind of measurement of attitude change that persists over time after the trainee has been trained in a structured purposeful way to master affective tasks.

Value development often is tied to standards. It is often demonstrated by creation of and adherence to new, higher standards, fairer procedures, more equitable opportunity, and more openness in processes like communication. Affective task mastery plays a role in sales training, customer service training, quality awareness training, and in training to work in teams. The stock broker's sales pitch is usually a good example of mastery of successive levels of affective tasks as he or she leads the client to the close of a deal. Peer training offers an excellent venue for teaching and learning affective tasks because of its very personal characteristics and natural use of feedback.

The following list of affective tasks is based on the book referenced above. Tasks are listed lowest to highest. Attitude change has a better chance of persisting when lower level tasks are mastered before advanced tasks are tackled.

(low)	**1.**	**Focusing one's interest**
(mid)	**2.**	**Responding with appreciation**
(mid)	**3.**	**Accepting, valuing, making a commitment**
(high)	**4.**	**Organizing or fitting the value into one's own value system**
(high)	**5.**	**Integrating the value, living the value, choosing it**

DEVELOPMENT STRUCTURES AND TECHNIQUES FOR PEER TRAINING

Presentation Options

Problem: A basic problem in implementing any peer training program is to get the peer trainers, and indeed the entire workforce, to think creatively and expansively about how to teach. A good train-the-peer-trainer program must have some lessons on presentation options. Peer trainers need some variety in their "bag of training tricks." There are some obvious and some not-so-obvious reasons for this.

The obvious reason is that trainees get bored when lessons are boring. Along with this is the obvious reason that it's easier to teach and keep on teaching when lessons are interesting; that is, learning has a better chance of happening when there's a good fit between the learner, the instructor, and the material to be learned. Another obvious reason is that timing might be right for one kind of presentation and totally wrong for another kind of presentation. Another obvious reason is that a peer trainer might be an ace at teaching one way, and a total disaster at teaching another way.

A not-so-obvious reason why peer trainers need to have a variety of presentation options available to them is that a major reason why trainees get bored is the problem of learning style. There are countless resources on the market today regarding style—management style, leadership style, team member style, negotiation style, and learning style, to name a few. Most of these resources trace their genesis back to Swiss psychologist Carl Jung and his study of personality. A major thread of Jung's work dealt with the theories and practices of creating a "harmony of the conscious and unconscious," a search for practical learning structures that can help individuals become integrated wholes, according to their unique personality characteristics and individual differences. At a recent conference I attended, the human resources consulting company, Drake, Beam, Morin handed out buttons and a quick pencil and paper survey which were supposed to help attendees determine their "communication" styles. My buttons said "Thinker" and "Intuitor"; other choices were "Feeler" and "Senser."[3] There are many models, matrices, charts, and checklists to help individuals identify and value their own unique learning styles. Peer trainers must recognize that individual learners have different styles of learning; one size never fits all in training. The real task of peer training is to develop lessons and the way of presenting them so that one size fits *one*. Often the best training begins with a trainer's simply asking a trainee how he or she learns best. Remember, again, that in teaching an adult, a teacher is dealing with an *experienced learner,* an individual who has had a lot of practice learning. Chances are that this person knows himself or herself well enough to know what those preferences for learning are. The peer trainer's job is to have available a variety of teaching techniques so that the trainer can choose which one might be the best way of presenting this information to this trainee at this time.

Another not-so-obvious reason why a trainer needs a "bagful of tricks" is that training often needs to be "just in time" training, delivered on the spot very shortly before it needs to be integrated in real work by the trainee. Peer training is absolutely the best way to deliver training "just in time," but it too must be designed and deliberately presented in such a way as to encourage maximum learning and immediate transfer to work. Peer trainers with a variety of presentation options at their disposal can do this "just in time" kind of training with style and grace.

A final reason why variety in presentation techniques is necessary is that employees at all levels and in all jobs in businesses and organizations of all sorts in today's fast changing workplace must continually re-identify jobs and job tasks anywhere in their companies which they feel interested and competent to do. The major organizational changes affecting the structure of so many of our workplaces often have the effect of creating what some are calling "transitioned work"—work that formerly was orderly and secure becomes flexible and in need of enhancement, extrapolation into something else, and very insecure. Trainers need to help employees tackle the new work that must be done and match their interests and talents to the work that's left over after rightsizing, downsizing, re-engineering, corporate takeovers, employee ownership, organizing into teams, and a host of other organizational re-directions that are so often happening in today's workplaces. Workers on the job before restructuring hits a company need help in seeing what possibilities are out there throughout the company; peer trainers with a variety of presentation options can be extremely helpful to individuals trying to see possibilities in their relationships to the company's new work. In fact, this kind of sometimes seemingly desperate and dissonant working environment is often the kind of scene in which peer training as a corporate-wide way of learning can be at its best. Accepting the fact of individual differences as learners is the first step.

Plan of action: Worksheets 2 - 16 through 2 - 20 outline twelve different, yet related, presentation options for improving performance one by one. These presentation options are:

Mentoring	Small Group
Coaching	Team
Storytelling	Correspondence course
One to One (supervisor or SME as trainer)	Laboratory
Cross training	Conference
Apprenticeship	Self-directed learning

The worksheets are organized in like fashion for each technique; similar options are grouped together on one worksheet. Each is organized this way:

Description of the peers
Features of the presentation option
Advantages of this option from the learner's perspective
Disadvantages of this option from the learner's perspective.

The plan of action regarding the problem of embracing a variety of presentation options must be to study the options suggested here on these worksheets and to practice using each on appropriate students. The topic of "Peer Training Presentation Options" should be part of any train-the-trainer class or training program prior to starting peer training.

Examples: Individuals showing each other how to do things at work have been part of teaching and learning in many workplaces for many years. In fact, there are a number of studies that suggest that some kind of peer training has been going on informally, unstructured, unmeasured, unevaluated, and largely unappreciated in both large and small companies in every sector of business and industry. When training statistics get compiled and reported in government studies and in magazine articles, these one-to-one efforts seldom get counted, and the training statistics therefore largely apply to only classroom training.

The fact remains that there are companies who have had some experience with peer training of various sorts, and some have documented and evaluated their experiences. The following examples are some of these.

The American Management Association's *Small Business Reports* in a recent issue[4] contained an article about a small manufacturing company in Ohio, Will-Burt, who literally re-invented itself in about five years' time. Hounded by lawsuits over an industrial accident, a shrinking customer base related to defense industry downsizing, a whopping reject and rework rate, an unhappy workforce and other problems, Will-Burt decided to develop a pervasive education and training program in order to save the company.

Among the techniques they used was peer training in the quality improvement area associated with reject and rework. Will-Burt management took the approach to inspection—an often dreaded process—of using "quality consultants" who were actually not outsiders but instead came from the ranks of the company's top workers. These quality inspectors were given the role of "troubleshooter" rather than "enforcer," and were promoted into the position of "inspector" from among the regular employees on the shop floor. The vice-president in charge of the changes has been credited with "changing the whole corporate culture." He says, in the AMA article, "I found that education creates involvement, and involvement creates knowledge, and knowledge says I want more education so I can get more involved." "Where quality was once a management imperative, now it is embraced by all employees (associates, as they are now called) . . ." He notes, "We have formed a team, a solidarity—from our janitor to our salesperson to our clerk—when it comes to our customers." In Will-Burt's case, peer training was a part of the total training effort that included classroom training and off-site courses at a local university, but a part that paid off handsomely in just a few years: only *two* faulty parts *per million*,—better than Motorola's famous six sigma— and a remake-time measurement of just 25 hours per 30,000 hours of labor.

Another venture into peer training is being made by Canyon Ranch, a top quality health spa with headquarters in Arizona and a branch in Massachusetts. This company's experience with cross-training is described in the book, *How to Start a Training Program in Your Growing Business*.[5] In such a business, where turnover is high and the nature of the highly personal services provided is very demanding, it is critical that employees know many different jobs in order to keep the work going at an acceptable level of service quality, and it is critical that employees be brought up to speed quickly and thoroughly.

In order to rise to these two critical training challenges, Canyon Ranch developed a peer training program of cross training, in which every employee learns the critical tasks of many other employees' jobs in related areas, so that customers with unique and specialized needs can be served efficiently and effectively. To implement this kind of training, a checklist of skills to be learned is used, the peer trainer establishes a schedule for learning each skill, and documents when the skill has actually been mastered. An employee's first 40 hours on the job are considered learning time, and the trainer and trainee together develop a 40-hour program of learning. The learning program is structured, documented, and evaluated. Peer trainers can be "a department head, a supervisor, or a co-worker." The secret to the program's success—and it's a company-wide program—is the time-based, skills-based documentation and evaluation form.

Finally, here's an example of a company who is using a mentoring and coaching peer training program to help its employees through difficult transition years. Bank of Boston in Massachusetts is using a structured mentoring and coaching program to help employees deal with recent rightsizing and reengineering efforts that left many workers unsure about how to do their jobs, and even, what their jobs really were after all the changes.

The manager of organization development there said that mentors and coaches needed to be "models and cheerleaders" for the new mindsets and work styles required by the changes, and that those in charge of training the mentors and coaches had to provide them with detailed support material such as lists of job tasks, learning objectives, workflow diagrams, job aids, CBT learning tools, reference materials, and so forth. She clearly indicates that training the peer trainer, in this instance mentors and coaches, is a corporate responsibility, just as developing viable training for individual workers is the mentor's or coach's responsibility.[6]

Each of these three examples is from a different type of business, and each develops the concept of peer training slightly differently. Each illustrates a viable option in the presentation of peer training. Each is real, current, planned, structured, documented, and evaluated. Worksheets that follow on the next pages outline these development techniques and other peer training presentation options which your peer trainers should have in their "stable of winners" as they embark upon peer training design and development.

WORKSHEET 2 - 16

MENTORING, COACHING, AND STORYTELLING

Description of the peers

Mentors, coaches, and storytellers can be anyone in an organization. Often they are workers who have been around for awhile, often old-timers in terms of experience on the job for which they are being asked to be trainers. The peers, in this case, are the trainees who need to know more than just the tasks or techniques or procedures of a job and the trainers who can provide the essentials of doing the job plus an accurate "education" in the unwritten rules and standards—the culture—of a company.

Features of mentoring, coaching, and storytelling

Mentoring, coaching, and storytelling have several important characteristics in common. All require both trainer and trainee to listen to each other in such a way that the "culture" comes through. Both must be willing and able to be "tuned in" to the other in a kind of emotional, holistic relationship; both must be willing to learn from the gestalt of the relationship. Both must be open to sharing experiences.

Mentoring, coaching, and storytelling all have disciplines that are not characterized primarily by logical analysis. They are, rather, forms of training that encourage community-building through the trainer's encouragement of the trainee's problem-solving efforts or deepening personal awareness of codes of conduct. These forms of peer training make use of the tangible artifacts of a corporate culture and its intangible stories, lessons, and "truths." All require belief, faith, commitment, and imagination in addition to whatever documentation "crutches" that are required by accountability-seekers. All require corporate support in the form of time for training, a belief that personal development pays off, help in setting appropriate success standards for the training, monitoring and assessment of the training efforts, a place in which to learn, and resource and reference material support.

Advantages of mentoring, coaching, and storytelling

- Experienced employees can quickly pass on information that's hard to transfer in classrooms or through purely logical, procedural types of instruction.
- New or inexperienced employees can find a helpful, lasting friend if trainer and trainee are well matched.
- A support system built on trust, hope, confidence, and personal understanding can result if trainer and trainee are well matched.

Disadvantages of mentoring, coaching, and storytelling

- Trainees can get stereotyped as "belonging" to their trainers.
- Trainees can feel isolated if their trainers find that they are not suitably tuned in.
- Trainees can get "dumped" if their trainers get tired of the soft-side of training.

WORKSHEET 2 - 17

ONE TO ONE (SUPERVISOR OR SME AS TRAINER), CROSS-TRAINING, AND APPRENTICESHIP

Description of the peers
Peers in these kinds of training are at different levels in terms of the clear tasks of a job; that is, the trainer knows how to do something at a mastery level and the trainee needs to be similarly competent at the end of training. Trainers who are supervisors, subject matter experts (SMEs), cross-trainers in related organizations or jobs, and apprentice coordinators are all co-workers who are differentiated from their trainees by a criterion-based performance indicator that sets them up as those who know and can do, and defines the trainees as those who need to know. These peer trainers represent the "hard side" of training as contrasted with the "soft side" of mentors, coaches, and storytellers.

Features of one to one, cross-training, and apprenticeship
Training via these options is very focused, often uses checklists and graded task lists, features sign-off spaces to indicate someone's verification that the task has been learned, and frequently carries with it a grade-level jump, a certification, or a move upward towards higher pay or status. It is the kind of training often associated with having to learn new machinery, procedures, or the psychomotor skills associated with manufacturing. This kind of training is characterized by obvious and well-defined things that must be learned, and once they have been learned, there's generally no expectation of a future relationship between trainer and trainee. It is competency-based, and generally has not much spinoff in terms of learning "the culture."

Advantages of one to one, cross-training, and apprenticeship

- Trainees can look up to trainers recognized as competent in specific tasks.
- Trainees have a clear indication of what they are supposed to be able to do.
- Trainees generally get good feedback regarding their performance progress.
- It is usually very efficient training.
- The administration of it is predictable, engendering a sense of security.

Disadvantages of one to one, cross-training, and apprenticeship

- Some more "right-brained" trainees often find it tedious.
- Trainees can suffer if the trainer is so competent and "above it all" that he or she doesn't want to take the time or have the interest in being a trainer.

WORKSHEET 2 - 18

SMALL GROUPS AND TEAMS

Description of the peers
Workers who are called upon to teach small groups of their co-workers or who become a "trainer-of-the-week" within a team are generally persons at the same level or job description as their trainees. They have the added burden of managing a group instruction situation, even if they have only two or three other peers to train.

Features of small group peer training and peer training within teams
Peer training in small groups or teams generally has an immediate problem driving the need for training. Someone who is deemed able gets asked by a supervisor or team leader to become a trainer for a brief time focused on a specific problem. Those who need to learn gather around and some consensus is reached about when and where training will happen.

If the trainer is smart, he or she will insist on some planning time to draft a few lesson plans, have the objectives verified by the supervisor or team leader, line up any clerical, materials or media support, and request "coverage" of the trainees' jobs—and their own jobs—while they are in training. Trainers need some time to think about who the trainees will be and to plan for their different learning styles, even though they are all focused on the same issue or problem. The rest of the organization must be made aware that training is special, different from work at this time, and requires preparation on the part of the trainer if learning is to occur.

Advantages of small group and team training

- It has a good chance of quickly being used ("transferred to") on the job.
- This kind of "just-in-time" training tends to motivate learners.
- Interactions of several peer learners over a focused problem tends to yield solutions quickly, or at least lead to action.
- Trainees are usually comfortable with a peer trainer in this kind of problem-focused learning situation.

Disadvantages of small group and team training

- Without preparation, this kind of training can degenerate into a gripe session or a bad show.
- Peer trainers are often pressed into service too quickly without adequate train-the-trainer preparation—emotionally as well as from a presentation skills perspective.
- Peer trainers, if unprepared as instructors, often try to teach by lecture or by end-of process evaluation rather than by questioning, give-and-take, and continuous progress toward achievement of objectives for learning.

WORKSHEET 2 - 19

CORRESPONDENCE COURSES AND LABORATORIES

Description of the peers
These two kinds of training are included here as presentation options because in both instances, peers or co-workers often become trainers or designers of instruction. In each case, the role of the peer trainer is that of facilitator and sometimes administrator. In each case, the trainer relies heavily on the nature of independent work done by the trainee. The role of the trainer is often to guide, give assurance, provide evaluative feedback during learning, set up training materials, and take care of entry and exit details. In both these kinds of training, the learner is expected to do independent work and seek assistance from the trainer when he or she needs it.

Features of correspondence courses and laboratories
Both of these types of training feature analysis, parts and sub-parts, and content divided up into small units. In both types of training, the organization of the material tends to encourage its management by a peer facilitator or administrator who often functions in the role of trainer—directing next steps, providing materials at the right times, and so forth. Peer trainers/administrators also often design the instruction and the written lesson materials, in effect, functioning as a behind-the-scenes instructor.

Advantages of correspondence courses and laboratories

- Many trainees can be managed at once using the same lessons, yet one by one.
- Trainees work at their own pace.
- Shy trainees don't have to worry about getting too personal with a trainer.
- Evaluative feedback is continuous, and generally written to correspond with sub-parts of content, increasing its probability of being used to make improvements as the learning progresses.

Disadvantages of correspondence courses and laboratories

- Trainees sometimes go off on tangents and don't get the point.
- Trainees at the base level of understanding or skill often need more interaction with a trainer than is typically possible in either correspondence courses or in laboratories.
- Insecure trainees need constant interaction with trainers; trial and error and "doing it yourself" frightens some people and sabotages learning.

WORKSHEET 2 - 20

CONFERENCES AND SELF-DIRECTED LEARNING

Description of the peers

In conferences and self-directed learning, the trainee chooses to learn what seems interesting. In both types of training, the trainee's preparation for the learning encounter is very important. Expectations play a major part in the trainee's success in learning via these two options: conference brochures and self-directed learning manuals help build enthusiasm and spark a trainee's expectations for success in learning. The trainers, in these options, are often designed into the medium for presentation; that is, the instructional design of a conference session and a self-directed learning session is instrumental to and facilitative of what and how the trainee learns. In both of these options, a third party presenter or progress monitor play key facilitative roles, but the real peer trainer in these options is usually the instructional design of the chosen medium for learning. In both cases, there is no instructor, per se.

Features of conferences and self-directed learning

These learning options present the challenge of the learner's becoming mentally "set" for learning. We've all gone to conferences that were fun but hardly produced lasting learning; we've all set about learning something on our own only to get frustrated, bored, or side-tracked. These less than optimal results were probably due to our lack of attention to our own learning objectives and our consequent lack of focus on the tasks of learning itself. Australian adult educator J.B. Biggs suggests that anyone who sets out to learn anything should ask himself or herself these questions:[7]

"What do I want? (motives)
What will it look like when I've got there? (goals)
What do I need to get there? (task demands)
What resources have I got to use? What constraints must I contend with? (context)
What am I capable of doing? (abilities)
Well, then, How do I go about it?" (strategies)

The essential features of both conferences and self-directed learning opportunities are that the possibilities and potential stimulations for learning are almost overwhelming, and this demands that the learner structure his or her expectations for learning ahead of the encounter. Biggs' questions are a good place to start.

Advantages of conferences and self-directed learning

- They capitalize on the trainee's readiness to learn.
- Instructors don't have to be trained.
- The trainee chooses a topic of interest.

Disadvantages of conferences and self-directed learning

- Most trainees need help in developing appropriate, "deep" learning strategies for learning on their own.

Endnotes for Chapter 6
Notes 1 through 7

1. Federal policy options are discussed in "Training and the Feds" by *Training* magazine's managing editor in the November 1993 issue, pp. 43-45.

2. Bob Filipczak, "Frick Teaches Frack," in *Training,* June 1993, pp. 30-34.

3. Communication style buttons can be ordered at 75 cents each from DBM Publishing, Order Department, 100 Park Avenue, 4th Floor, New York, NY 10164, or by phoning at 1-800-345-5627. Choices are Senser, Feeler, Thinker, Intuitor.

4. "A Little Education Goes A Long Way" by Donna Brown Hogarty, in *Small Business Reports,* December 1993, pp. 47-55.

5. Carolyn Nilson, *How to Start a Training Program in Your Growing Business,* New York: AMACOM, 1992, pp. 164-166.

6. Robin Grumman-Vogt, "What Needs to Happen Before Learning?", presentation notes from the Ziff Institute On-The-Job Learning Conference, Boston, MA, 1993.

7. Biggs list reproduced in Philip C. Candy's *Self-Direction for Lifelong Learning,* San Francisco: Jossey-Bass, 1991, p. 297.

CHAPTER 7

IMPLEMENTATION AIDS FOR LEARNING ONE BY ONE

By now it should be obvious that this book is not talking about the haphazard kind of "quick, show me how you do it" last-minute training that sometimes gets labeled peer training. Rather, the peer training of this book is a carefully planned, designed, and developed set of learning encounters. From the discussion and examples of options in presenting peer training found in the last chapter, the reader can see that as much effort and development thought must go into these kinds of training as goes into the development of classroom training.

An essential part of implementing training of any sort, including peer training, is the use of audial, tactile, visual, and interactive learning aids that expand upon parts of the lesson or that stimulate thought or demonstrate points in the lesson. These kinds of instructional aids have typically been present in teacher-dominated classrooms; they should also be an integral part of learner-controlled training. These aids help to establish a comfortable context for learning and they help bring students to the brink of learning.

Particularly in training one by one, trainers and trainees both need the full range of instructional media available to them to help the learning along. Problem statements and worksheets that follow deal with these implementation aids in two groups: the traditional audio and visual aids, and multi media training aids.

IMPLEMENTATION AIDS FOR LEARNING ONE BY ONE

Instructional Aids (Traditional Audio and Visual Aids)

Problem: We've all heard the numbers from conventional training media wisdom: people are said to retain approximately:

only 10 percent of what they read,

only 20 percent of what they hear,

only 30 percent of what they see,

but. . .

50 percent of what they hear and see together,

70 percent of what they say,

and a whopping

90 percent of what they say and do.

These numbers have been used to both discredit the lecture as a training delivery choice and at the same time encourage the student's note-taking during lectures in order to get the learner "doing" something as well as "seeing" something. They have been used to encourage teachers to assign projects as homework rather than just plain reading. They have been used to justify creating media libraries, media centers, and spending thousands of dollars on the latest and greatest audio and visual equipment. They have even been used to discredit "linear" media altogether in favor of more "problem solving"-type learning experiences such as role play and "show and tell" demonstrations.

One of the problems to be overcome in dealing with traditional audio and visual media is the problem of thinking it's old-fashioned and perhaps not choosing it for that reason only. The surest way to deal with this problem is to think in terms of the hierarchies for learning (cognitive, psychomotor, affective)—see Worksheets 2-13, 2-14, and 2-15. Try to figure out what it is that you're training your learner to know, to do, or to believe, and choose media that will help the learner along. Often a simple transparency or drawing on a flipchart will be just the thing that's needed to help the learner connect with a familiar procedure, or to see clearly the four critical concepts of the lesson. Sometimes introducing a working model for the trainee to manipulate, or having a blank form for the trainee to fill out under your direction will be exactly the thing that creates that learning moment.

The surest way to not "get snowed" into buying the latest bells and whistles is to keep the objectives for the learner foremost in your mind as you are designing and developing the instructional experience for your trainee.

The other problem, obviously, is which implementation aid to choose.

Plan of action: The first step in choosing media is to say to yourself over and over and over again, **"Media aids support instruction, not supplant it."** Media aids are just that—aids to instruction; they should never be considered instruction in and of themselves. One of the biggest mistakes that many, many trainers make is to buy videotapes and send them back to the office or media center with a trainee in the name of "training." Most videotapes are simply information; often they are entertainment. Seldom are they training media. Realize that a videotape is not instruction; it can be an *aid* to instruction if it fits in with your well planned objectives for your specific learner. Always preview any video you intend to purchase with your learner's objectives in mind. Never buy a video on the strength of its advertising alone. Misuse of videotapes is probably the biggest error that trainers make, and one which peer trainers are particularly prone to making. The other common mistake trainers make with traditional media is the misuse of overhead transparencies; that is, many trainers crowd their overheads with too much information, and worse, often "teach" the lesson by simply reading the overhead to the—naturally—bored trainee.

The next step in deciding which media to choose is to remind yourself that the traditional audio and visual media are essentially print-related, or, said another way, they involve similar cognitive skills such as skills required for understanding of reading—skills such as recognize, define, list, organize. They are essentially linear, as is reading. They can be chosen and used effectively to complement and reinforce lower and mid-level cognitive skills. They can be chosen and used effectively to guide a trainee's actions in psychomotor skills training. They can be chosen and used effectively to persuade or illustrate effects of belief and adoption of ideas in affective skills training.

Examples: These are the traditional audio and visual media that support instruction; all should be considered useful in learning one by one:

Job aids	Flipcharts	Audiotapes
Manuals	Transparencies and slides	Videotapes
Handouts		

Training manuals, for example, can be used effectively to reinforce instruction by providing space for the trainee to practice, check answers against an answer key, or list steps of a procedure as a reference to be returned to as needed. Transparencies are often a very effective way of testing a trainee on details or concepts by engaging the trainee in an interactive question and answer exercise by covering up the "answer" on the transparency until the trainee gets it right; then uncovering it to reinforce the trainee's correct response. Audiotapes can be used effectively in providing background or context information, or in assisting with rote memory tasks such as those required for learning a foreign language. They can also go home with a trainee to be used in a car tape player, at home at the trainee's leisure, or to be played in the trainee's office while the trainee does some routine task like opens mail. Media can be used to encourage a trainee to engage in "parallel processing" mind training.

As a workforce becomes used to learning from each other—to alternately being peer trainers and peer trainees—employees will begin to take more responsibility for their own learning, and they will become self-directed learners. This doesn't happen quickly or automatically by magic. Learners learn best when their learning is supported, reinforced, complimented, rewarded, and continuously encouraged. Choosing traditional audio and visual media can help provide learning crutches, cues, and support. Use it often, and use it always as an adjunct to training, not in place of it. Worksheets that follow provide decision-making guidance.

WORKSHEET 2 - 21

JOB AIDS CHECKLIST

Directions: Review this entire worksheet before deciding to choose a job aid as an aid to instruction.

Reasons for choosing this learning aid

_____ 1. It is a good memory cue.

_____ 2. It can be used over and over again on the job.

_____ 3. The learner chooses to use a job aid at the moment it is needed, enhancing the learner's motivation to learn.

_____ 4. Its use on the job reminds the learner of accomplishments during training.

_____ 5. The essence of a lesson can be synthesized and abbreviated into a chart, card, graphic representation, or model.

Design features that affect learning

_____ 1. A job aid is more graphic than narrative. Principles of good graphic design affect its design.

_____ 2. A job aid tells or shows what to do.

_____ 3. A job aid represents generic or standardized information.

_____ 4. A job aid uses specific terms applied to single tasks or concepts.

_____ 5. A job aid stands on its own apart from related narrative material.

_____ 6. A job aid is a good reference that is easy to use.

_____ 7. A job aid's graphic elements appeal to more than one sense; a job aid can be an excellent stimulus to deeper learning.

WORKSHEET 2 - 22

MANUALS CHECKLIST

Directions: Review this entire worksheet before deciding to choose a manual as an aid to instruction.

Reasons for choosing this learning aid

_____ 1. It sets up the trainee for receiving the instruction upon which it is based.

_____ 2. It is a reference to be used throughout training as well as back on the job.

_____ 3. It contains an entire lesson or course of instruction, providing an overview and a summary of related instruction. It helps with ''big picture'' understanding.

_____ 4. It lists learner objectives and content outline, providing a crutch to the trainee as the trainee becomes increasingly more involved in the lesson.

_____ 5. It is in the familiar form of a book, increasing the learner's comfort level with it as an instructional aid.

_____ 6. It can be used again and again at the learner's initiative whenever a refresher on any part of its contents is needed.

Design features that affect learning

_____ 1. The manual's size and scope are flexible, increasing its appeal.

_____ 2. The manual relies on the familiar principles of print design, making it easy to produce quickly on most office word processing systems.

_____ 3. The manual provides opportunity to create a context for learning through narrative sections of text; to exercise the trainee in definition, recall, and discrimination tasks; to present lists of steps and outline procedures; and to provide elaborations through explanation, metaphor, case studies, and examples that lead to higher level conceptual learning and problem solving.

_____ 4. The manual is personal; it can be written in, notated, and possessed by the trainee.

WORKSHEET 2 - 23

HANDOUTS CHECKLIST

Directions: Review this entire worksheet before deciding to choose handouts as an instructional aid.

Reasons for choosing this learning aid

_____ 1. The "third party" authorship of most handouts helps to create value regarding the topic of the lesson.

_____ 2. Handouts expand one's grasp of the topic.

_____ 3. Handouts appeal to various "frames of mind" by presenting contrasting points of view or different ways to look at the topic.

_____ 4. Handouts can be assembled and filed for accessibility at any time according to the trainee's interest and need to know.

_____ 5. Choice of handouts can be tailored to a trainee's special preferred learning style.

_____ 6. Handouts can motivate and turn a trainee on to action.

Design features that affect learning

_____ 1. Handouts can help learners form associations that are necessary to building new concepts.

_____ 2. Handouts can be directly related to levels of skills in the cognitive and affective domains (Worksheets 2 - 13 and 2 - 15), reinforcing learning.

_____ 3. Handouts can create background or context information required for problem definition or evaluation activities; they can appeal to high-level skills.

_____ 4. Handouts can supplement outlined lesson plans with full text; handouts can fill in the information gaps.

_____ 5. Handouts can be used as references, memory joggers, and conceptual triggers to creative thinking and innovation. They supplement lessons in both convergent thinking and divergent thinking.

WORKSHEET 2 - 24

FLIPCHARTS CHECKLIST

Directions: Review this entire worksheet before deciding to choose flipcharts as an instructional aid.

Reasons for choosing this learning aid

_____ 1. It is inexpensive.

_____ 2. It is flexible in terms of being capable of encouraging interactivity on the part of the trainee as well as the trainer.

_____ 3. It forces the variation of viewing distance from "up close and personal" to a farther-away comfort level that is attractive to many trainees.

_____ 4. Sheets can be ripped off, taken back to the office or the job site, or posted on walls as a reminder of key points of training.

_____ 5. It's easy to use and easy to customize for one person or a small group.

_____ 6. Its use connotes a certain formality regarding training that some peer trainers and trainees find helpful as they get used to the act of teaching; it can be a "methodology crutch" to beginning trainers.

Design features that affect learning

_____ 1. Flipchart writing must be legible, with large, clearly formed letters of consistent size.

_____ 2. Flipcharts should contain plenty of white space so that the key points of content are easily read. It's tempting to crowd the page; don't. Learners will quickly turn off if you do, and soon prefer to read it themselves out of the book. Poorly executed flipcharts can sabotage teaching.

_____ 3. Bleeding markers can cause graphic garbage on subsequent pages if they bleed through from one page to another. Graphic garbage creates waste in terms of message clarity and appeal.

_____ 4. Flipcharts are flexible in terms of right-brain as well as left-brain appeal—they can accommodate drawings, colors, lines, shapes, as well as numbers, letters, and words and word-related lists, points, rules, and definitions.

TRANSPARENCIES AND SLIDES CHECKLIST

Directions: Review this entire worksheet before deciding to choose transparencies and slides as an aid to instruction.

Reasons for choosing this learning aid

_____ 1. They have the added media appeal of color, large scale, and projected light through them.

_____ 2. They can be photographic, presenting real images of people, place, and things.

_____ 3. They can be projected at the trainer's or the trainee's own preferred pace, allowing for explanatory pauses and clarifications.

_____ 4. Their media effects can be judiciously and specifically tied to points of content giving the content added emphasis.

_____ 5. The transparencies or slides can be quickly and easily adjusted to the trainer's presentation; items can be eliminated easily, or referred back to easily.

_____ 6. They are inexpensive to produce, yet can often provide the same multi-sensory stimulation and learning support as computer-based multi-media aids.

Design features that affect learning

_____ 1. Each item in a transparency pack or slide show is a unit, and is therefore flexible in terms of time spent viewing it. The element of time can be customized to the learner's advantage.

_____ 2. Sound can accompany slides or transparencies via audiotape.

_____ 3. Their use requires the room to be darkened, often suggesting sleep; don't use these media after a meal or at the end of the day when the trainee is tired.

_____ 4. They are more appropriate for use in teams or small groups than in one-to-one peer training. The large scale is generally inappropriate for one-to-one situations.

_____ 5. Trainees can interact with transparencies, but generally, these are instructor-controlled learning aids.

WORKSHEET 2 - 26

AUDIOTAPES CHECKLIST

Directions: Review this entire worksheet before deciding to choose audiotapes as an instructional aid.

Reasons for choosing this learning aid

_____ 1. Audio stimulation is critical to learning: to memory, to cueing, to pattern recognition.

_____ 2. Time is at a premium and information can be presented via audiotape while the trainee is doing something else (like driving a car, drinking coffee, exercising).

_____ 3. Rote memorization or drill and practice need to be done, as in foreign language study.

_____ 4. A conceptual preview is required prior to problem definition.

_____ 5. It is inexpensive to produce and use.

Design features that affect learning

_____ 1. Audiotape is linear and can be segmented, counted, and identified by number for selective listening.

_____ 2. Audiotapes can be privately listened to via earphones, and therefore customized for specific learners.

_____ 3. Audiotapes can be interactive.

_____ 4. Audiotapes are limited to audio stimulation. Combine them with visual media for more complete memory enhancement.

_____ 5. Audiotape is good at capturing the totality of verbal information: a speech, what was said at a meeting, an interview, or dialogue between key players. It is a reliable documentation and informational device.

_____ 6. The quality of audiotape is affected by temperature and humidity, the volume of recording, and the quality of microphones, speakers, and recording and playback equipment.

WORKSHEET 2 - 27

VIDEOTAPES CHECKLIST

Directions: Review this entire worksheet before deciding to choose videotapes as an instructional aid.

Reasons for choosing this learning aid

_____ 1. Videotape is multi-sensory and moving, increasing its power to captivate a viewer/listener.

_____ 2. It is inexpensive to produce; "home" video cameras are of better and better quality, widely available, and can be used effectively in capturing images.

_____ 3. Wide angle shots and detailed close-up shots can present a range of visual information.

_____ 4. Still photos, action, and animation graphics can be combined for a combined entertainment effect.

Design features that affect learning

_____ 1. The powerful combination of sound, color, graphics, fantasy, and motion added to words attracts and "hooks" viewers/listeners.

_____ 2. Videotapes can be viewed/listened to at the trainee's convenience.

_____ 3. Purchased videotapes are seldom precisely appropriate for your learning objectives. They are difficult to customize and can be a costly waste of time and money.

_____ 4. Videotapes are excellent at presenting information, providing context, and helping to change attitudes at the lowest level of awareness. They are generally pitched at the lowest levels of skills, being especially good at defining and explaining, illustrating and giving examples.

_____ 5. Videotapes are all too often designed for their entertainment value and have very little to do with learning. Trainers must preview all videotapes for their capacity to enhance objectives for learning. It is unconscionable for trainers to purchase videotapes that entertain and call it training, wasting the company's money and employees' time. Videos are generally inactive training.

IMPLEMENTATION AIDS FOR LEARNING ONE BY ONE

Multi Media Training Delivery

Problem: There's an old saying in the advertising business that "information does not equal behavior," meaning that the behavior change that's sought because of effective "catchy" advertising can't be expected to happen because of information alone. That consumer decision to purchase and use happens because of a well-planned, orchestrated strategy to lead the consumer to the sale. In learning too, information does not equal behavior—there's a huge amount of design and development that must precede that change in behavior that is the moment of learning—not to mention the careful strategies that must be carried out to make that learning last beyond the "Aha!" moment. Our linear, print-based world of the 20th century has come to grips with the relationship between information and behavior in a variety of ways, including our disciplined systems approach to the design of instruction. The notion of "instruct" is a constructionist idea, a building little by little, step by measured step.

What's happening as the century closes is an enormous technological revolution in our access to information—total information, not just print-based information. The combination of digitized data production and laser "transportation" lines has enabled our businesses, governments, homes, individuals, and organizations of all sorts to accumulate, search, and share great volumes of information in print-related formats, and also to experience new images, sounds, and tactile information in astonishing quantity and variety. Through computer, video, and laser technology we have exponentially increased the information base of society, particularly the access to information. We have also designed and developed amazing machines, electronic hardware that takes us into and through information. We are paying a great deal of attention to our information infrastructure.

Our problems come when we talk about the social effects of information, the dislocation effects and disenfranchisement effects of those that won't or that can't deal with it, the political dynamic that's set up when those who are displaced by technology are not the ones who benefit from it, the new economic development issues that arise from a new class of information-have-nots versus the ruling class of the information-haves. The imperatives are powerful for better education at early ages and in all schools, for training in all workplaces, and for practice of the skills of self-directed learning in all aspects of our lives.

We have entered a brave new world in a lopsided way, with great promise in the technology itself but with little understanding of how to learn within it. Translated into training-speak, we need to keep learning objectives foremost as we engage with new media. We need to continue to build on what we know about how to learn, to embrace the power of the digital bit and the laser beam and continue to learn in ways that make us masters of information. It is very easy to become mastered by information, especially since we have an overload of it and our information highways are getting bigger and more sophisticated minute by minute. The role of capable self-directed learners will become increasingly more important as we travel these highways. The workplace focus on peer training can be instrumental in creating individuals who know how to learn and continue learning.

Technologies like interactive videodisc, CD ROM, and virtual environments have great promise as aids to training. If they are to advance beyond being mega-information providers, we must be able to rise above being seduced by their entertainment value and develop the skills to perceive, organize, and use information efficiently and effectively. This is the challenge of multi media.

Plan of action: Several key writers of the past generation provide us with some guidance regarding how we should deal with information as learners and as masters. Our first task in devising an appropriate plan of action is to frame our thinking about information. These creative thinkers can help; their books are:

(1) MARSHALL MCLUHAN AND QUENTIN FIORE, *The Medium Is the Massage: An Inventory of Effects*, New York: Bantam Books, 1967;
(2) J. P. GUILFORD, *Intelligence, Creativity, and Their Educational Implications*, San Diego: Knapp, 1968;
(3) SHOSHANA ZUBOFF, *In the Age of the Smart Machine: The Future of Work and Power*, New York : Basic Books, 1984;
(4) ANTHONY PATRICK CARNEVALE, *America and the New Economy*, San Francisco: Jossey-Bass, 1991; and
(5) DONALD A. NORMAN, *Things That Make Us Smart*, Reading, MA: Addison-Wesley, 1993.

McLuhan, a professor at the University of Toronto, and his graphic artist colleague Fiore, catapulted us into thinking differently about how we receive information. McLuhan's extraordinary little book on "electric technology" came out at a time when many of us were just beginning to experience the wonder and power of computers. His juxtaposition of letters in words we normally use to give them new information-age meanings tantalized us to think about information in new ways. McLuhan used the term *"massage"* in place of the term message; he spoke of the *"world* pool of information" instead of the whirlpool; and he noted that "all the world's a *sage"* instead of a stage. McLuhan forced us to connect the semantics of both spellings to bring new meaning to our ideas of communication and information.

McLuhan made the point that whereas the technology of print created the public—a collection of individual persons interacting in the marketplace, the technology of electricity, namely, electronics, has created the mass—a flowing, unified, fused interdependence of persons. He called for an awareness of the effects of the continuous flow of information—messages—on society. He causes us to think about how we disconnect from the mass in order to process information and ultimately use it according to our own personal needs and for our own good. McLuhan suggested that if the "technique" of the 19th century were "invention," then perhaps the "technique" of the 20th century has been "suspended judgment."

McLuhan's shakeup of our complacency and naiveté regarding information can help us devise a plan of action regarding today's multi media that involves the higher level cognitive skills of evaluation, reflection, and suspended judgment as we try to customize and personalize our way out of the immersion of information in which we find ourselves today.

The idea that creative responses require an ability to connect and interrelate information is akin to McLuhan's call to explore and probe information. J.P. Guilford, an Air Force psychologist and former president of the American Psychological Association, wrote extensively on the structure of intellect and the requirements of creative action. Guilford's "SI Cube" is a familiar representation to students of educational psychology. Guilford identified four basic kinds of material which we use as categories for information: these are *behavioral, symbolic, figural* or concrete, and *semantic* or verbal. Guilford challenges us to logically organize and reorganize our thinking in each of these areas, and to "transform" our thoughts into other interrelated ideas to create different information. Guilford challenges us to apply lower and mid-level cognitive skills to the task of devising something new out of the continuously accumulating stores of information in his four essential categories of intellectual material. Guilford, like McLuhan is a builder. They both encourage initiative and action regarding information.

Shoshana Zuboff, a professor at Harvard Business School, talks specifically about the effects of large-scale computerization of work. In her very important book, she makes the case that the computer has fostered an "abstraction of work," leading many workers to a great sense of loss of personal power over their work. Throughout the book, she calls for a definition of the new skills workers need in order to deal with this abstraction. Among these skills are: dialogue, inquiry, monitoring, procedural reasoning, ability to conceptualize, ability to infer, ability to engage in the context of systems, ability to manage information, and the ability to interpret data. She notes that workers must have *attention* to the stimuli of information as well as *intention* regarding their involvement with the information-based, computer-wise abstraction of work. Zuboff's list of essential workplace skills in the age of the smart machine takes us into a new world of workplace learning and skill development.

Anthony Patrick Carnevale, an economist and ASTD's executive director of the Institute for Workplace Learning, echoes Zuboff's clarion cry for skills of adaptability in the face of technology's rapid advance into the nature of work. In addition to skills in the academic basics and communication, personal development and leadership, Carnevale calls for skill development in problem solving, creativity, and learning to learn. He devotes considerable space to a discussion of the notion that continuous learning is the "cornerstone of economic progress." He is, after all, an economist, and takes the economist's perspective that economic growth is fueled by learning, with inquiry leading to invention which leads to investment and creation of new jobs. He makes a good case for a re-direction of strategic economic initiatives towards the learning capacity of the American workforce.

It sounds like we're talking about survival as human beings, here, and the dramatic reasons why we should invest in the learning potential of the human resource base of the workforce. Surely another supporter of the constructionist point of view regarding information is Donald Norman, professor at University of California, San Diego. Indeed, Norman boldly states that we are in danger of using technology "to amuse ourselves to death." He is particularly critical of television which he defines as a medium which controls its own pace and is largely for "display." He presents the cognitive psychologist's case for exercising the mind as a "compositional medium" requiring periods of reflection in order to do its best work of re-grouping, transforming, and re-directing action. Sociologist, psychologist, and economist alike focus on our involvement with information as the critical variable in communicating, learning, working, and mastering our destinies as sentient, intelligent creatures.

So we enter the training arena of CD ROM, Interactive Video Disc (IVD), and Virtual Environments, key structures in the evolution of multi media information in the workplace. Above all, our plans of action for mastering the surround of messages through these media must be plans of:

> **initiative,**
> **inquiry,**
> **reflection,**
> **evaluation, and**
> **reconstruction.**

At the very least, these five approaches must be directed at information delivered via multi media devices. We are too smart to allow ourselves to amuse ourselves to death. Our economic survival depends on our ability to use these instructional technologies to advance our capacities to learn and to continuously improve work.

Examples: Popular magazines and the business press are beginning to be full of articles about how companies are moving away from "traditional" classroom training and sending people across country to seminars and instead using some of these new technologies as aids to instruction, essentially creating learning one by one. The next several pages will highlight some of these recent experiments and adventures into the brave new world of information bombardment and their effects. Worksheets 2 - 28, 2 - 29, and 2 - 30 give details about each of these three multi media aids to learning.

First, we need to get specific about some of the problems. *Newsweek* magazine's cover story in the May 31, 1993[1] issue was entitled, "inter-active." *Newsweek*'s own definition of the word, also on the front cover, was "new technology that will change the way you shop, play, and learn; a zillion-dollar industry (maybe)." There's always the 'maybe.' The section began with a suggestion that information today is what land was yesterday to the restless American capitalist—the metaphor of the frontier as a shaper of the American character is as applicable today as it was in yesteryear; only the object of the drive toward it has changed. *Newsweek* says there's big money on the table, and the race is on to find the bonanza vein hidden in interactive technology. The lead article in the group contained a chart (p. 41) full of dizzying numbers and seemingly unlikely partnerships of corporate giants who believe they see the future of information movement and management—and profit—clearly. A McLuhan-like "mass" is certainly the angel hovering over the giants as they try to steer their enterprises toward their goals.

Millions of dollars are being spent in business arrangements that combine computer software and hardware, cable, video, telecommunications, and motion pictures. Three examples from this scramble to cash in on information are:

1. April 1993—Intel (computer chips) creates a partnership with Microsoft (software) and General Instrument (cable equipment) to make a hand-held personal computer that will function much as a television remote control device, an information-age controller that will allow the user—note *"user,"* not viewer—to manage the vast store of information available from one's position on the old couch.

2. December 1992—Tele-communications, Inc., the nation's largest cable operator, announces that it will use digital technology developed by General Instrument to create 500-channel television.

3. March 1993—*Newsweek* itself began issuing discs for Sony's interactive CD-ROM players.

These are businesses that five years decade ago would have been classified in different industries. My own publisher's letterhead over the past six months while I have been writing this book has evolved into its latest version which simply says "Paramount Communications." *Information* is today's umbrella—not chips, not software, not cable, not telecommunications, not news, not entertainment, not publishing.

The new frontier is beckoning brightly: AT&T has 80 million customers; Time Warner and new partner US West together have customers in 43 of the 50 states; three corporate investors put up $15 million to fund development of an interactive disc player; cable is in 60 percent of US homes now. The vision seems clear; what's not so clear is whether the consumer will be willing to pay for what's available: more to the point, whether the consumer knows how to use the information that's available. So we return to the need for a constructionist view of the mind in tandem with "the long drive" of capitalist America to the wild frontier of the 21st century.

Other questions the *Newsweek* story raises are: Through what device will we control data—telephone, TV, PC, or something else? When will it be available? Will everyone be able to afford it? How will we find time to do anything else but cruise through information? Will government regulate information or information highways? and Really, what do we need all this stuff for anyway? (p. 42) The huge success of the Home Shopping Network is causing many information gurus to predict that there will be two parallel interactive home markets, one for entertainment and one that caters to business done at home or on the road. Apple's Newton is a move in anticipation of the latter notion. The possibilities for enhancing learning are legion: there is no question that the availability of and access to information—images, sounds, words, numbers, sensations, maybe even smells and tastes—can be powerful aids to learning. Information in its many forms can be there for learners who need to branch to other sources in order to complete their learning objectives, or for learners who are just plain interested in finding something new. The key problem will come when we tout information range-riding as learning itself; we must continue to be honest in instructional design and not allow slick advertising or entertainment's psychological hooks to promote information as something it is not. Remember, information never equals behavior. Learning must be constructed; built; continuously improved upon.

The frontier metaphor is not only the purview of the popular press. The November-December 1993 issue of *Harvard Business Review*[2] ran an interview with Silicon Graphics' CEO, Ed McCracken. The article's title is "Mastering Chaos at the High-Tech Frontier" and its main message is that the companies who are on 'the long drive' have to remain entrepreneurial in order to keep moving swiftly ahead. Inventing, creating, and learning are essential workplace skills. As McCracken says, "The key to achieving competitive advantage isn't reacting to chaos, it's producing that chaos" (p. 135). McCracken's view of his workplace is that workers have freedom and support, pushed by belief in their potential for innovation. His workforce has a shortened view of time and strategic planning—HBR says they maintain a "climate of urgency." McCracken acknowledges this entrepreneurship is tough in a large and growing business (earnings of $92.5 million last year); he says he thinks Silicon Graphics can pull off getting bigger without getting boring.

Being on the producing end of the multi media information business challenges companies to find, hire, and nurture workers who are flexible and can continuously learn on the job. Information workers must be able to be stimulated by the challenges of the nature of information work. Self-directed learning and peer training are certainly the modalities of choice in such environments. The corporate-training-operation-of-the-past's catalog of courses seems like a dinosaur or artifact of an ancient civilization in such a workplace. It seems like a quaint and fanciful notion to think that training could be planned a year in advance. "Faster even than just-in-time" is a better idea for training of information workers.

We've talked about the market, the mass consumer, and even the producer; but what about the mind of the individual user of multi media? MIT's November-December 1993 issue of *Technology Review*[3] contained an article called "Video Games That Teach?," the gist of which is that the combination of education and entertainment must get beyond the trite and trivial, elementary level rewards for correct responses—"visual candy" and "mechanized praise" the article calls them—(p. 57), to providing an experience of building "real knowledge and the chance to learn even more." The fear written between the lines of the article is that our businesses are so quick to rush into what appears to be a willing market that they are not taking the time to thoughtfully and carefully design into their products the educational strategies that they know are possible to build in. Today's information tools have the capability to be learning tools, but the market drives them to concentrate on their entertainment value.

The article's author notes that a recent collaboration between AT&T, Time Warner, and Matsushita has the ability "to provide both the sizzle of entertainment and the steak of education" (p. 57). He also points out that learning is not a dull and unappealing chore that requires external flashy images and sound to entice people into it; learning is natural and exciting to most people, and especially to children. Parents and training-budget-watchers rightfully are wary of whiz-bang packages that addict users with entertainment only. Time will soon tell whether we have the corporate will to use multi media to enhance learning, or whether we'll blow off the opportunity and ultimately fail both to do business and to provide training as consumers—ever wise and knowing and right—will simply not buy products that are all fluff and bluster.

Then, of course, there are the R&D problems of the technologies themselves. The November 15, 1993 issue of *Information Week* talks about the design problems with Artificial Intelligence—problems today that are the same as they were in the late 1960s when corporate development organizations put so much hope in the technology. In an article, "Shades of Gray Matter," the author describes a major design problem: AI programs typically can't discriminate between true and false input, and they process erroneous data as if it were correct. Sounds like a pretty major problem; no wonder consumers didn't buy. As in so many other long drives to the frontier, this one had to pull back, re-group, and get real. The "little AI" trend in recent years is more realistic, more useful, and more market-wise. Beyond of Cambridge, Mass., for example, has developed a rule-based AI system to route and even automatically answer electronic-mail messages.[4] This smaller, more focused AI applications movement is commendable, but we always need to be on guard that our fantasy worlds don't overtake our actual world that is so grounded in economics.

The same article referenced above talks about Apple's noisy promise that its Newton would be able to recognize casually entered cursive handwriting. Even the *Doonesbury* cartoon blasted Apple when the promise turned out to be untrue (p. 104). The *Technology Review* article previously cited speaks of a "multi media extravaganza" from Software Toolworks in which zoo animals are presented in still pictures, video clips, and audio segments. The problem is that it takes up so much memory for its images that its text is superficial— only a fraction of the amount of information available from an encyclopedia (p. 54). Programs and information that require super computers to load them will simply remain on store—or laboratory—shelves. Consumers will ultimately not buy products, in spite of their hype, that are not designed for consumers. Even the popular "Carmen Sandiego" geography learning games from Broderbund, according to the article, contains "factoids" that are irrelevant to learning geography; and worse, the medium sets up "contrived barriers" to the enjoyment of the game itself (p. 55). The product is, after all, billed as a game. An article in *Forbes ASAP*,[5] October 25, 1993, devoted to videoconferencing products says that the "technology is way ahead of the acceptance level of the average meeting goer" (p. 48), in spite of the dismal statistics that senior executives, for example, spend 53 percent of their time in meetings—many without agendas, conclusions, or influence—at an average hourly rate of $320 (p. 46). Products with names such as LANtastic or Option Finder seek to help meeting-goers through electronic brainstorming sessions with their global colleagues. One small item that some designers overlooked—extroverts (and that's many executives) tend to drop out of electronic meetings because they can't type fast enough and the medium is not suited to their personalities that prefer to communicate by using their strongly-developed verbal and eyeball-to-eyeball skills (p. 54). Licensing costs alone for some of these meeting support systems can start at $30,000— definitely a deterrent to many small and mid-size companies. Even highly acclaimed virtual reality or virtual environment (VE) systems can hardly claim to simulate reality when the effects of touch on the skin seem to elude VE designers. The cover story,[6] "Virtual Reality: The Next Best Thing to

Being There?'' in the October 1993 issue of *Technology Review* says that ''the shortcomings of today's VE systems mean that it will be many years, if ever, before a computer simulation will be indistinguishable from physical reality'' (p. 27), and ''like the space program in the 1950s, research on virtual environments holds great promise but has little to show for itself so far'' (p. 28).

All of this doesn't mean that we shouldn't be open to the possibilities of multi media technology both for improving work environments and for improving work. Indeed many companies have successfully used interactive technologies. An ASTD book, *The Application of Emerging Training Technologies*,[7] cautions trainers not to simply ''repackage'' old methodologies into electronic wrappings—for example, ''instructional television'' of the 1960s simply used videocameras to take and show pictures of people giving lectures—hardly an educationally sound approach to the potential of the medium of video; ''rethinking'' is a better approach (p. 63). At the other end of the spectrum is the possibility that the new technologies will become increasingly transparent as trainees interact with systems without being aware that their behavior is changing or is being modified by the software. Learning systems, of course, can have the power to enhance the cognitive, psychomotor, and affective processes of learning. Information can be presented in such a way as to foster creativity and innovation—to be designed with such care and elegance that our own ways of thinking are emulated and we are led to greater heights and depths of insight and action (p. 19). As trainers, we must explore multi media with all senses ready and our design knowledge base well-tuned.

Here are several examples of CD-ROM, Interactive Video Disc, and Virtual Environments; as with all previous long drives to the west, the jury is still out on the validity of the land claims and the quality of the gold!:

CD-ROM—CD-ROM is a technology featuring compact discs with read-only-memory that hold video clips, sound, and text. At present, they require specialized players to allow browsers to search through the information contained on them. They play through either a computer screen or a television screen.

The Smithsonian Institution is captured on a Philips Interactive system which encourages the user to select which corridor in the museum and then which displays he or she wants to view. Encyclopedias and college archives are conveniently stored and accessed in CD-ROM systems. CD-ROM discs are relatively inexpensive to reproduce and have the advantage of being able to store massive amounts of data—more than 600 MB by today's estimates according to *Training* magazine[8] (p. 6). It should be recognized and appreciated for what it is, an excellent storage device that can provide information to support learning.

Interactive Video Disc (IVD)—IVD is an optical disc technology that is capable of high quality audio, graphics, and full motion video and the interactivity of computer-based instruction. All information on videodisc is randomly accessible, with search times of 3 seconds or less.

A 1984 study by IBM showed that IVD training was three times more effective than an instructor, and that IVD was capable of simulations that effectively took the place of hands-on practice and testing, making truly individualized instruction possible.[9] Forward-looking companies in human resources development like IBM, Ford, Xerox, and Federal Express were early users of IVD. Massachusetts Mutual Insurance Company uses interactive video to train more than 4,000 agents nationwide. Mass Mutual's IVD training programs include such topics as financial design, recruiting and coaching skills, and selling. Results of the IVD program were encouraging: one trainer reported that it saved him 10 hours per week, and agents posted significant increases in commissions during their first year in business.[10] In my mail last week was a catalog of IVD training programs of technical topics such as "Air Compressor Repair," "Pipefitting," and "Instrument Calibration" from the ITC company in Herndon, VA. The technology, marketed as *Activ*™ is described in the front matter of the catalog thus:

> "*Activ*™'s laser disc technology remains the most sophisticated platform available for multimedia applications—preferred above all others because of its ability to capture and permit real-time manipulation of full motion video, and provide high quality, sharp resolution images. Laser disc platforms also incorporate rapid, powerful data storage and retrieval capabilities."

On the same page is a testimonial from a user at Weyerhaeuser Corporation who says, "With traditional classroom training, the more you use it, the more it costs. Interactive multimedia training systems have proved to be a more cost effective training method over time. The more you use them, the less they cost."[11] The federal government agrees: A major study in 1990 by the Institute for Defense Analysis determined that with IVD training, student achievement improved by up to 25 percent, while the time required to reach equivalent levels of achievement was reduced by 31 percent over traditional classroom training in the same subjects.[12] Trainers generally agree that IVD is a good training medium to enhance the learning procedures, equipment maintenance and repair, troubleshooting, and for simulation of high-risk tasks such as those found in medicine, law enforcement, and dangerous plant operations. In addition, Americans love video format: in 1992, Americans rented 3.6 billion videos from stores.[13] IVD capitalizes on this, for training, and for other commercial uses such as interactive video merchandising in direct competition with catalog houses and direct marketers.

Virtual Environments (VE)—Virtual environments are computer programs that simulate the sights, sounds, and feel of imaginary worlds. Computerized head gear, goggles, and gloves work together to make the sensations seem real. Trainees suit themselves up to be trained in virtual environments. The entire virtual environment is conveyed and communicated entirely through computer displays.

Researchers at the NEC Lab outside Tokyo are developing a prototype VE system to train skiers. The "Virtual Reality Check" article in the October 1993 *Technology Review* describes the training process thus:[14]

> "The skier stands on a platform in front of a huge projection screen that shows a simple computer-generated model of a ski slope. While the skier twists and turns down the imaginary slope, two force plates in the platform measure the pressures exerted by each foot and signal the computer to update the screen display accordingly. As the skier holds onto two rigid ski poles fixed to the training platform, a tiny cuff attached to the right index finger measures blood-flow. If the bloodflow is slow and steady, the computer assumes the course is not challenging enough, and makes the slope steeper. If bloodflow is strong and rapid, the computer assumes the skier is nervous and struggling and makes the slope more gentle."

Like the IVD training described above, this VE training is probably rather classic psychomotor skills training, depending on sensory cues and patterning of muscles to achieve success. Another example of VE learning, described in the same *Technology Review* article, is a NASA "planet simulator" in which a user can create a "virtual landscape" on another planet by using data collected by satellite flyby of the planet. Unlike the psychomotor context of the skier training, the planet simulation depends on cognitive skill development and use. Workers designing planet landscapes, no doubt, are monitoring, analyzing, and synthesizing data continuously as they work and collect and access more data; they are probably constantly defining and redefining design problems, solving sub problems, and approaching solutions to problems through many different paths.

Virtual environments are expensive to create and use, and the future of the technology is just beginning. What we know and experience today will certainly be different from the VE that we will know and experience tomorrow.

WORKSHEET 2 - 28

CD-ROM CHECKLIST

Directions: Review this entire worksheet before deciding to choose CD-ROM as an instructional aid.

Reasons for choosing this learning aid

_____ 1. Massive capacity for storage (at least 600MB of data).
_____ 2. Easy to duplicate and distribute widely.
_____ 3. Easy to handle, transport, use.
_____ 4. Your computer is ready to receive it.
_____ 5. Your objectives for learning include the need to branch to numerous reference sources.

Design features that affect learning

_____ 1. CD-ROM greatly increases a learner's access to information.
_____ 2. CD-ROM is easy to use, but requires guidance in why it should be used.
_____ 3. CD-ROM is not a self-teacher; it is primarily an information storage device.
_____ 4. CD-ROM is an excellent medium for informational or awareness training because it can contain and present a great number of informational options and allow the trainee to choose what he or she needs to know.
_____ 5. CD-ROM is easy to distribute in a hurry, so training can be conducted with consistency quickly around the country or world, wherever appropriate hardware is installed.
_____ 6. If CD-ROM is developed with full-motion video, it is very expensive and generally of lesser quality than IVD. CD-ROM is most effective for storage of text and for training applications that are text-dependent.

WORKSHEET 2 - 29

INTERACTIVE VIDEO DISC (IVD) CHECKLIST

Directions: Review this entire worksheet before deciding to choose IVD as an instructional aid.

Reasons for choosing this learning aid

_____ 1. High in entertainment value.

_____ 2. Appeals to and reinforces sight and sound.

_____ 3. Excellent for learning procedures, troubleshooting, technical, and mechanical subjects.

_____ 4. Video format and conventions are familiar and comfortable for trainees.

_____ 5. You have the appropriate equipment to use it.

Design features that affect learning

_____ 1. IVD enables the learner to control pace, content, and approach to problems.

_____ 2. IVD can provide monitoring and feedback continuously reinforcing learning and motivating the trainee to continue.

_____ 3. IVD can present experts describing and explaining their points of view, adding credibility to lessons.

_____ 4. IVD has strong graphic elements that many learners need for cues and to help them establish patterns for understanding or action.

_____ 5. IVD can facilitate continuous improvement in a learner's capacity for self-directed learning.

_____ 6. IVD can contain opportunities for appeal to many learning styles, presenting information simultaneously through words, pictures, animation, charts, sounds.

_____ 7. IVD can contain expert system/intelligent tutorials to evaluate and provide customized remedial exercises.

_____ 8. IVD has great potential for abuse and degeneration into only entertainment.

WORKSHEET 2 - 30

VIRTUAL ENVIRONMENTS (VE) CHECKLIST

Directions: Review this entire worksheet before deciding to choose VE as an instructional aid.

Reasons for choosing this learning aid

_____ 1. Learning objectives can best be met through simulation.
_____ 2. The trainee is comfortable in techno-space; can tolerate the ambiguity of virtual reality and technical aids affixed to one's person.
_____ 3. Your company has plenty of money for this kind of training.
_____ 4. Your company is a research and development organization and open to learning experimentation.
_____ 5. You have the spaces and equipment for creating virtual environments.

Design features that affect learning

_____ 1. The trainee must be mentally able to objectify his or her learning, knowing that learning is occurring in virtual, not actual, reality. Almost real is not real, and some learners cannot make the leap to objectivity.
_____ 2. The medium is exceptional for providing simulation training. Problems involving safety, danger, multiple effects are all handled well in VE training.
_____ 3. Learning objectives must be clearly designed into VE training, otherwise the experience will feel like a video arcade orgy or amusement park ride.
_____ 4. VE training can take a trainee into a total situation involving events, context, tools, evaluation, and remediation all at once.
_____ 5. A learner just getting used to VE training might need extra help from a peer trainer—a real person—to sort out and reflect upon what happened during learning. VE can be an excellent and ultimate medium for peer training.

Endnotes for Chapter 7
Notes 1 through 14

1. *Newsweek*, May 31, 1993, a series of articles in the "society" section around the theme, "Eyes on the Future." Authors contributing were: Bill Powell, Anne Underwood, Seema Nayyar, Charles Fleming, Barbara Kantrowitz, Joshua Cooper Ramo, David Kaplan, Sharon Begley, Jolie Solomon, Patricia King, Ray Sawhill, Jennifer Foote, Michael Meyer, Richard Ernsberger, Jr., pp. 39-50.

2. Steven E. Prokesch, "Mastering Chaos at the High-Tech Frontier," in *Harvard Business Review*, November-December 1993, pp. 135-144.

3. Herb Brody, "Video Games That Teach?," in *Technology Review*, November-December 1993, pp. 50-57.

4. Richard Dalton, "Shades of Gray Matter," in *Information Week*, November 15, 1993, p. 104.

5. Alice LaPlante, "90s Style Brainstorming," in *Forbes ASAP*, October 25, 1993, pp. 44-61.

6. Thomas B. Sheridan and David Zeltzer, "Virtual Reality Check," in *Technology Review*, October 1993, pp. 20-28.

7. Wallace Hannum, *The Application of Emerging Training Technology*. Alexandria, VA: American Society for Training and Development, 1990.

8. LaTresa Pearson, "Is CD-ROM About to Bloom?" in *Presentation Technologies*, a supplement to *Training* magazine, November 1993.

9. Hannum, *op.cit.*, p. 48.

10. *Ibid.*, p. 49.

11. Training catalog, *Interactive Innovations from ITC*, Herndon, VA. Telephone: (800) 638-3757, p. 10.

12. LaTresa Pearson, *op.cit.*, p. 6.

13. *Newsweek*, May 31, 1993, p. 44.

14. *Technology Review*, op.cit., October 1993, p. 28.

SECTION III

EVALUATION OF PEER TRAINING

This is the last major section of this book, a consideration of the function of evaluation in the learning cycle—more precisely, a consideration of evaluation as a critical and connecting element in the design of instruction. A review of the Instructional System Design model for peer training is useful. The ISD figure from Worksheet 2 - 1 is reproduced here to refresh your memory:

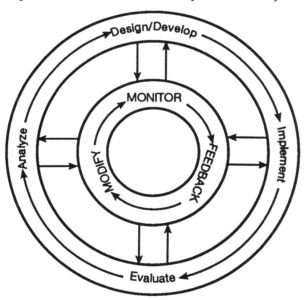

Recall that action in this cycle proceeds from evaluation to analysis, then to design, development, and implementation—and on and on and on, with continuous monitoring, feedback, and modification at every process. This is an active model, a systems model of interacting processes that change and are caused to be changed by effects and purposeful decisions about the effects.

DEFINITIONS OF EVALUATION

Said most simply, evaluation is the process of gathering information in order to make a decision. It is also frequently defined as a systematic search into variables that determine merit or worth. Evaluation seeks to promote understanding and to be a springboard to improvement. An evaluator must be a communicator, a documenter, and a facilitator.

Evaluation is carried out by anyone in an organization who understands the positive, continuous improvement intent of the process. In the evaluation of peer training and learning one by one, a strong component of self-evaluation is essential to validity, accuracy, and utility. Peers can make very good evaluators for each other because of their proximity and accessibility to, and knowledge and trust of, each other.

STANDARDS FOR EVALUATION

Traditional standards for the process of evaluation include:

- Service for a specific, identified audience,
- Useful scope and selection of information to be evaluated,
- Valid information upon which to focus,
- Preparation of the evaluator to ensure informed choices,
- Use of systematic, consistent, clear procedures,
- Control of variables to yield uncontaminated results,
- Communication during all phases of evaluation.

Evaluation is not a silent, negative, sleuthing hunt for deviations from imaginary norms. Standards of performance should be well defined and understood by learner and evaluator, and, in fact, should be developed together. In peer training, of course, this process is direct and effective; in peer training, one half of the pair knows how to do something which the other half of the pair needs to know how to do. Standard-setting in peer training is a non-equivocal endeavor. If jobs and tasks are well-defined, the question of what constitutes good work is obvious to answer. And after evaluation, it is a relatively easy assignment to re-define the analysis to account for standards that haven't been met by training. Thus, the learning cycle continues.

The processes of evaluation requires that "results information" be collected in an organized way, sorted, summarized, synthesized, and verified according to standards. In peer training, these evaluation functions are done *during the process of* instruction, and, in fact, are instrumental in propelling learning forward during training time. That's what the inner circle of the ISD model is all about—it's how the essential results-oriented functions of evaluation are continuously and personally being used to foster learning. The integrated, intimate, continuous characteristics of evaluation during peer training are strong variables that support and recommend peer training as a work process that has the potential for helping to create organizations of individuals who know how to learn from each other.

TYPES OF EVALUATION

When we think of evaluation, we often first think of being tested and given a grade. This limited and fearsome image from our pasts needs to be put into context and updated. School learning a generation ago, and even now to a large extent, has been a "mass production" type of enterprise. Evaluation activities in that setting were mainly driven by norms, and especially by the normal curve under which a statistical number of us were expected to excel and a statistical number of us were expected to fail. The dreaded standardized tests were imposed on our classrooms around the country to see how our schools, and indeed ourselves, stacked up against national norms for our grade level. Our parents got letters about which percentile we "fell into." Our science books and our history books were meant for us to "cover" during the course of a semester or two—that is, our learning took us literally, from cover to cover. And then we had a final exam, and then the dreaded grade for the exam and for the course, and then the even worse news about where we stood in relationship to our peers and to that bell-shaped curve. If we were better than everybody else, everyone hated us; if we were worse, we were ignored. This is the model of evaluation which most of us have experienced and remember. It's probably one of the major reasons why we're having such a hard time as a workforce dealing with the concept of *continuous* anything—continuous progress, continuous process, continuous improvement, continuous quality, continuous learning. The norm-referenced model of evaluation waits until the end of the process of instruction, and then all at once collects the information upon which to make that decision regarding worth.

No wonder we question how this emotionally-shaped, experience-grounded view of evaluation can ever hope to be a process that can help produce "goodness." The truth of the matter is that it can't, and the model must be changed. We need a new definition of what to measure and when to do it. We need a context for evaluation that suggests "making better," "building," and "creating." We need an explanation of a useful process, so that we can begin to comprehend what continuous improvement can mean to the cohesiveness and strength of a workforce.

Earlier admonitions in this book to consider errors as your friends in the relentless search for quality in all work processes and products are worth repeating here. Look again at the inner circle of the ISD cycle for peer training. Monitor, feedback, and modify are all actions focused on making something better as it *continues* to occur. All of the quality improvement theories depend upon building quality into work as it is being done, of finding and fixing small problems and errors before they become big ones; study after study in major corporations shows in dollars and cents terms how inspecting quality in during development is a far better business practice than inspecting it out at the end. The obstacle to our comprehension and ultimate embrace of this idea is our troublesome norm-referenced gut-level remembrance of evaluation in schools. It's time we replaced those images from our childhood with something more useful in our collective adult memory.

One of the reasons why peer training has such promise for facilitating the learning organization is that the feeling that "we're all in this together" which peers tend to share can help support a new kind of evaluation that is continuous and is naturally focused on the small things that colleagues—buddies, partners—can fix because they're so close to them. The emotional, "affective" hooks into learning through structured, intentional, peer training can be forceful propellants into a continuous improvement/continuous learning way of doing business. The focused relationship of peers to *their work*—and not necessarily to the politics of their company's standing in relationship to global norms or last year's annual report—is the clue to effectively finding and fixing those errors, driving out fear, and making continuous progress. In peer training, there's the added advantage of communication and reinforcement—double the attention, double the experience, double the wisdom.

There is a name for this alternative kind of evaluation, and a body of literature out there for review and discussion. Instead of norm-referenced, this way of approaching the process of evaluation is criterion-referenced. It is what we've been talking about throughout this book and throughout the instructional design cycle. It's the system of making judgments basd on standards, objectives, and definition of individuals' needs to know. It is related to the kind of constructionist learning that is built from the bottom up, from having mastered elementary tasks before tackling more advanced ones. It is evaluation that is focused on many variables teased out of the nature of work itself by the persons who know the work best. Criterion-referenced evaluation makes judgments about progress toward goals, most of them small. Criterion-referenced evaluation yields a number which represents proximity to the standard, and also which, as a by-product, identifies specifically which error must be fixed and how it should be approached. It is convergent thinking which systematically zeros in on what can be changed; it requires well-tuned skills of analysis which then expand into the needs assessment phase of the instructional design cycle. Small is definitely beautiful in criterion-referenced evaluation. It is a paradigm shift from norm-referenced evaluation.

OBJECTS OF EVALUATION

Part of understanding this shift in evaluation thinking is an expansion of your idea of the object(s) of evaluation. The old model simply evaluated people—made a judgment about the worth of a person—and filled schools and dinner tables on report card day with fear and trembling. The new model has a long list of objects of evaluation; here are just a few:

- cognitive tasks,
- psychomotor tasks,
- affective tasks,
- processes,

- products,
- services,
- designs,
- supports,
- learning materials,
- learning environments.

The point is that in the continuous improvement mindset, each variable is valued and defined in such a way so as to isolate it in order to study it. This isolation of important variables is the key to finding and fixing errors early in development processes—and, of course, that includes the development process of learning.

How one goes about the act of evaluating requires some thought, some preparation, and the mastery of some evaluating skills. Who is an evaluator and what they evaluate also needs some attention prior to embarking upon evaluation processes. And finally, why the evaluation was done in the first place has to be discussed, and how results are to be used must figure into the design for evaluation. These who-what-when-where-why and how questions will be addressed in the last pages of this book.

CHAPTER **8**

EVALUATION OF LEARNING

The goal of the act of teaching is learning, and that's the primary consideration in discussing one of the "objects" of evaluation in peer training. Earlier chapters in this book dealt with the many kinds of things we learn, and how to analyze the things that we do at work into discreet and hierarchical tasks. The analysis function of instructional design, described and discussed previously, is fundamental to the ability of an evaluator to evaluate learning.

Making incremental, small, continuous improvements in work requires that we think of learning, not as an amorphous whole, but rather as a collection of units—different and unique objects—each of which can be evaluated for its rightness—accuracy, completeness, worth, quality, and so forth, according to its own standards. This kind of evaluation must be done as work is done, as new skills are being learned and practiced. This kind of evaluation requires evaluators who communicate, document, and facilitate.

Problem statements and worksheets that follow discuss issues related to evaluators whose task it is to evaluate learning. Pages that follow deal with self-evaluation, peer evaluation, and supervisory evaluation.

EVALUATION OF LEARNING

Self-Evaluation

Problem: As individuals learn to learn, they require at least two basic kinds of evaluation focus as they objectify their own progress toward their learning goals. This is sometimes a tough task—it's not always easy to take charge of one's learning, especially when the passivity of seminar or classroom training has been the mode of training operation for so long, and the specter of the normal curve has driven most of us into a "cover up" mentality. Self-evaluation requires self-disclosure—out of the closet and into the daylight; no more sweeping it under the rug; hiding it in the back of the bottom drawer. Errors are your friends, remember.

There are two kinds of self-evaluation, one, the task/product/content-based evaluation directly related to *what* one does at work; and two, the process-based evaluation related to *how* and *why* action is directed. Self-directed learners, and those learning to be self-directed learners, must create for themselves a systematic evaluation process—perhaps even using data collection and documentation forms—that can address these two dimensions of their work efforts. That's the problem: it's difficult, feels strange at first, and requires a willingness to face oneself honestly. It requires breaking old habits of blaming someone else, and establishing new habits of being responsible for one's own learning.

Plan of action: There is some help out there from companies that have been encouraging training one by one and the self-directed learning spin-off from it, and from researchers who have been analyzing the factors involved in self-learning and self-evaluation.

First, the self-evaluation of learning tasks: Worksheet 3 - 1, SELF-EVALUA-TION TASK RECORD, following, is one kind of documentation form that could be used. Various training companies have structured on-the-job training materials which can be purchased "off the shelf" and adapted for use. Industrial sites, factories and assembly operations generally have a wealth of diagnostic and evaluation materials available to them from training publishers.[1] These instruments and forms are based on an analysis of the tasks which comprise standard technical, scientific, or procedural jobs. In most cases, the generic job analysis and task lists are applicable as a foundation from which to customize your own forms. Don't hesitate to adapt the good materials available commercially or from the Federal government.

Remember, of course, that the purpose of self-evaluation is to use the results to make improvement in the work that *you* do. Generic off-the-shelf materials can provide guidance, but no one knows your work better than you do. Get a real head start on truly valid self-evaluation materials by developing them yourself. Previous worksheets in Chapter 5 on design methods and Worksheet 1 - 24 on training standards can also provide some guidance.

Another place to look for guidance regarding self-evaluation of task-based learning is to the acknowledged experts in their field—those persons who have excelled at work similar to yours. In a systematic way, ask them to do a self-evaluation of the way they do their work to identify for you the critical things they do that, if you did them too, would make improvements to work. Use these "SME tasks" as a basis for your own standard setting and self-evaluation. Worksheet 3 - 2, SME's SELF-EVALUATION FORM, suggests an approach.

Second, self-directed learners must focus on evaluation of the processes that make their work valuable. Tasks are a bit easier to deal with; most people don't pay much attention to quality in the way things are done. At issue here is the fast-approaching time when most work will be "knowledge work" and will not result in "products" that are more easily defined in terms of the tasks that must be mastered to produce tangible output. Knowledge work must be concerned with process quality, process standards, and self-evaluation of knowledge workers in order to find and fix errors in the how and the why of work. Knowing yourself is the first step in being able to articulate to yourself how and why it is that you must do better in order to continuously improve your work. Worksheet 3 - 3, KNOW YOURSELF QUIZ, is one kind of structured form to document your own understanding of yourself as a worker.

Finally, a self-directed learner can be helped greatly during self-evaluation by having a personalized learning plan on which to base judgments about his or her progress through a learning enterprise. Keeping your own timetable or action plan handy where you can refer to it often to keep on target is a good idea. It allows you to monitor not only your learning but also your self-management as you engage in the various processes necessary for support of learning. Worksheet 3 - 4 suggests a flowchart format, the INDIVIDUAL LEARNING PLAN FLOWCHART.

Examples: The first example that illustrates an organization's interest in tasks appropriate for self-evaluation is the New York State Board of Cooperative Education Services (BOCES), a high school and post-high school educational consortium funded primarily by Federal vocational education funding. In its heyday in the early 1980s, BOCES in conjunction with the Federal CETA legislation and funding created vocational Assessment Centers throughout the state. The following list comes from a BOCES-CETA publication at that time. It is a list of "work factors and worker characteristics" that the developers believe are "specific" to some work samples and not to others, meaning that it is these factors that can account for quality in work or stand-out performance on the part of any individual that demonstrates competency in them. In the language of test design, these are the factors that account for individual differences, or discriminate among learners. Achievement of standards of performance in tasks delineated within each of these factors would probably identify superior performers. These factors would make a good starting point for development of a self-evaluation checklist or task record.

color discrimination	following written instructions
counting ability	form perception
eye-hand-foot coordination	motor coordination
finger dexterity	manual dexterity
following diagrammatic instructions	measuring ability
following a model	numerical ability

These high performance factors are defined thus:

Color discrimination: The ability to perceive or recognize similarities or differences in colors, or in shades or other values of the same color; to identify a particular color, or to recognize harmonious or contrasting color combinations, or to match colors accurately.

Counting ability: The ability to correctly recognize and/or name numbers in sequence.

Eye-hand-foot coordination: The ability to coordinate simultaneous movements of the eyes, hands, and feet rapidly and accurately.

Finger dexterity: The ability to move the fingers and manipulate small objects with the fingers rapidly and accurately.

Following diagrammatic instructions: The ability to comprehend and effectively utilize a drawing or a sketch.

Following a model: The ability to effectively utilize a demonstrated sample made by the evaluator.

Following written instructions: The ability to comprehend and effectively utilize written materials at a minimal reading level.

Form perception: The ability to perceive pertinent detail in objects or in pictorial or graphic material; to make visual comparisons and discriminations and see slight differences in shapes and shadings of figures and widths and lengths of lines.

Motor coordination: The ability to coordinate eyes and hands or fingers rapidly and accurately making precise movements with speed.

Manual dexterity: The ability to move the hands easily and skillfully; to work with the hands in placing and turning motions.

Measuring ability: The ability to utilize a ruler to accurately determine the length of specific distances and/or objects.

Numerical ability: The ability to perform arithmetic operations rapidly and accurately.

"Learning from experience" is a phrase that has been around for a long time. But just what does this mean in terms of self-evaluation? Surely it must be related to the notion of continuous improvement; surely there must be a way to systematize or "intentionalize" the individual worker's ability to do just this. The bad news is that we typically have paid very little attention to learning from experience—in spite of John Dewey and W. Edwards Deming—and so have missed countless opportunities to learn and to become better learners. The good news is that help is beginning to show up in the form of materials developed recently in response to pleas from corporate America and government alike for us to organize ourselves into "learning organizations."

One such source of materials to help individuals learn from their experience is a periodic flyer mailed to a large mailing list of trainers, human resources development, and organization development practitioners called the *HRD Quarterly*. It is usually full of various inventories, surveys, and questionnaires which can be purchased singly or in quantity. For at least a decade since the renewed interest in adult learning following the important work of Malcolm Knowles in the 1970s, it has been the source of numerous materials on learning, teaching, and management styles. A recent issue contains the description of a "Learning Diagnostic Questionnaire" and accompanying workbook, "Capitalizing on Your Learning Opportunities." These pieces, and others similar to them, talk about aspects of learning such as:

- "converting accidental learning to integrated learning activities,
- factors influencing learning in the organization,
- attitudinal and emotional influences on learning,
- the skills of learning, and
- how to find help in the organization."

These and other materials from this source can be used in groups or by individuals interested in self-evaluation.[2]

These kinds of process skills are often the ones that make the critical difference between adequate and extraordinary performance. When we involve subject matter experts (SMEs) in job and task analysis for the purpose of capturing their special know-how, we often focus especially on the specificity and depth of their process skills. If you are an SME, by all means help others in your organization who are not by doing a focused self-evaluation of not only the content-related skills that make you outstanding but also of the process skills which you do differently from the simply adequate performers. Worksheet 3 - 2 can give you some ideas about how to go about doing this. The following process-related tasks are some that vocational researchers have deemed important tasks in which expert behavior can be demonstrated:

elaboration skill	illustration skill
expansive thinking	summarizing skill
ability to infer	symbolic representation
memorization and recall	translating
organization	visualizing

The important work of J.P. Guilford, referenced earlier, regarding the "structure of intellect," suggests that there are six major "products" of ways of thinking. That is, the processes by which we think (remember, solve problems, focus in on things, expand with metaphors, etc.) act upon certain elements of content and result in one or more of these six products of our thinking. These six are "units, classes, relations, systems, transformations, and implications."[3] Intelligence researchers from Alfred Binet at the turn of the 19th century to present-day academics such as John B.Carroll at North Carolina (Chapel Hill), Robert Sternberg at Yale, and Howard Gardner at Harvard have tried to determine the factors or components of mind whose *exercise* makes a difference in terms of the quality of a person's performance. We believe that there is such a thing as process quality, and we try to identify its critical tasks by talking with SMEs and learning from our experience.

My own work at several times during my career was directly involved with instructional design based on work with subject matter experts. At Combustion Engineering (now part of Asea Brown Boveri, an international energy corporation), one of my projects in the mid-1980s was to develop an expert system in learner evaluation in simulation training. The computer's enormous capacity for remembering, storing, branching, accessing, and giving feedback—all in split seconds—was going to be harnessed for use in an elaborate corporate training system, of which evaluation was a key component. My work with a corporate team from around the country involved a heavy-duty intellectual relationship with our "SME" simulation training instructor and several SME software engineers.

My job was fascinating; our knowledge engineering sessions using expert system authoring software taught us all a great deal about what made expert instructional behavior, and, in turn, what intentional, instructional factors helped learners to continue to learn. We found out which learner evaluation strategies were related to outstanding learner performance. My doctoral research included studies of SMEs in auto mechanics and accounting, and in using the computer for factor analysis of achievement tests to isolate and capture cognitive elements that made a difference to outstanding performance; my later work at AT&T Bell Laboratories included work with UNIX and C-Language SMEs. SMEs are found everywhere: in hotel maintenance departments, in retail establishments, in hospitals, in brokerage houses, at drafting tables, in schools, in police departments, in kitchens. We know them when we experience the effects of their work, and we are grateful for their *doing* what they do in the way that they do it. Working with SMEs in a systematic way can be a great boon to self-evaluation. If you are not an SME, be sure to find someone who is and get to know his or her approach to the process skills of the job; if you are an SME, by all means allow others to learn from your experience at work.

A final word needs to be said about one more area of personal competency that can be a critical area of investigation during self-evaluation of learning, and that is the area of self-esteem or "self-concept." Interest in structured adult education, continuing education, and self-directed learning in the 1980s, worldwide, sparked an interest and numerous studies in the United States and particularly in Australia in the area of self-esteem. Researchers noted that high performers often had a higher measure of moral and emotional autonomy about themselves, and were thus able to be innovative, take risks regarding learning challenges, and persevere. Philip Candy, of Queensland University of Technology in Brisbane, says it this way:

> ". . . arguably the most important yet most elusive aspect (is) the development of a sense of personal control or of 'learning competence.' . . . In order to behave autonomously in a learning situation, a person requires not merely intellectual but also moral and emotional autonomy. This involves a robust self-concept, along with a strong sense of purpose and an emerging commitment to the value of the learning experience. It is in this domain, perhaps more than any other, that attempts to enhance self-direction in learning 'spill over' into attempts to enhance self-determination more generally."[4]

The Rev. Martin Luther King, Jr. said it this way: "One day we will learn that the heart can never be totally right if the head is totally wrong. Only through the bringing together of head and heart—intelligence and goodness—shall man rise to a fulfillment of his true nature."[5] Self-determination, self-direction, self-learning, self-evaluation—all require comfort with the practice of monitoring oneself for those elements of both "head and heart." This too requires individuals at work to practice in a systematic, purposeful way. "Knowing thyself"—as Shakespeare and numerous other sages have said—is of utmost importance in love, in warfare, in work, in one's performance in living. As part of self-evaluation, develop some kinds of personal skills, "skills of the heart" inventory, which you monitor yourself on a regular basis, such as at the end of each week, month, or quarter. Develop your own "5 Year Strategic Plan" for personal "goodness" development. Realize that content, process, and self-esteem are integrally related in superior performers. Help yourself to an integrated approach to life by systematically paying attention to continuous improvement in all three areas. Something like Worksheet 3 - 3, KNOW YOURSELF QUIZ, can get you started.

In addition, you might find it useful to map your learning needs for the next week, month, or year on a flowchart or other graphic display and documentation device. I have personally seen this done: a new training manager at the Torrington Company, a division of Ingersoll Rand, had his own personal "quality training" program mapped onto four pages of an interconnecting flowchart taped to the side of his office lateral file. A colleague at AT&T, the director of a large operation, had a "war room"—a whole room full of strategy charts and results charts for individuals in his organization. A person monitored *the charts*, and notified individuals when they should be updated, just in case they forgot (which they didn't often do). The war room became a lively place for individuals to monitor themselves and each other. A friend of mine is famous for her "10 year plans" which have successfully taken her through career change, major investments, business partnerships, and middle age! The graphic nature and systematic structure of a visual display or planning device can be a great tool for self-monitoring.

An example of this is found in the October 1990 issue of ASTD's *Technical & Skills Training* magazine[6]; Worksheet 3 - 4, following, is based on the concept described in the magazine article. The article, "Individualized Literacy Improvement: A Case Study in Success" was written by two management employees at the US Department of Agriculture in Washington, DC. It includes a flowchart of an individual learner's intended progress through literacy training, from "pre-assessment" actions and "counseling" to various kinds of selection options which the trainee controls. Like apprentice training which tends to be skill based and personalized, this kind of training can be readily charted to help the learner see his or her "place in the program." The graphics can help a learner feel in charge.

SELF-EVALUATION TASK RECORD

Directions: This form is an example of one way to establish the habit of self-evaluation regarding specific tasks of your job, especially of new tasks you are trying to learn or of tasks that can improve your present way of doing things. Use a stack of these forms to record your efforts in many different tasks. Use one form per task. The discipline of recording your "time on task" will guide your progress. The goal is to accomplish the task well in only as much time as is necessary, and without help. This is a record of your learning a task for use in your job. A completed sample is included on the next page.

Identification of the task to be learned: _____

_____

date	practice time	with help	without help	self-evaluation of mastery level (high) 5 4 3 2 1 (low)

Notes/comments: _____

_____

_____

WORKSHEET 3 - 1 (SAMPLE)
SELF-EVALUATION TASK RECORD

Identification of the task to be learned: *learn the accusative case personal pronouns in German by next Wednesday*

date	practice time	with help	without help	self-evaluation of mastery level (high) 5 4 3 2 1 (low)
12/8	noon-1:45 p.m.		X	2 (they all sound alike)
12/10	7 - 9 p.m.		X	2 (drawing a chart helps)
12/11	10:30-11 p.m.	X		2+ (used partner's chart too)
12/13	7-8 a.m.	X		3 (used tapes: listening helps)

Notes/comments: *I think I like learning aids to learn a new skill like this—they seem to give me more confidence*

WORKSHEET 3 - 2

SME'S SELF-EVALUATION

Directions: Use this form to get ideas about what the subject matter expert (SME) does and the factors that affect how well the job is done. The SME is not a self-proclaimed expert; he or she has earned the designation by the acclaim or judgment of colleagues. The SME has demonstrated consistently high performance over time, shown an adoption of—not just an appreciation for—job standards or task requirements, and has usually had a positive impact on the work of others and the profit profile or prestige of the company. SMEs sometimes need help in sharing what they know and can do. Systematizing the self-evaluation process can help.

Have the SME complete the form by first listing 10 - 20 critical tasks of doing this job; then complete the matrix by checking the boxes appropriate to the kinds of training required to accomplish each task. Add other factors across the top of the matrix as appropriate.

Critical Tasks	Creativity	Math/Number Facility	Memorization/Recall	Muscle Coordination	Oral/Verbal Expression	Organization	Reasoning	Speed	Teamwork	Written Expression	
	Kinds of Training Needed										
1.											
2.											
3.											
4.											
5.											
6.											

Matrix was originally published in *Training Program Workbook & Kit* by Carolyn Nilson, Englewood Cliffs, NJ: Prentice Hall, 1989, pp. 41 and 43.

SME'S SELF-EVALUATION

Job of programmer

Critical Tasks	Creativity	Math/Number Facility	Memorization/Recall	Muscle Coordination	Oral/Verbal Expression	Organization	Reasoning	Speed	Teamwork	Written Expression
	Kinds of Training Needed									
1. choose the precisely appropriate language for the job	✓	✓	✓			✓				✓
2. flowchart the program to establish logic, although it takes time					✓		✓	✓		✓
3. maintain regular, periodic personal contact with originator of the request for program					✓				✓	
4. seek regular periodic review of code, especially at decision points					✓		✓		✓	
5. verify system specs with peers and management as parts of the program are finished					✓		✓		✓	✓
6. analyze all expressions for clarity, leanness, and sufficiency	✓	✓				✓	✓			✓
7. construct a spare program	✓	✓				✓	✓	✓		✓
8. produce code sheets that are clean and neat										✓
9. pre-test completed sections before system test						✓	✓			

Matrix was originally published in *Training Program Workbook & Kit* by Carolyn Nilson, Englewood Cliffs, NJ: Prentice Hall, 1989, pp. 41 and 43.

WORKSHEET 3 - 3

KNOW YOURSELF QUIZ

Directions: As you enter a period of learning, growth, or change, take stock of your personal work characteristics. The simple act of facing yourself with these simple twenty questions (and others you might add) can help you to become a better learner by focusing your attention on the behaviors and things you value. Effective lifelong learners are integrated personalities—with knowledge, skills, and attitudes in alignment, individuals who pay attention to tasks, content, processes and approaches, and beliefs and ethical behavior.

Date: _____ The defined challenge: _____

		Comments
1. What results do I want?	1.	
2. How much recognition do I need?	2.	
3. How much energy do I have?	3.	
4. What factors release my energy?	4.	
5. How does working environment affect me?	5.	
6. Do I work best alone or in groups?	6.	
7. How do I respond to criticism?	7.	
8. What do I do to turn others off?	8.	
9. Am I a good listener?	9.	
10. Do I work slowly or quickly?	10.	
11. Do I like to learn?	11.	
12. What is my best learning style?	12.	
13. What do I value on the job?	13.	
14. Can I give and receive feedback?	14.	
15. Do I like to compete?	15.	
16. Why should the company value me?	16.	
17. What are my personal goals?	17.	
18. Do I prefer to lead or be led?	18.	
19. What are my weaknesses?	19.	
20. What are my strengths?	20.	

This checklist was first published in *Training Program Workbook & Kit* by Carolyn Nilson, Englewood Cliffs, NJ: Prentice Hall, 1989, p. 51.

WORKSHEET 3 - 4

INDIVIDUAL LEARNING PLAN FLOWCHART

Directions: Use this type of graphic as a reminder to yourself about your learning plan. Such a plan can cover a specified period of time (e.g., over the next year, next 3 months, next month, etc.) or a specific new complex job (e.g., learn to sell real estate, become a registered nurse, or work the hotel's front desk). Often a graphic will be a strong incentive and reminder to periodically evaluate one's progress through the boxes on the chart. Adapt the chart to your own learning plan.

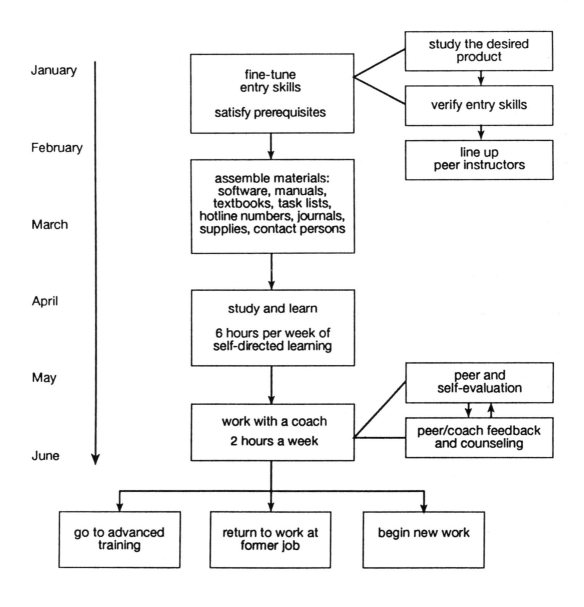

EVALUATION OF LEARNING

Peer Evaluation

Problem: There are two typical problems when peers evaluate peers. One is that they are uncomfortable making a judgment about the "goodness" of another person's learning—probably a discomfort arising out of an old negative association with getting the report card in high school. The other problem is that people at work typically have no experience with evaluation techniques, and they need to learn how to do effective evaluations.

Solving the first problem with peer evaluation is usually harder than solving the second one because there are both subtle and overt changes that must be made in the working environment/culture for a comfort level about peer evaluation to be established. The issue of time, which we discussed previously in this book, is the major issue: how the company culture values time is the first issue to be dealt with if peer training is to be successful. Seeing people teaching and learning on the job should look and feel right to any observer—co-worker, supervisor, CEO, stockholder, visitor. Training time must be seen and accounted for *not* as time away from the job.

Having said this, the objective of these next few pages is to suggest some ways in which peers can evaluate peers with comfort and competence, knowing that their learning is their work. Mastering a few essential training evaluation techniques to be practiced one by one to improve performance is not as hard as one might think.

Plan of action: Standardizing the documentation process can be one way to help peer trainers/evaluators to feel more comfortable about doing evaluation. Developing forms for monitoring, feedback, and reporting evaluative results is the first step. There is no great mystery to this; the forms themselves should meet these minimum standards:

1. Based on tasks of the job
2. Based on important, that is, non-trivial, tasks of the job
3. Include criteria or standards for the content of the task
4. Include criteria or standards for the processes required for good work
5. Include a place for written comments by either trainer or trainee
6. Be easy to use (cue lists, checklists, charts, etc.)
7. Be agreed on by everyone involved in the use of the form
8. Be available to trainer and trainee at all times.

Using the forms consistently and systematically is the next step.

Learning to use the techniques of peer evaluation will probably require some practice with feedback in a role play situation before peer evaluation begins. This should be an essential part of a peer training train-the-trainer program. These are some of the considerations regarding techniques of evaluation:

- Peer evaluation is a critical part of instruction
- It should be conceptualized as an element within a teaching/learning loop
- It is "in-process" evaluation, not end-of-process evaluation
- Its purpose is to make decisions that contribute to improvement.

Worksheets 3 - 5, 3 - 6, and 3 - 7 provide guidance regarding several evaluation techniques and are the kinds of forms that can be used during evaluation. However, before thinking too specifically about the design of forms, here are some general considerations about the approach to peer training. These ideas should frame your plan of action.

Trainer and trainee should focus "deeply" on the task at hand, searching for meaning inherent in the work itself at its smallest levels; always ask 'why?' in addition to 'what?' Trainer and trainee should develop an appreciation for the act of learning; learning should be seen as growth and personal development, continuous and cumulative, not simply as something that must be done in order to climb some arbitrary success ladder or get some grade. Try to relate what's new to something in the past experience of both trainer and trainee; the effects of evaluation mean more in the context of workers' experiences. Building the future almost always is enriched by a consideration of the joys and sorrows of the past. Try to always see the parts in relationship to the whole; see the whole in each of its parts. Peers are generally very good at helping each other achieve integration and alignment; in these endeavors, two heads are definitely better than one!

Keep in mind that peer evaluation should always be tightly connected to instruction. Peer evaluation ("that's good, that's bad, that's almost right, think of it this way instead") is best done at the time the trainee takes action. The feedback idea is closest to what the act of peer evaluation should be. Evaluation should happen every few minutes during training, as a way to help the trainee make a decision about improving his or her work. If you think of evaluation as many small acts of intervention to help the trainee to continue to learn, you'll be on the right beam. Giving the trainee a cue is one small type of evaluative action: by giving a cue, you are also fundamentally saying something evaluative, such as 'no, that's not the best approach—go down a different path, like this one . . .' Reinforcing a good action or a brilliant deduction with an exclamatory 'Terrific!' is also an evaluative—in-process—judgment that can help a trainee keep doing that wonderful thing he or she just did or said. Leading a trainee into a hands-on involvement with a learning task, such as helping/guiding the trainee in filling out a form correctly or assembling some parts into a working whole can be a teaching action that is grounded in formative evaluation. Working side by side with a learner and then trusting that learner to continue doing the task correctly is an evaluative act. Knowing when to back off is an evaluative judgment. It bears repeating to note that:

- giving cues,
- reinforcing good action or judgment, and
- leading hands-on

are three ways to be a better peer evaluator. Just as learning itself is a constructionist process, so is evaluation. They must be part of an integrated, purposeful, meaningful work. Continuous improvement is the probable outcome of this kind of work.

Some other spinoff techniques involved in effective peer evaluation include:

- *Tell the trainee why* something was wrong or inadequate. Never make an evaluative judgment that doesn't also suggest an avenue to improvement.
- *Listen a lot;* don't talk too much. Evaluation is an interactive process; this is one major reason why peer evaluation holds so much promise as part of the new learning cycle. Instruction that is "information dumping" seldom works; evaluation that follows the same emotional model of the "all-knowing one" dispensing wisdom and judgment never works either. Evaluation one by one, up close and personal, has great potential to truly improve learning and work. It is as close to work as is possible, it is efficient, it is done within an atmosphere of collegiality and trust, and it is constructed bit by bit and 'entered' into the memory bank of experience. Think more of guiding, facilitating, and monitoring a trainee's action—making evaluative comments *in response to* the trainee, not in front of or at the trainee.
- *Use logical or procedural aids.* Follow checklists, outlines, procedures, steps so that both you and the trainee focus together on what's right. Use these evaluation aids (they are not just teaching aids) to de-personalize the standards piece of evaluation. In this way, the act of evaluation doesn't degenerate into 'he said/she said' type of dialogue. It's not one person's opinion against another's; it's behavior in approximation of the standard.
- *Show the trainee the standards;* evaluation should never be a surprise. In fact, get agreement from the trainee regarding what the standards should be, and help the trainee reach or surpass them.
- *Use 'big picture' approaches and 'rules of thumb'* in addition to task-related detailed approaches to instruction and to evaluation. Your experience as a worker is invaluable to the trainee at this level of generality. This

is often overlooked in the desire to be thorough in coverage of the specifics.

- *Monitor your own performance as an evaluator.* Guard against a "holier than thou" attitude; realize that you're both in this together. Guard against being too social; guard against just doing the work and not concentrating on the evaluation tasks of giving cues, giving reinforcement, and leading the trainee into the exercise of new skills. Evaluation requires interaction of a specialized sort; check yourself from time to time to be sure that you are acting this way and not some other way.

- *Give the trainee a chance to evaluate the learning too.* Remember again and again and again that evaluation, like instruction, is interactive. If you are going to be a peer pair for weeks or months, you will certainly benefit from knowing as much about the trainee's learning preferences as you can. You'll be a better evaluator if you understand and can evaluate to the trainee's preferred way of learning (e.g., visual, tactile, graphic, verbal, procedural, holistic, seeing means and ends, etc.) Talk about learning with your trainee, not just about the content of the job.

Examples: Last year, I did some field research prior to publishing the book, *How To Start A Training Program in Your Growing Business* (New York: Amacom, 1992). One of the small companies I visited was Sterling Engineering, a family-owned-and-operated defense industry subcontractor in northwestern Connecticut. As the CEO walked me through the factory, I was struck by the number of informal "bunches" of people gathered around some piece of equipment or computer display or huddled over a manual or spec sheet. These people were engaged in peer training and peer evaluation as an integrated function of working. This was teaching and learning on the job; and this pervasive practice was probably one of the major reasons that this small, job-shop, high-end engineering company has been able to stay in business since the early 1940s in a business that has never been all that predictable.

These small learning groups were not casual, nor were they social. They were highly focused on the tasks at hand and highly interactive among peers. My host and I were hardly noticed as we walked through the factory, the workers were so intent on their work. It was explained to me that at Sterling Engineering, everybody was expected to be a learner; in fact, the employee manual specifically stated that it was the employee's job "to pay attention." Training was delivered just-in-time, an operational principle that seems to fit well with the nature of the business.

At the other end of the range of businesses is the large factory for car and truck manufacture. Sterling Engineering's 150 employee base is contrasted with Subaru-Isuzu Automotive (SIA) Inc.'s 2000 employee base; Sterling Engineering sits on an acre or two of land in the Northeast; SIA, on 55 acres in the Midwest. Sterling Engineering is constantly faced with having to practice strategies for longevity; Subaru-Isuzu is looking for ways to survive the heady start-up times associated with global joint-venturing. An article in *Technical & Skills*, October 1991, describes SIA's choice and development of "on-the-job training" with an essential peer training and evaluation component as the key to its complicated maintenance training for the start up of such a sprawling technical enterprise.[7] Both companies have made the same choice.

The article presents a clear picture of the major decisions human resources managers had to make regarding how to train a maintenance workforce faced with a huge amount of new and different equipment and numerous facilities with varying maintenance requirements. Maintenance training in this kind of situation can be a nightmare.

Among the spinoffs from designing a peer and self-training program, on-the-job, were these: as a result of the job and task analysis and design activity, SIA found that there were many similarities among the pieces of equipment; there were similarities in usage, maintenance, and troubleshooting of systems that, at first glance, seemed different. Discovering these similarities and designing training around the similarities saved training time, and focusing the training exercises on the critical differences encouraged a deeper understanding of each unique equipment situation or configuration. The HRD folks at SIA computerized the data base of critical skills, using structured questions for subject matter expert (SME) design involvement. Self-training and peer training using the task lists and process requirements out of the data base allowed training to be flexible and accessible when it was needed. Instructor's guides and an "OJT Guide and Record" documentation manual were created to help the teachers and the learners to stay on the right target. Doing the right thing right was the goal. Each OJT trainee's guide had a place for the designated trainer (the "authorized person") to sign off on a particular task or process. Worksheet 3 - 6 contains some of the elements of the Subaru-Isuzu Automotive Inc. documentation form. Clearly, in this system of training, evaluation is a necessary and structured function within the learning system.

And finally, here's an example of how peer evaluation works in a non-manufacturing endeavor. IBM for years used an evaluation system for software development that makes use of in-process "reviews" and "inspections" and "walkthroughs" of finished sections of products before panels of peers. AT&T Bell Laboratories adapted this in-process peer review, inspection, and walkthrough for use in creating new courses.[8] Software development and course development are "soft" endeavors, as contrasted with the "hard" work of machining and engineering parts for defense and space equipment or manufacturing trucks and cars. That the structured peer evaluation model can serve progress in both kinds of work is a tribute to the viability of the very simple truth that improved performance does happen one by one and one to one.

One of the most important features of this peer evaluation process of review and inspection is its "structured" format. Peer evaluation meetings are called when products are ready for review or inspection—logical sections of programming code or logical pieces of a course-under-construction. Documentation forms are given to each peer evaluator present at a review or inspection meeting; persons are invited on an ad hoc basis to be evaluators based on their business interest in the product being examined. Evaluation group size and composition varies from meeting to meeting: the examination process is standards-driven, not personality driven.

IBM consultants and authors Freedman and Weinberg, in their book referenced in endnote number 8, on the previous page, *Handbook of Walkthroughs, Inspections, and Technical Reviews,* include a section of samples of the documentation forms used in the work there. Some of the standards against which the software product is evaluated by the peer review team are: reliability, maintainability, availability, cost, portability, security, performance, ease of learning, and market appeal.[9] Each evaluator rates the product on these characteristics, according to some numerical range or quality of goodness, and documents the finding on the form. Errors or problems discovered this way are easily found and fixed before work goes forward. A quotation near the end of the book sums up author Weinberg's point of view: "We do not know through our experience with egoless programming that there is no particular reason why your friend cannot also be your sternest critic" (p. 425). Likewise, the AT&T adaptation of the IBM model has peer evaluators meeting in small ad hoc groups to rate course products on content accuracy, instructional design validity, readability, consistency, and other factors appropriate to the way a course is constructed. Reports from both companies' experiences with structured reviews, inspections, and walkthroughs indicate that errors are definitely caught and fixed earlier in the design and development processes, and that therefore quality is being built into the "soft" products of programming and course development.

The downside is that the process takes time at the front-end of business, and businesses are not used to getting what they perceive as a "slow start." One way to control the time variable somewhat is to limit the length of review meetings, and to distribute materials for review in time for the peer evaluators to look them over in a "big picture" mode prior to coming together for evaluation. Another time-saving strategy is to structure the facilitation of the evaluation meeting with named leaders and recorders; knowing one's facilitation role ahead of time often helps one prepare mentally for it, tending to sharpen one's facilitation skills *at entry to the task* of evaluation. Our old friend, Benjamin Bloom, from the University of Chicago, has important things to say both about the phenomenon of "time on task" and "cognitive entry variables"[10] as key factors that contribute to the learner's "amazing potential for learning" (p. 382). His article on "alterable variables" in the February 1980 *Phi Delta Kappan* magazine is worth digging out of the archives.

WORKSHEET 3 - 5

PEER PAIRS FEEDBACK AND DISCUSSION WORKSHEET

Directions: This worksheet is meant to be used at the end of a peer training session in which one peer must evaluate the other based on his or her observations on the trainee's learning progress during that specific training session. The form is designed as a *discussion worksheet,* and should not be construed as a "test." It works like this: (1) At the start of the training, with the trainee, list up to 10 work-related behaviors that you agree should be observed; (2) Match up these behaviors with lines on the worksheet; (3) At the end of the training session, give the worksheet to the trainee first, and have the trainee rate himself or herself on each behavior according to the 5-point scale, giving a number to each behavioral item; (4) Fold the worksheet vertically on the dotted line so that you can't see the trainee's ratings; (5) As the peer evaluator, now, do a similar rating on each behavior, using the blank half of the worksheet on which to record your evaluations; (6) Open the worksheet so that you see the trainee's self-evaluation and your peer evaluation side by side. Discuss similarities and differences, and use your findings to improve instruction the next time you meet for peer training.

work-related behaviors	rating scale				
	to a very small extent	to a small extent	to some extent	to a great extent	to a very great extent
	1	2	3	4	5

	1 2 3 4 5 |	1 2 3 4 5
1. _____	1. _____ |	1. _____
2. _____	2. _____ |	2. _____
3. _____	3. _____ |	3. _____
4. _____	4. _____ |	4. _____
5. _____	5. _____ |	5. _____
6. _____	6. _____ |	6. _____
7. _____	7. _____ |	7. _____
8. _____	8. _____ |	8. _____
9. _____	9. _____ |	9. _____
10. _____	10. _____ |	10. _____

WORKSHEET 3 - 6

PEER TRAINER'S SIGN-OFF FORM

Directions: This kind of form is very useful in technical training, and has been used for many years by companies who have relied on task lists to guide their training. Similar forms have often been used by "top down" organizations in which "the boss" or supervisor must sign off. Its adaptation for use in peer evaluation is an evolutionary thing: this particular form is for use by peer trainers and evaluators only. Its structured dependence on task analysis makes it an easy form to use, particularly for those new to the role of evaluator. The idea behind this form can be adapted to other kinds of training besides technical training. The form is essentially a listing of specific, small training objectives in a columnar form with a special place for the evaluator's "sign-off" initials and date of sign-off. Using engineering numeration (1.), (1.1), (1.1.1), and so forth, can make formatting the column of objectives easier and clearer.

1.0 LESSON TITLE	SIGN-OFF	DATE
1.1 Objective #1		
1.1.1 Task, part of Objective #1		
1.1.2 Task, part of Objective #1		
1.2 Objective #2		
1.2.1 Task, part of Objective #2		
..... and so forth......		

WORKSHEET 3 - 7

ASKING EVALUATIVE QUESTIONS

Directions: This worksheet is a set of guidelines for asking questions. One of the easiest ways of getting good information upon which to base an evaluation is to use the technique of questioning with some forethought and intention. Both "closed questions" and "open questions" are useful in peer evaluation.

TEN GOOD REASONS FOR USING CLOSED QUESTIONS

1. They tend to be easy to answer.
2. They generally lead to "the facts."
3. There is usually no argument about the answer.
4. They generally do not intimidate.
5. They generally do not confuse.
6. They usually can be answered quickly.
7. They generally yield correct answers.
8. They generally do not need explanation.
9. They help build the respondent's confidence regarding answering questionnaires.
10. Responses to them are generally usable immediately.

FIVE RULES OF THUMB TO HELP YOU GET GOOD INFORMATION DURING OPEN QUESTIONING

1. Keep the questioning and responding going when you are getting good responses—use short, positive words of encouragement at short intervals such as "good," "I appreciate where you're coming from," "yes," "that's a valuable insight," "your comments are excellent."
2. Maintain smiling eye contact during questions and answers—don't let your respondent wander. Your eye contact can help motivate the respondent to keep focused on the question at hand.
3. Don't allow responses to degenerate into gripes. If your respondent begins to lose focus and starts to complain or "dump" on you, gently bring the respondent back on tack by asking him or her to "define that a little better," or to "explain that more, please." Use the terms "define" and "explain" to focus attention on a specific subject, thereby helping the respondent elaborate rather than digress into a gripe.
4. Keep your opinions to yourself. Don't be tempted to indicate agreement or disagreement with your respondent. Your role is to encourage the respondent's free response—be careful not to jeopardize this.
5. Verify any response that seems different or potentially controversial. Read it back to the respondent and say, "Do I have this response recorded correctly?"

These guidelines were first published in *Training Program Workbook & Kit,* by Carolyn Nilson, Englewood Cliffs, NJ: Prentice Hall, 1989, pages 34 and 38.

EVALUATION OF LEARNING

Supervisory Evaluation

Problem: While the major responsibility for evaluation in peer training belongs to peers who are part of the training program, supervisors will want to and should have some responsibility in the evaluation of learning. As long as there are supervisors, their roles in evaluation must be defined and implemented so that all types of on-going evaluation are complementary.

Supervisors generally play a major role in the motivation aspect of training: they are close to those whom they supervise in terms of knowing the reasons people work, what turns them on to work, and what their career goals are. Supervisors have had a traditional part to play regarding a worker's pay and continued employ in the company. Supervisors have traditionally had decision-making responsibility over workers' incentives, punishments, social rewards, and recognition connected with the work that workers do. Supervisors have traditionally been charged with providing the tools and organizational supports, the data and the schedules, to enable good work to occur.

While these traditional supervisory functions don't seem very directly involved with the nature of an employee's learning, they are nevertheless instrumental in facilitating learning. The trick for supervisors is to restrict their evaluative efforts to the supports framework, and leave the evaluation that derives from the tasks of the work itself to the front-line peer. It behooves the supervisor to clearly differentiate the learning-focused evaluation that leads to further learning from the kinds of work environment evaluative decision-making that also plays a part in an organization's ability to become a learning organization. The supervisor's problem in an organization of teachers and learners is to maintain the proper distance yet at the same time be very near at hand with organizational supports for learning.

Plan of action: Probably the best help a supervisor can give an employee is to know him or her so well that meaningful—"learningful"—discussions and plans regarding career development can be implemented. Improved performance can and must be facilitated by supervisors, and to be most effective and long-lasting, it should be facilitated one by one. The increasingly more narrow, uniquely defined work of many people, the increasing diversity of the workforce, the increasing specialization of tools and work environments all lead to a tremendous need for persons' supervisors to really get to know them at the "learning needs" level.

This is most often done through management by wandering around, active listening, and a set of well-designed personnel forms for skills analysis, self-analysis, peer review, and career path planning. Supervisors who don't have these things in place should get busy. Time is changing, and old verities are being questioned from all quarters. Supervisors generally know what makes good workers, and their scope of the workplace is necessarily broader than the peer trainer's view. Supervisors stand in a good position to evaluate the environmental/organizational factors that affect persons; they generally should not evaluate the learning tasks that individuals working closely together daily know much better.

Example: A fascinating study of both peer evaluation and supervisory evaluation is reported by Chris Argyris of Harvard University in his recent book, *Knowledge for Action: A Guide to Overcoming Organizational Change.*[11] In this book, he annotates the transcript of a consulting assignment with a 'knowledge work' kind of organization of management consultants. He, of course, references his "double loop" learning model which he developed in the mid 1970s, and which others such as Peter Senge in Massachusetts and Richard Chang in California have adapted to their work. Argyris's notion is that real organizational change can't occur until the underlying framework or "master program" at work in an organization changes; lasting change—including lasting learning—can't happen by just changing the surface actions, or what Argyris calls the single loop. The entire book is an in-depth case study of his work with the management consulting company as they try to figure out what their "master program" really is and then take some small steps to make lasting, incremental changes in it.

In standard consultant fashion, individuals are interviewed, peer groups and vertical work groups are interviewed, and finally the CEO is brought into the interview process. Many pages in the book are devoted to the peer group sessions, in which they evaluate each other and the organization's ability to be an organization of learners. Argyris spends a lot of time talking about the seemingly universal workplace behavior of "cover-up and bypass," those actions that seem to speak louder than the good words so many knowledge workers speak about openness and teamwork. Argyris found that supervisors around the world—in North America, Europe, South America, Africa, and the Far East (p. 51)—all shared the unfortunate characteristics of defensive strategizing, in spite of their good words to the contrary. Argyris contrasts the "theories in use" with the "espoused theories" of many of the leaders he has worked with around the globe. Those in the book were no exception.

The purpose of these pages here is not to review Argyris's book, but rather to suggest that his study points up the need for supervisors of all sorts in all kinds of companies to insist on alignment of the theory in use with the espoused theory—or, to say it simply, to be honest in evaluation of an organization's capacity to become an organization of builders, of learners, and not of people who tear down and create obstacles. Supervisors have an opportunity by virtue of their position in proximity to both individual workers and corporate resources to make evaluative judgments and to take direct action to build stronger organizations based on those decisions.

WORKSHEET 3 - 8

SUPERVISOR'S CONCERNS REGARDING IMPROVEMENT

Directions: If you as a supervisor are serious about helping those who report to you to become an organization of learners, use this worksheet as a set of guidelines for your facilitative behavior.

1. *Know yourself as a supervisor.*

_____ Parameters of my job are clear.
_____ I respect the work I do.
_____ I respect the people whom I supervise.
_____ I believe that everyone can be a learner.
_____ I believe that everyone can contribute something significant to work.
_____ I 'practice what I preach.'

2. *Know your employees.*

_____ I have asked individuals what they need to know.
_____ I have asked individuals what they want to learn.
_____ I know what motivates individuals to do better work.
_____ I separate discussions about pay from discussions about individual development.
_____ I keep individual development plans for persons whom I supervise.
_____ I listen when employees talk to me.

3. *Evaluate the organization you represent.*

_____ Are we an organization of winners/ losers? Is this a productive way to look at it?
_____ To what extent do we practice being defensive and covering-up bad decisions?
_____ To what extent are leaders expected to admit mistakes?
_____ To what extent are ordinary workers expected to admit mistakes?
_____ Have we ever tried to build quality in by finding errors early and fixing them early?
_____ To what extent are the personal moral principles by which our employees live in alignment with the way that they behave or are expected to behave at work?
_____ Is the information upon which we make choices valid information? Verifiable?
_____ Are resources for learning available in this organization and equally accessible to all employees?

4. *Take action to facilitate learning.*

_____ Analyze information accuracy, flow, and timeliness. Correct problems, and institute self-correcting systems to maintain information.
_____ Support risk-takers who admit early errors. Punish those who cover up and blame others for their mistakes.
_____ Make yourself be a person who wants to hear the truth; encourage this in others.
_____ Communicate. Give and receive feedback. Take overt steps to keep communication open in all directions—forms, suggestion boxes, e-mail, prizes, etc.

CONCLUSION: THE USES OF EVALUATION

A few words of conclusion should be said about the outcomes or results of the many processes of evaluation. In its simplest definition, evaluation is a systematic look for variables that make a difference in the worth of something. Once we have found these variables, it's our job as responsible workers to continuously modify them to make our work better. The decisions for which we use evaluation data will be the measures of our organizational worth. Evaluation decisions feed into the analysis phases of our design systems, and development planning begins in a renewed cycle. Outcomes of evaluation help us set new standards and plan ways by which to achieve them. Formative evaluation, or in-process evaluation, is our best hope for program renewal. Systematically making evaluation a collegial endeavor through a facilitated peer to peer teaching and learning relationship holds great potential for creating and maintaining viable and successful workplaces.

TRANSFER OF LEARNING TO THE JOB

The issue of "transfer" has been a concern of trainers ever since the invention of instructional design. We believe that the way in which we organize learning opportunities will make a difference in terms of the competency of a worker to actually do better work. Questions of "how much?" "in what depth?" and "how soon?" are those which trainees, trainers, and managers have traditionally asked about the transfer of learned skills from the training situation to the work situation.

In businesses where training is done primarily in classrooms, the concern over transfer understandably has been greater than in businesses where training is frequently done on-the-job. Union worker training, or apprentice training, for example, can show us many good examples of training that supports efficient transfer to the job. The problem of transfer is compounded, however, the farther we go from the job. For example, training via watching inspirational videotapes, if it can be called training at all, has almost no chance of being transferred to the job. Particularly if videos have been designed for their entertainment value, there will be no transfer—entertainment, after all, is an escape from reality, not an embracing of it. Videos have their place in training as information vehicles, and sometimes as motivational vehicles, but not as vehicles that carry skills over into work.

Peer training, on the other hand, if designed with learning in mind, if constructed out of the evaluation decisions about an individual's workplace skills—learning skills, communication skills, problem solving skills, mathematical skills, manipulative skills, personal skills, and so forth—can be the most efficient and effective, direct and deep, transfer vehicle for learning. If work itself in all its complexity and variation provides the data base from which to draw learning objectives for individual workers, the training that is focused on an individual's work can be expected to transfer well to the job. When learning and working are integrated, better work and better learning happen.

PLANNING FOR CONTINUOUS IMPROVEMENT

And so, the instructional design cycle moves from the inside out: continuous monitoring, feedback, and modification affect each phase. Persons who are in charge of their working and their learning have *learned* to take charge: they are not afraid of errors, they listen to others, they share, they are good work analysts, and they know themselves. Individual learners who make continuous improvements to work have *learned* to evaluate their learning, they've *learned* to ask for help, and they've *learned* to assemble resources to continue to learn. Continuous learners know that survival and success both depend on a constructionist approach to work processes, systems, organization structures, and even stakeholders. Continuous improvement of work is built one step at a time.

Peer training as a systematic structure and support for learning deserves a renaissance as the new century challenges our proximity to fellow workers and our accessibility to information. Continuous improvement happens because individuals have the will and the wisdom, the structures and techniques to *make* it happen. This book will help you get started on the courageous and heady endeavor of improving performance one by one.

Endnotes for Chapter 8
Notes 1 through 11

1. One example of a publisher of diagnostic and evaluation task-based materials is Schoolcraft Publishers, 1-800 837-1255. In addition, the National Center for Research in Vocational Education at Ohio State University has a wealth of information on task analysis and evaluation of on-the-job training; phone them at (800) 848-4815. Also contact the National Occupational Competency Testing Institute at Ferris State University at Big Rapids, MI at (800) 334-6283 for information on criterion-referenced task-based testing and evaluation.

2. *HRD Quarterly* is available by phoning (800) 633-4533. *Learning Diagnostic Questionnaire* was developed by Peter Honey and Alan Mumford.

3. J.P. Guilford, *Intelligence, Creativity, and Their Educational Implications*, San Diego: Knapp, 1968, p. 10.

4. Philip C. Candy, *Self-Direction for Lifelong Learning*, San Francisco: Jossey-Bass, 1991, p. 314.

5. Martin Luther King, Jr. quotation from a postcard purchased in Atlanta, GA in 1993 at the Martin Luther King Jr. Center for Social Change.

6. Nancy Goudreau and Andrew Leighton, "Individualized Literacy Improvement: A Case Study in Success," in *Technical & Skills Training*, October 1990, pp. 47-51.

7. Barry J. Martin, "A System for On-the-Job Training," *Technical & Skills Training*, October 1991, pp. 24-27.

8. IBM consultants Daniel P. Freedman and Gerald M. Weinberg detailed the peer review process used by IBM and other corporations in their book, *Handbook of Walkthroughs, Inspections, and Technical Reviews*, Boston: Little, Brown and Company, 1982. AT&T's adaptation of this process is described in a book by Carolyn Nilson, *IQPM User Guide*, published by AT&T Bell Laboratories, Kelly Education and Training Center, Middletown, NJ, 1986. Numerous articles in the *IBM Systems Journal* throughout the 1970s describe peer review at IBM; numerous IEEE publications during those years also report on structured technical reviews and peer evaluations, especially in software development. These are referenced in the bibliography of the Freedman and Weinberg book named above in this endnote.

9. Freedman and Weinberg, *op. cit.*, p. 323.

10. Benjamin S. Bloom, "The New Direction in Educational Research: Alterable Variables" in *Phi Delta Kappan*, February 1980, pp. 382-385.

11. Chris Argyris, *Knowledge for Action*, San Francisco: Jossey-Bass, 1993.

INDEX

326

INDEX

Small Business Reports, 28, 188, 246
small groups, 246, 251
Smithsonian Institution, 274
Sony, 270
Southwest Airlines, 59
Spectrum Control, 36
Sterling Engineering, 306
Sternberg, Robert, 294
storytelling, 249
Subaru Isuzu Automotive, 113, 306, 307
subject matter expert (SME), 246, 250, 291, 294, 295, 299, 300, 307 (*See also* job analysis)
systems thinking, 13, 70, 71, 111-113, 122-123, 129, 130, 141-143, 149-153, 212, 266, 304, 316, 317

T

teams, 17, 55, 58, 96, 257
Technical & Skills Training, 296, 307
Technology Review (MIT), 86, 272-274, 276
Telecommunications Inc., 270
Time Warner, 271, 272
T.J. Maxx, 227
trainer competencies, 180
Training magazine, 55, 227, 274
training standards, 85-92
training tax, 217, 218
train-the-peer-trainer, 223-232, 244, 246-253, 303-306
transfer of learning, 316
transparencies, 257, 293
Tufte, E.R., 208

U

University of California, 269
University of Chicago, 205, 237
University of Pennsylvania, 182

University of Texas, 213
University of Toronto, 267
Upjohn Company, 207
US Department of Agriculture, 296
US Department of Commerce, 22, 23
US Department of Education, 12, 188
US Department of Labor, 83, 84, 191
US Department of the Navy, 13
US News & World Report, 66, 114
U.S. West, 271

V

videogames, 270-273
videotapes, 171, 257, 265
virtual environments, 117, 267, 269, 273-276, 279
Volvo, 57

W

Wallace Company, 26
Walt Disney World, 202, 227
The Washington Post, 95
Waterman, Robert, 57
Weyerhaeuser Corporation, 275
Will-Burt, 246, 247
Workplace Basics, 83, 84, 191

X

XEL Communication, 96
Xerox, 196, 275

Z

Ziff Institute, 213
Zuboff, Shoshana, 204, 208, 267, 268

NOTES

NOTES

NOTES

NOTES

NOTES